THE MEANING
OF TREASON

REBECCA WEST

Second enlarged and revised edition
containing two long additional chapters
on Atomic Espionage

THE REPRINT SOCIETY
LONDON

TO

HAROLD ROSS

NOTE

PARTS of this book relating to William Joyce and John Amery appeared in *The New Yorker,* and the Epilogue appeared in *Harper's Magazine,* and I reprint them here with a strong sense of gratitude to those periodicals. The material I collected for the most part by attending various civil trials and courts-martial, and I have supplemented this in certain cases by information supplied by friends and relatives of persons accused of treachery. Of these accused persons, some mentioned in the earlier editions of this book have come forward to help me, in several instances with great candour and magnanimity.

Since this book was first published, the Committee appointed in 1946 to investigate the court-martial system of the Army and Navy and Air Force has issued its report; and the passages referring to courts-martial on pages 159-161 therefore describe conditions which either have ceased to exist or will soon disappear. The amateurishness deplored there is to be remedied by a reconstitution of the office of the Judge-Advocate-General; the verdicts and sentences are to be announced in open court without delay; and on December 14, 1950, there was published the text of the Courts-martial (Appeals) Bill, which provides for the establishment of a court of appeal for the Navy, Army, and Air Force, to which every person convicted by a court-martial may, with the leave of the court, appeal against his conviction. These are advances for which we should all be grateful.

In cases where convicted persons seemed likely to return to the outer world after a short period, and had not received much mention in the press, I alluded to them in the earlier editions of this book by names other than their own. I have been reproached for this by certain readers who say I have thus placed obstacles in the way of students who are interested in the legal aspect of these cases. But I know no law, and I am not writing for lawyers, who have a right to despise me on their own field. I wrote this book because I wanted to describe the sufferings which overtake people who live unnaturally and cut the bonds which bind them to their own country. Patriotism may be the last refuge of a scoundrel; but since all of us are to some degree scoundrels we are foolish if we get rid of our last refuge.

I have also been asked by various kindly people to reassure them by giving particulars of what revisions of sentences have been granted in certain cases. But this is inadvisable. It is not possible for an unofficial person to learn the grounds on which certain prisoners have been released; and simply to state that they have been released would be to raise hopes, which often could not be realized, in the relatives of other prisoners whose circumstances were different. I can only record my personal opinion that the authorities, civil and military, have used their powers humanely: more humanely than any alien government treats the nationals of another country whom it seduces into its service.

R. W.

CONTENTS

For he was numbered with us, and had obtained part of this ministry. Now this man purchased a field with the reward of iniquity; and falling headlong, he burst asunder in the midst, and all his bowels gushed out. And it was known unto all the dwellers at Jerusalem; insomuch as that field is called in their proper tongue, Aceldama, that is to say, The field of blood. For it is written in the book of Psalms, Let his habitation be desolate, and let no man dwell therein: and his bishoprick let another take.

THE ACTS OF THE APOSTLES, I : 17-20

I

THE REVOLUTIONARY

I

EVERYBODY in London wanted to see William Joyce when he was brought to trial as a radio traitor, for he was something new in the history of the world. Not before have people known the voice of one they had never seen as well as if he had been a husband or a brother or a close friend; and if they had foreseen such a miracle they would not have imagined that the familiar unknown would speak to them only to prophesy their death and ruin. All of us in England had experienced that hideous novelty. It was difficult not to chance on Joyce's wavelength when one was tuning-in to the English stations, and there was an arresting quality about his voice which made it a sacrifice not to go on listening. It was a rasping yet rich voice, very like the voice of the American rabble-rouser, Father Coughlin, and it was convincing in its confidence. It seemed as if one had better hearken and take warning when he suggested that the destiny of the people he had left in England was death, and the destiny of his new masters in Germany life and conquest, and that, therefore, his listeners had better change sides and submit. This was often terrible to hear, for the news in the papers confirmed it. He was not only alarming, he was ugly; he opened a vista into a mean life; he always spoke as if he were better fed and better clothed than we were, and so, we now know, he was. He went further than that smug mockery of our plight. He sinned that sin which is the dark travesty of legitimate hatred because it is felt for kindred, just as incest is the dark travesty of legitimate love. When the U-boats were sinking so many of our ships that to open the newspapers was to see the faces of drowned sailors, he rolled the figures of our lost tonnage on his tongue. When we were facing the hazard of D-day, he rejoiced in the thought of the English dead that would soon lie under the West Wall.

So all the curious went off to the Central Criminal Court on

September 17, 1945, when he came up for trial. It looked odd
to those who had not seen it since the war. It had stood in a
congestion of unlovely commercial buildings; the blitz had now
converted it into a beautiful desert. Churches stood blackened
but apparently intact; birds, however, flew through the empty
sockets of the windows and long grass grew around their altars.
A red-brick Georgian mansion, hidden for a century by sordid
warehouses, looked at the great Renaissance dome of St. Paul's
across acres where willow-herb, its last purple flowers passing
into silver clouds of seed dust, grew with the yellow ragwort
from the ground plan of a lost city drawn in rubble. The courts
themselves startled the eye that knew them as they were, housed
in a solid building built of grey stone in the neo-classical style.
Its solidity had been sliced as if it were a cake, and the walls
of the slice were raw, new red brick. At the time of the trial,
because of the sealing-off of the bombed parts, and the heavy
black-out, not yet removed owing to the lack of labour, all
the halls and passages and stairs were in perpetual dusk. The
courtroom—the Court No. 1 where all the most famous criminal
trials of modern times have taken place—was lit by electric light,
for the shattered glass dome had not yet been rebuilt. Bare boards
filled it in, giving an odd-come-short look to what used to be
an austerely fine room.

The strong electric light was merciless to William Joyce,
whose appearance was a surprise to all of us who knew him only
on the air. His voice had suggested a large and flashy handsomeness.
But he was a tiny little creature and, though not very ugly, was
exhaustively so. His hair was mouse-coloured and grew thinly,
particularly above his ears. His nose was joined to his face at an
odd angle, and its bridge and its point and its nostrils were all
separately misshapen. Above his small dark-blue eyes, which
were hard and shiny, like pebbles, his eyebrows were thick and
pale and irregular. His neck was long and his shoulders were
narrow and sloping. His arms were very short and very thick, so
that his sleeves were like little bolsters. His body looked flimsy
yet coarse. There was nothing individual about him except a
deep scar running across his right cheek from his ear to the corner
of his mouth. But this did not create the savage and marred
distinction that it might suggest, for it gave a mincing immobility

4

to his mouth, which was extremely small. His smile was pinched and governessy. He was dressed with an intent and ambitious spruceness which did not succeed in giving any impression of well-being, but rather recalled some Eastern European peasant, newly driven off the land by poverty into a factory town and wearing his first suit of Western clothes. He moved with a jerky formality which would have been thought strange in any society. When he bowed to the judge, his bow seemed sincerely respectful but entirely inappropriate to the occasion, and it was difficult to think of any occasion to which it would have been appropriate.

At right angles to the dock, against the wall of the court, sat the jury, none of its members greatly blessed by nature, though there was one woman, slender and high-nosed, of the colonel's-daughter kind, who had an irresistible charm. Day by day the journalists who watched the case became more and more convinced, for no reason at all, that she was a very good sort. But the members of the jury were all middle-aged, since the armies had not come home, and though they were drawn from different ranks of life, there was then no rank in which English people were other than puffy or haggard. But at that they were all more pleasant to look at and more obviously trustworthy than the homely and eccentric little man in the dock; and, compared with the judicial bench which he faced, he was of course at an immense disadvantage, as we all should be, for its dignity is authentic. Against oak panels, columns ran up to a pediment framing the carved royal standard and the sword of justice, which is affixed to the wall in its jewelled scabbard. At the foot of the wall, in a high-backed chair, sat the judge, dressed in his scarlet robe, with its neck-band of fine white linen and its deep cuffs and sash of purplish-black taffeta. Beside him, their chairs set further back as a sign of their inferiority to him, sat the Lord Mayor of London and two aldermen, wearing their antique robes of black silk with flowing white cravats and gold chains hung with chased badges of office worked in precious metals and enamel. These two sorts of pompous trapping are always given some real meaning by the faces of the men who support them. Judges are chosen for a combination of intellect and character, city honours are usually earned by competence and character and the patience to carry out a routine of tedious

5

public duty over decades, and such qualities usually leave an imprint on the features.

Looking from the bench to the dock, it could be seen that not in any sane state would William Joyce have had the ghost of a chance of holding such offices as these. But when he was asked to plead he said, "Not guilty", and those two words were the most impressive uttered during the trial. The famous voice was let loose. For a fraction of a second we heard its familiar quality. It was as we had heard it for six years, it reverberated with the desire for power. Never was there a more perfect voice for a demagogue, for its reverberations were so strong that they were certain to awaken echoes in every heart that was tumid with the same appetite. What could the little man do—since he so passionately desired to exercise authority, and neither this nor any other state would give it to him—but use his trick of gathering together other luckless fellows, that they might overturn the sane state and substitute a mad one? That was the most profound cause which had brought him to the dock; but there was another which quickly became apparent.

This trial, like the great treason trial of the First World War, when Sir Roger Casement went to the gallows, was an Irish drama. From the first, rumours had been current that Joyce was Irish, but they had never been officially confirmed, and his accent was difficult to identify. But there was little doubt about it when one saw him in the dock. He had the real Donnybrook air. He was a not very fortunate example of the small, nippy, jig-dancing type of Irish peasant, and the appearance of his brother, who attended the court every day in a state of great suffering, was proof of the family's origin. Quentin Joyce, who was then twenty-eight, was eleven years William's junior. He was much better-looking, with a sturdy body, a fresh colour, thick and lustrous brown hair, and the soft eyes of a cow. Nobody in his senses could mistake him for anything but an Irishman from the provinces. There were also strong traces of Irish origin in the followers of Joyce who watched the trial. These were a singular crowd. There were also some women who especially attracted attention by an almost unearthly physical repulsiveness, notably an ageing and floozy blonde in a tight Air Force uniform, who sucked sweets and wept, as she swung an ankle creased with fat from

6

crossed knees that pressed up against her drooping bosom. But she and her like, it seemed probable, had been merely on the fringe of the British Fascist movement and were sympathizers with Joyce rather than his associates.

These could be seen every day gathered round Joyce's brother, and his solicitor and his clerk. The solicitor was a fragile, even childish, figure with blond hair and a pale sensitive face who was acting for Joyce not because he wished to have him as a client or had any sympathy with British fascism, but because Joyce, being without means on his return from Germany to England, had had to apply for the services of a lawyer under the Poor Prisoners' Defence Act when he first came up before the minor judge we call a magistrate for the preliminary stages of his trial. This meant that the magistrate had had to select at random the names of certain lawyers from a rota, and call on them to perform the duty of defending Joyce, a summons which they were not allowed to refuse. The task must have been extremely onerous for this lawyer, who was a practitioner of high standing and had no need for notoriety. But he could not have behaved with more exquisite loyalty to his client, nor soothed more kindly the grief of the many persons associated with the case which he must heartily have wished he never had seen. Each day he bore himself amiably towards them, aided by his clerk, a girl in her twenties, with long and elaborately curled hair, bareheaded and dressed as if for the beach walk of a summer resort, with flowered frock, fleecy coat, and light shoes. There could not have been a figure more discordant with the peculiar dry decorum of the English courts. But she too was conscientiously gracious to Joyce's friends, the chief of whom was a thin man with fierce black eyes blazing behind thick glasses, a tiny fuzz of black hair fancifully arranged on his prematurely bald head, and wrists and ankles as straight as lead piping in their emaciation.

He was a Scotsman named Angus MacNab, the editor of a Fascist paper and Joyce's best friend. He was plainly foredoomed to follow odd by-paths, and a variation in circumstances might have found him just as happily a spiritualist medium or a believer in the lost ten tribes of Israel. As for the rest of the followers, men of violent and unhappy appearance, with a look of animal shyness and ferocity, and, in some cases, a measure of animal beauty, they were for the most part darker in complexion than one would expect in subscribers to the Aryan theory. One, especially, looked like a true gipsy. Many of them had an Irish cast of feature and some bore Irish names. It must be remembered that most of these men were not followers of Sir Oswald Mosley, who picked a more varied and more cheerfully brutal type. Joyce had seceded from Mosley's movement some years before the war and started his own. This was his private army, part of his individual hell.

The story developed during the first day and the morning of the second, and it was certainly an Irish story. At first our attention wandered from Joyce's personality because the lawyer for the Crown was Sir Hartley Shawcross, the Attorney-General appointed by the new Labour Government. He was young for the post, charming in manner and voice, and he set out a beautifully lucid argument, and we were pleased, and pleased to be pleased. For the English were eager to approve of whatever the new government did; we were tired out by such excitements as had produced this trial, and what we wanted was to hear the machine ticking over. But the interest presently shifted to an ironical story of a family who, for obscure reasons springing from one convulsion of history, engaged in disingenuous conduct which, long after, brought their dearest member a nonsensical doom in another historical convulsion.

That the proceedings were to be odd was indicated by the three counts of the indictment brought against him. He had offended, it seemed, against the root of the law against treason: a Statute in which Edward III, in the year 1351, "at the request of the lords and commons" declared that "if a man do levy war against our Lord the King in his realm or be adherent to the King's enemies in his realm, giving them aid and comfort in the realm or elsewhere", he was guilty of treason. So the Clerk of the Court, Sir Wilfrid Knops, said: "William Joyce, you are charged in an indictment containing three counts with high treason. The particulars in the first count are that on the 18th September 1939, and on other days between that day and the 29th May 1945, you, being a person owing allegiance to our lord the King, and when a war was being carried on by the German realm against our King, did traitorously adhere to the

8

King's enemies, in parts beyond the seas, that is to say in Germany, by broadcasting propaganda. In a second count of the same indictment, it is charged that you, on the 26th September 1940, being a person owing allegiance as in the other count, adhered to the King's enemies by purporting to become naturalized as a subject of Germany. And in a third count, the particulars are the same as in the first count, that is to say, you are charged with broadcasting propaganda, but the dates are different, and the dates in this case are the 18th September 1939, and on days between that day and the 2nd July 1940." Later the first two counts were amended, for reasons emerging during the trial, and he was described in them as "a British subject", but, significantly, no such change was made in the third.

It seemed, in the early stages of the trial, as if William Joyce must be convicted on these two first indictments. He himself had again and again described himself as a British subject, and his father had done the same. The first evidence to this effect came from a comely and pleasant-voiced lady in early and spruce middle age with marcelled grey hair and a spirited red straw hat, the kind of lady who is photographed in women's magazines as having taken a prize for preserves at a Women's Institute fair, who, oddly enough, turned out to be the assistant secretary of the Committee for Military Education in the University of London. When one thought of the blond and boar-like young man or the Brünhilde-like young woman who would have held such a post in a German University, it became a better joke than ever that we had won the war. She was present because someone with a prodigious memory had recalled that in August 1922 William Joyce, then a boy of sixteen, had sent a letter of application for entrance to the London University Officers' Training Corps, in which he had described himself as a British subject, a description which was supported by his father, Michael Joyce. The boy's letter threw a light on the inner ferment that had brought him to the dock. In this letter he had said that he wanted to study with a view to being nominated by the University for a commission in the Regular Army; but it was obvious that he would find difficulty in following that road. His letter was a little too high-falutin, even for a boy of sixteen. Doubt would have crossed the mind of anybody who read it. And the letter from his father, the loving letter of a father eager to do his best for his son, was too illiterate. But they made themselves plain enough on the subject-matter of the correspondence.

"I must now", wrote the young Joyce, "mention a point which I hope will not give rise to difficulties. I was born in America, but of British parents. I left America when two years of age, have not returned since, and do not propose to return. I was informed, at the brigade headquarters of the district in which I was stationed in Ireland, that I possessed the same rights and privileges as I would if of natural British birth. I can obtain testimonials as to my loyalty to the Crown. I am in no way connected with the United States of America, against which, as against all other nations, I am prepared to draw the sword in British interests. As a young man of pure British descent, some of whose forefathers have held high position in the British army, I have always been desirous of devoting what little capability and energy I may possess to the country which I love so dearly. I ask that you may inform me if the accident of my birth, to which I refer above, will affect my position. I shall be in London for the September Matriculation Examination and I hope to commence studies at the London University at the beginning of the next academic year. I trust that you will reply as soon as possible, and that your reply will be favourable to my aspirations." At an interview with an official of the O.T.C. he conveyed that he was "in doubt as to whether he was a 'British subject of pure European descent'", a doubt which must have been honest if he expressed it at all in view of the ardent hope expressed in his letter; but he asserted that his father had never been naturalized. This the father confirmed when the official wrote to him for further particulars. "Dear Sir, your letter of 23rd October received. Would have replied sooner, but have been away from home. With regard to my son William. He was born in America, I was born in Ireland. His mother was born in England. We are all British and not American citizens."

But why, when William Joyce was making later declarations that he was a British subject, had he sometimes said that he was a British subject, and he sometimes said that he was born in Ireland and sometimes that he was born in America, when he had a birth certificate which gave his birthplace as Brooklyn?

The answer is that he was probably never sure of the real facts regarding his own and his father's status till he learned them from his own defence lawyers just before the trial. In the statement he made to the Intelligence officers on his arrest he expressed himself uncertainly. "I understand, though I have no documents to prove any statement, that my father was American by naturalization at the time of my birth, and I believe he lost his American citizenship later through failing to renew it, because we left America in 1909 when I was three years old. We were generally treated as British subjects during our stay in Ireland and England. I was in Ireland from 1909 till 1921 when I came to England. We were always treated as British during the period of my stay in England whether we were or not." But the truth was disclosed when Mr. Gerald Slade, K.C.,[1] counsel for the defence, got going with the case for Joyce and told—with a curious dry and ascetic fervour which recalled that in his spare time he is a temperance advocate—a story which would have charmed a snake if read to it at dictation speed. For it turned out that William Joyce's father, Michael Joyce, had been a naturalized American long before William Joyce had been born at 1377 Herkimer Street, Brooklyn. Therefore William Joyce was by birth an American citizen and owed the King of England no allegiance arising out of British nationality. All his life he had described himself as a British subject, and his father had done the like; and they had been lying. There was no doubt about it. The documents of naturalization were present in good order, dated in 1894, and a torn certificate, printed in that early nineteenth-century type which we used to regard as hideous and now nostalgically think charming, proved that Michael Francis Joyce and Gertrude Emily Brooke had been married in All Saints Church, at 129th Street and Madison Avenue, New York, by Roman Catholic rites, on the 2nd of May 1902.

Then, to confirm all this, came Mr. Frank Holland, who was a difficult witness. An old gentleman, white-haired and shrivelled and deaf and palsied and quavering, he stoutly gave evidence that he had been born in 1883; and there was apparently no mistake about it. Added to this, he was Irish beyond the normal provisions of nature, with the emphasis of art; he might have been one

[1] Now Sir Gerald Slade, since June 1948 a judge of the High Court.

of the Dublin players taking part in a Sean O'Casey play. He also suffered from an eerie form of deafness, the inverse of a banshee's wail; one saw even the baritone of Sir Hartley Shawcross, which is as audible as an actor's voice, come to his ear and be attenuated and disappear into nothingness. Added to that, he had a mind which, in one sense fragile, was in another vigorous. He did not fly off at a tangent—flying things can be brought down—but he crept off at tangents, and not the entire forces of the Central Criminal Court could bring him home. The defending counsel had announced that he was calling Mr. Holland to certify that when Michael Joyce was leaving America for England, his passport had arrived after he had left his home in Brooklyn to go down to the steamer, and that Mr. Holland had waited to take it from the postman and had carried it down to his friend at a Hoboken pier, and that Mr. Holland had then seen it was an American passport. But when the relevant questions were put to the old man, he bridled. They appeared to him to cast aspersions on his gentlemanliness. Yes, he had helped his friend by fetching him his passport, but how was he to know what kind of passport? His attitude sharply indicated that other people might know no better than to be inquisitive, but he had his manners. As the examination went on, old age could be seen shifting itself from the shoulders of Mr. Holland to those of the examining counsel; yet Mr. Holland contributed enough.

Long ago he had known a girl named Gertrude Emily Brooke. She was called Queenie, he told us, with a sudden affectionate chuckle. She had married a man named Michael Joyce, who worked in America. It was on Michael Joyce's advice that Mr. Holland himself had gone to America and followed his calling of civil engineer under the employment of the Pennsylvania Railway Company. He and his wife had seen much of the Joyces in America; they had liked them, and even if they had not, would have been inclined to visit them frequently for the simple reason that they were the only people they knew anywhere near New York. And indeed they were lucky to have friends with such a pleasant home. For the Joyces' house, which has since been reconstructed and is now an estate agent's office, stood on a corner lot in a broad street planted with trees, which is now occupied at one end by Negroes and at the other by Italians, but was then a centre of the

Irish community. The German quarter was not far away. He went on to describe how Michael Joyce had told him that he had become an American citizen and advised him to do the same. He took the advice, but came home to England after the outbreak of the First World War; he was greatly inconvenienced by his American citizenship, for he had to register under the Aliens Act which was passed in 1915 and report all his movements to the police. At this time he had visited Queenie, then settled in Lancashire, and had exchanged commiserations with her, because she was incommoded in the same way. His cracked old voice evoked two people grumbling together thirty years ago. That they had so grumbled could not be doubted.

This witness's evidence recalled the acting of Sir Henry Irving. It was impossible to hear a word of what Irving said for years before he left the stage, and as his memory had gone that was just as well; but the melodic line of his murmurs and the gesture of his gauntness never failed to evoke the truth concerning Shylock, because he knew that truth and charged such means of expression as still remained to him with instructions to transmit it. Mr. Holland was as bewildering a witness as could be imagined. The name of Gertrude Emily Brooke's birthplace, the town of Shaw in Lancashire, inspired him to dazzling feats. Through his deafness he appeared to swear that he had been born there, that he had never been there, that he had seen the Joyces there, and that he had not seen them there, and that he had visited the Joyces in 1919 at a house in which they had in fact settled in 1923. But he had known the Joyces for fifty years; he did recognize the prisoner in the dock as the William Joyce who had been a baby in Herkimer Street, Brooklyn; he had heard Michael Joyce say he was an American and Gertrude Emily Joyce grumble about the necessity to register as an alien; and he was telling the truth. It showed in the irritable twitch of his eyebrows when he was asked to put what he said into a form more likely to convince the jury, the impatient wail of his voice as he made what seemed to him the superfluous repetition. The case against William Joyce, so far as it depended on his British nationality, lay dead on the courtroom floor when Mr. Holland left the witness-box.

There came to confirm that evidence a police official named Woodmansey, who proved that in the last war Mr. and Mrs.

Michael Joyce, oscillating between Galway and Lancashire with their children, had been registered as Americans. They had broken the rules by failing to report their movements and this had produced an illuminating correspondence between the police in Lancashire and the Royal Irish Constabulary in Galway. This revealed that both Michael Joyce and his wife had oddly met the situation with the nonsensical tale which we had heard before, that they were not really aliens, because Michael had failed to re-register as an American citizen within two years after leaving the United States. What was odder still was that the Galway constabulary—which must have known that it was nonsense, for there was nothing that an Irish policeman knew better than the American laws that affected Irish emigrants—recommended this preposterous story sympathetically to the Lancashire police, urging that Michael Joyce was "one of the most respectable, law-abiding, and loyal men in the locality, and one who has been consistently an advocate of the 'pro-Allied' cause since the beginning of the war", and expressing doubt "whether these people are aliens at all". The Lancashire police crisply resisted the suggestion, but dealt with the case by a caution. The Galway constable who had administered the admonition came to give evidence—a thin and aged giant, so disabled by blindness and partial paralysis that he had to be led to the witness-box and propped up in it, a tall blanched obelisk. It was odd to find that to this incident Mrs. Joyce, who was by all accounts a person of scrupulous character, had contributed her own lie. She told the police that though her husband had been in the United States he was "only three or four years there altogether". It seems unlikely that she should not have known that he had lived there for eighteen years preceding their marriage.

The oddity of the situation was emphasized by the evidence of Quentin Joyce. There passed between him and the man in the dock a nod and a smile of pure love. One realized that life in this strange family must sometimes have been great fun. But it evidently had not been fun lately. Quentin told the court that his father had died in 1941, shortly after the house in which he had lived for eighteen years had been destroyed by a bomb, and his mother had died in 1944. Out of the wreckage of the house there had been recovered a few boxes full of papers, but none had any bearing on the question of the family's nationality, and there was a reason for that. Michael Joyce had told young Quentin, when he was ten years old, that he and all the family were American citizens but had bade him never speak of it, and had in later years often reiterated this warning. Finally, in 1934, the boy, who was then sixteen, had seen him burn a number of papers, including what appeared to be an American passport. He had given a reason for what he was doing, but the witness was not required to repeat it. The date suggested what that reason may have been. By that time the police knew William Joyce as a troublesome instigator of street-fighting and attacks on Communists and Jews, and in November 1934 Joyce was prosecuted, together with Sir Oswald Mosley and two other Fascists, on a charge of riotous assembly at Worthing; and though this prosecution failed, it indicated a serious attempt by the authorities to rid themselves of the nuisance of Fascist-planned disorder. Michael Joyce had every reason to fear that, if the police ever got an inkling of his secret, they would deport his son and not improbably the whole family.

The courtroom was by now in a state that would have puzzled those Americans who think of the British as a comfortably homogeneous people; for some of the spectators could not make head or tail of this old story, and some of them knew perfectly well where they were, even if they did not know exactly what was going on in that peculiar field. The people who knew where they were had two characteristics in common: they had Irish antecedents and they were not young. They knew what Ireland was before it was Eire, and the dreary round by which men, often brave and good men, kept in check, by a complicated mechanism of oppression and espionage, other men, also often brave and good, who retorted by shooting them from behind stone walls and burning down their houses. Because Michael Joyce had been married in a Roman Catholic church, and because of the surname he bore, which is extremely common in certain counties, it could be known that he was one of the native Irish, the mass of whom were against the English and on the side of the people who shot the English from behind stone walls. But when an officer of the Royal Irish Constabulary described him as one of the loyalest men in Galway, it meant that he was on the side of England. There were many such native Irish who turned against their own kind and worked with the alien oppressor, and we forget now how many of them were passionately sincere. Doubtless some were seduced by the bribery dispensed by Dublin Castle. But many, and among those we must include Michael Joyce, were people who honestly loved law and order and preferred the smart uniforms and the soldierly bearing of the English garrisons and the Royal Irish Constabulary to the furtive slouching of a peasantry distracted with poverty and revolutionary fever. The error of such people was insufficient inquiry into first causes, but for simple natures who went by surface indications their choice was very natural. It must have come very natural indeed to the Joyce family, who, as could be seen from the nervous neatness of both William and Quentin Joyce, and their bearing in court, had been reared to cultivate military smartness and to appreciate ceremonial to such a degree that their appreciation did not entirely desert them even when the ceremonial belonged to a trial at which one of them stood charged with a capital offence. These native Irish who had made that choice often felt a love of England which struck English people as excessive and theatrical: such a love as William Joyce had, at sixteen, expressed in his letters to the secretary of the London University Committee for Military Education, such a love as often led him in after-life to make a demand—which struck many of his English acquaintances as a sign of insanity—that any quiet social evening he spent with his friends should end with the singing of the national anthem.

There was, in that letter he wrote when he was sixteen, an astonishing sentence. "I have served with the irregular forces of the Crown in an Intelligence capacity, against the Irish guerrillas", wrote the boy. "In command of a squad of sub-agents I was subordinate to the late Capt. P. W. Keating, 2nd R.U.R., who was drowned in the *Egypt* accident. I have a knowledge of the rudiments of Musketry, Bayonet Fighting, and Squad Drill." The *Egypt* was sunk off Ushant in May 1922; which meant that if this story were true the boy was engaged in guerrilla fighting with the Black and Tans when he was fifteen years old. That story was true. A photograph of him at this time shows him in battle-dress, and many persons still living remember this phase of his life. He repeated the statement later on an official form, giving the duration of his service as four months, and the name of the regiment with which he had been associated as the Worcestershires, and during his trial at the Old Bailey an old man from County Galway stood in the crowd outside and gave rambling confirmation to this claim. He illustrated the Irish conception of consistency by expressing to bystanders his hearty desire that William Joyce should be hanged for treason against the King of England, on the ground that when he was a boy he had worked with the Black and Tans in persecuting the Irish when they were revolting against the English. The crowd, with that tolerance which foreigners, possibly correctly, suspect of being a form of smugness, was amused and sympathetic. It is typical of the irony which determined William Joyce's life that not only did that service he thought he rendered England mean ultimately nothing, since now we see the severance of England and Ireland as a historical necessity, but even at the time it can have recommended him hardly at all to the Englishmen who read his letter. The Black and Tans were terrified men, set down in a country where it was impossible to tell friend and foe, and assassination was the only art of the people; they burned and slew with the ferocity of fear. Even those who thought that England should not have relinquished Ireland were ashamed at this reminder of the inevitable impudicity of the conqueror's sword; and to all, a child who had partaken, even with gallantry, in such deeds, would have seemed to have had his childhood outraged.

To the end of his life this love of an obsolete England persisted in William Joyce, to be rebuffed by contemporary England. Its climax was related at the trial by an officer with the superb name of Alexander Adrian Lickorish, who described how it came about that William Joyce fell into the hands of justice at the end of the war. He might never have been arrested had it not been for his desire to do a service to two English officers whom he did not know, whose only value to him can have been that they were English officers. In November 1944 he had been given a fake passport, apparently for the purpose of enabling him to escape recognition if he fell into the hands of the British. The Germans provided these passports for all the traitors who had been broadcasters for them; but this one was not a very convincing document. It was made out to Wilhelm Hansen, but the holder was stated to have been born in Galway, Ireland, a detail which would have been likely to arouse the interest of any Intelligence officer. After William Joyce had made his last broadcast on April 30, 1945, a broadcast in which, not without dignity, he acknowledged the coming of the night, he took this false passport and with his wife went into hiding. On May 28, when evening was falling, Captain Lickorish and a Lieutenant Perry were walking in a wood near Flensburg, on the Danish frontier, looking for some branches to make a fire, when they came on a man who was wandering aimlessly among the trees. He watched them for a time, and then called to them in French, "Here are a few more pieces." Presently he said in English, "There are a few more pieces here." At once the voice betrayed him. The two officers conferred together, and then Lieutenant Perry said to him, "You wouldn't happen to be William Joyce, would you?" The man put his hand in his pocket, and Lieutenant Perry, thinking he was about to draw a revolver, shot him in the leg. He fell to the ground, saying, "My name is Fritz Hansen." Fritz is not an abbreviation of Wilhelm; but the slip did not matter, for when they searched him they found not only the civil passport (*Reisepass*) made out to Hansen but a military passport (*Wehrpass*) made out in the name of William Joyce.

It was his love of England, slanting across time, which made him a Fascist. He had been brought up to believe in an England who held Ireland by force, and felt betrayed when Home Rule was given. This meant an actual, material betrayal. The family had to leave Ireland, like many other loyalist Irishmen. Thus William Joyce found himself exiled from his real motherland, Ireland, which his blood must have loved, and confined in England, for love of which he had betrayed Ireland, and which showed no gratitude for that sacrifice. Though the loyalists often received financial aid, Michael Joyce plainly suffered heavy loss through his exile. He was a builder and contractor who had come back from America with handsome means and owned, at the time of the First World War, considerable house property in County Mayo and County Galway, as well as managing the horse-tramway system in Galway town. He came to England for three very good reasons of diverse sorts: the horse-tramways in Galway were abolished; his British sympathies were known and his house had been burned down; and, perhaps the most cogent reason of all, he was confused in many people's minds with an informer, also named Michael Joyce, who had denounced to the Black and Tans a priest whom they murdered. It should be noted that no such action is attributed to William Joyce's father even by his most stubborn enemies. With exile he entered on a declining scale of prosperity and on his death in 1941 left nothing but effects valued at six hundred and fifty pounds. He himself attributed his impoverishment to the failure of the British Government to give him adequate compensation for the burning of his house and the destruction of other property belonging to him by the Sinn Feiners. This complaint was, in the opinion of a detached observer with some knowledge of practical affairs, well founded. Michael Joyce's children were, therefore, brought up to consider the existing British Government as the shabby and dishonest heir of great ancestors. William Joyce himself could not restore the family fortunes—in spite of his intellectual equipment, which was sufficient to give him a degree at the University of London, with first-class honours in English language and literature— because of his personal limitations, the clownish extravagance which left him, even after he had played a uniquely sinister part in history, with the comic nickname of Lord Haw-Haw, the odd vulgarity which made it almost impossible to believe, looking at him or listening to him, that he was a University graduate or the child of people with a position in a community. After finishing his studies he at once gained a position, and not an unremunerative one, in a tutorial college, but it would have been inconceivable that he could have arrived at any position of distinction in the academic world. He had in early youth joined the Conservative Party and spoken for it, but it would have been inconceivable that any local committee could have nominated him as Parliamentary candidate. If he had remained innocent as snow he would still have looked a gangster, and, what was worse for him, a comic gangster.

Therefore the Fascist movement was a godsend to him. Its leader was himself on the grotesque side; and he was determined not to modify but to obliterate all those standards by which Joyce would have been excluded. In 1931 Sir Oswald Mosley appeared at a by-election at Ashton-under-Lyne to support the candidature of a member of his New Party, which was to be a socialist party more drastic and dashing than the Labour Party. His supporter was standing against a Conservative and an orthodox Labour candidate. When the results were announced at the town hall on election night he looked down at a sea of jeering faces who were exulting at this defeat; for several reasons some were guffawing because a rich baronet should profess socialism and because a man who was brilliant and handsome had suffered disappointment and humiliation; others because such a man had split the orthodox Labour vote and let in the Conservative; and he said to a friend, "These are the people who have got in the way of everybody who has tried to do anything since the last war." It was a sensible enough observation; but, making it, Mosley fell into the sin of Lucifer. In his pride he violated the just pride of others. He abandoned the attempt to wrestle with the vulgarity of the vulgar by argument and by example. Thereafter his agitation might have deceived the vulgar into crediting himself with a like vulgarity, and it looked as if he might seize power through their support. Joyce was therefore valuable to Mosley for those very qualities which would have prevented his becoming an army officer or a don. So the Fascist movement gave him a place in a hierarchy, with which there went acclamation, a certain amount of money, travel abroad, and company which was of a certain distinction. It also gave Joyce an opportunity to use that superb courage which his people have wrung out of their terrible history, and to gratify that itch for plotting and intrigue which is another product of Irish history. It also gave him the hope that under fascism England might become what Ireland had been to him and his family before there was Home Rule, a police state where spruce tyrants held down the unworthy and rewarded those who submitted to them. It also gave him cause to use that voice, that really extraordinary voice, in which his discontents were fused into a powerful demon able to call all like demons in other men's hearts and stir them into comradeship.

It must have also nourished a strain in William Joyce that was implanted in him by his family life. Michael Joyce was a mysterious person. It is difficult to see why, loving England as he did, he went to America and stayed there for many years. In the nineteenth century it was still economically advantageous to emigrate to England, and emigration to America was more commonly the resort of the anti-English Irish. There were, of course, some pro-English Irish who went to America to act as informers on the anti-English Irish, who at that time were very actively supporting the Fenian and other separatist movements. It is said that Michael Joyce was a candid and honourable man, but even such could, even against their own wish, be entangled in the fierce intrigues and counter-intrigues of those days. It is very difficult to see why, when Michael Joyce returned to England and found his American citizenship such a burden that he warned his children to keep it a deadly secret, he never took the simple steps which would have readmitted him to British nationality. It would have cost him only a few pounds, and he was in those years well-to-do. It cannot have been the legal technicalities which baffled him; his wife's brother was a solicitor. The official resistance to the process was not great. His friend Mr. Holland described his readmission to British nationality without any of the complaint for which he had a natural turn. Can Michael Joyce have feared to remind either the British or the American government of his existence? Had he once been involved in some imbroglio and got a black mark against his name? Was he working his passage home when he gained the good opinion of the Royal Irish Constabulary? There is probably nobody alive now who knows. All that we can be sure of is that the story was probably incredibly complicated. Nothing was simple in that world of espionage and counter-espionage, treachery and counter-treachery, vengeance and vendetta; and complication is to the soul what condiments are to the palate and alcohol is to the nervous system. During the last century Europe has been debauched with an increasing debauchery by this particular form of complication. Sweet it is to be not what the next man thinks one, but far more powerful; to know what he wrote in the letter he was so careful to seal before he sent it for quite a different person's reading; to charm the confidences from the unsuspecting stranger; to put up one's finger through the whimsical darkness and touch the fabric of the state, and feel the unstable structure rock, and know it one's own doing and not a soul suspecting it; and to do all this for nobility's sake. It is the misfortune of our age, with its high degree of political fluidity, that the life of the political conspirator offers the man of restricted capacity but imaginative energy greater excitements and satisfactions than he can ever derive from overt activities.

In the complexities of that life, the shifts and disguises and evasions, William Joyce nearly found shelter from justice. For he owed the Crown no allegiance at all of the sort which springs from British birth. The immunity he had for the moment established by proof of his American birthright can be realized better if his position in regard to the second indictment is considered first. He had, it now appeared, committed no offence whatsoever in becoming a naturalized German subject on the 26th of September 1940. That would have been high treason had he been a British subject, for a British subject is forbidden by law to become the naturalized subject of an enemy country in war-time. But when he took out his naturalization papers in Germany he was an American citizen, and even the American government could not have questioned his action, being then at peace with Germany, which did not declare war on the United States until the 11th of December 1941. It followed then that his broadcasting was, if only his nationality had to be considered, an offence against nobody. Up till the 26th of September 1940 he had been an American working for a neutral state; and after that he had been a good German working for the fatherland. He would have walked out of the court scot-free if society had been conducted on lines as arbitrary as is imagined by those who are Fascist, who desire, that is to say, government by a minority on a non-contractual basis. Allegiance is not exacted by the Crown from a subject simply because the Crown is the Crown. The idea of the divine right of kings is a comparatively modern vulgarity. According to tradition and logic, the state gives protection to all men within its confines, and in return exacts their obedience to its laws; and the process is reciprocal. When men within the confines of the state are obedient to its laws they have a right to claim its protection. It is a maxim of the law, quoted by Coke in the sixteenth century, that "protection draws allegiance, and allegiance draws protection" (*protectio trahit subjectionem, et subjectio protectionem*). It was laid down in 1608, by reference to the case of Sherley, a Frenchman who had come to England and joined in a conspiracy against the King and Queen, that such a man "owed to the King obedience, that is, so long as he was within the King's protection". That is fair enough; and indeed very fair, if the limitations which were applied to this proposition were considered. For in Hale's *History of the Pleas of the Crown*, in the seventeenth century, it was written: "Because as the subject hath his protection from the King and his laws, so on the other side the subject is bound by his allegiance to be true and faithful to the King. And hence it is, that if an alien enemy come into this kingdom hostilely to invade it, if he be taken, he shall be dealt with as an enemy, but not as a traitor, because he violates no trust nor allegiance. But if an alien, the subject of a foreign prince in amity with the King, live here, and enjoy the benefit of the King's protection, and commit a treason, he shall be judged and executed, as a traitor, for he owes a local allegiance."

There could be no doubt whatsoever that William Joyce owed that kind of allegiance. He had certainly enjoyed the protection of the English law for some thirty years preceding his departure to Germany. The lawyers for the defence, in proving that he did not owe the natural kind of allegiance which springs from British birth, had found themselves under the necessity of proving beyond all doubt that he owed this other acquired kind; and there were the two damning sentences in his statement: "We were generally counted as British subjects during our stay in Ireland and England. . . . We were always treated as British during the period of my stay in England whether we were or not." Thus, though an alien, William Joyce owed the Crown allegiance and was capable of committing treason against it. But a further question arose. In the reference to Sherley it was defined that such an alien "owed the King local obedience, that is, so long as he was within the King's protection". Obviously this condition opened the door wider and wider, as communications improved, to conduct which no nation could tolerate, and in 1707 an assembly of judges laid it down that "if such alien seeking the Protection of the Crown having a Family and Effects here should during a War with his Native Country go thither and there Adhere to the King's Enemies for purposes of Hostility, He might be dealt with as a Traitor. For he came and settled here under the Protection of the Crown. And though his Person was removed for a time, his Effects and Family continued still under the same Protection."

Now, the letter of this judgment did not apply to William Joyce. He had taken his wife with him to Germany, and by that marriage he was childless. He had two children by a former marriage, but they were in the care of their mother and did not enter into this case. If he possessed any effects when he quitted England they were sure to be of such a trifling nature that it would have been fairer to regard them as abandoned rather than left under the protection of the Crown. Had he retained any substantial property in the country he would not have had to avail himself of the provisions of the Poor Prisoners' Defence Act. But he was within the sphere of the spirit of the judgment. Joyce disappeared from England at some time between August 29, 1939—when he issued an order dissolving the National Socialist League, the Fascist organization of which he was the head—and September 18, when he entered the service of the German radio. He was the holder of a British passport; it was part of his lifelong masquerade as a British subject. He had declared on the application papers that he had been born in Galway, and had not "lost the status of British subject thus acquired". He obtained this passport on the 6th of July 1933, and there is perhaps some significance in that date. He had become a member of the British Fascists in 1923, when he was seventeen, but had left this organization after two years, to become later an active member of the Conservative Party. In January 1933 Hitler seized power, and later in the year Mosley formed the British Union of Fascists, which William Joyce joined. This passport was, like all British passports, valid for five years. When July 1938 came round he let it lapse, but applied on September 24, 1938, for a renewal for the customary period of one year; and there is, perhaps, some significance in that date also, for the Munich Agreement was signed on the 29th of September. The next year he was careful not to let it lapse. He made an application for renewal over a month before its expiry on the 24th of August 1939, and there was certainly some significance in that date, for war broke out on the 3rd of September. Each of these renewals was dated as if the application had been made when the passport expired. So when William Joyce went to Germany he was the holder of a British passport which was valid until the beginning of July 1940. That was why the third count of an indictment charged him with committing high treason by broadcasting between "the eighteenth day of September 1939, and on divers other days thereafter, and between that day and the second day of July 1940, being then to wit, on the said several days, a person owing allegiance to our lord the King". It was, in fact, the case for the prosecution that a person obtaining a passport placed himself thereby under the protection of the Crown and owed it allegiance until the passport expired.

No ruling on the point existed, because no case of treason involving temporary allegiance had been tried during the comparatively recent period when passports, in their modern sense, have been in use, so the judge had to make a new ruling; and for one sultry afternoon and a sultrier morning the prosecuting and defending counsel bobbed up and down in front of the bench, putting the arguments for and against the broadening of the law by inclusion of this modern circumstance. People with legal minds were entranced, and others slept. Joyce enjoyed this part of the trial very much, and frequently passed down to his counsel notes that were characteristically odd. Like all prisoners in the dock, he had been given octavo sheets to write on, and could certainly have had as many as he wanted. But when he wrote a note he tore off irregularly shaped pieces and covered them with grotesquely large handwriting, so large that it could be read by people sitting in the gallery. One ended with the words, "but it is not important". His enjoyment of the argument was not unnatural in one who loved complications, for no stage of it was simple. Much depended on the nature of a passport, and this had never been defined by the law, for a passport has been different things at different times and has never been merely one thing at a time. It was originally a licence given by the Crown to a subject who wished to leave the realm, an act as a rule prohibited because it deprived the King of a man's military services; but it was also a licence given to an alien to travel through the realm; and it was a pass given to soldiers going home on leave, or paupers discharged from a hospital. Through the ages it changed its character to a demand by the issuing state that the person and property of one of its subjects shall be respected by other states when he travels in their realms; a voucher of his respectability, demanded by the states he intends to visit, as a precaution against crime and political conspiracy; and a source of revenue to the states, which charged heavily for such permits. But of its protective nature in our day there can be little doubt, since the preamble on every passport announces that "we", the Foreign Secretary of the day, "request and require in the Name of His Majesty all those whom it may concern to allow the bearer to pass freely without let or hindrance, and to afford him or her every assistance and protection of which he or she may stand in need". In 1905 the Lord Chief Justice of that day, Lord Alverstone, defined a passport as "a document, issued in the name of a Sovereign, on the responsibility of a Minister of the Crown, to a named individual, intended to be presented to the governments of foreign nations and to be used for that individual's protection as a British subject in foreign countries".

The arguments that Joyce's counsel brought against the obvious inference were peculiarly masculine; they were tainted with that decadence which befalls all human activities, art, literature, science, medicine, and law, when the game becomes less important than the rules. This was not due to the imperfection of Mr. Slade's mind, which is an admirable machine. It happened because the case against Joyce rested on principles evolved in the classic phases of the law, when rules were laid down in order that the game should be the more sporting. The argument that William Joyce, an alien by birth who had acquired a temporary and local allegiance, extended its sphere by taking a passport with him when he went to the Continent could not be met on its own plane of forthrightness. It had to be met by the incomplete plea that a British court has no right to try an alien for a crime committed abroad, which was obviously true, but not applicable, since William Joyce was not simply an alien, he was an alien who had acquired a temporary allegiance to Great Britain. This plea involved maintaining that a temporary allegiance could in no circumstances be carried over by an alien to the Continent, that he must divest himself of it by the mere act of passing beyond the three-mile territorial limit; which committed Mr. Slade to the view that an alien who had been a resident of England and was the holder of a British passport could pop across the Channel, conspire with an enemy of England at Calais, and pop back again, not only once but hundreds of times, and never be tried for treason, because at three miles' distance from Dover he lost his duty of allegiance.

There was another fantastic argument which was appropriate to the case, because it went back to the Ireland of Michael Joyce and the transatlantic journeys made alike by his kind and their enemies. Just after the 1914-18 war an Irishman named Johnson, who was a naturalized American, returned to Ireland and took part in the treasonable activities of the Sinn Fein. He was discovered, and some property of his was confiscated by the government as "an act of State", which is a process not applicable to British subjects but only to aliens. He then sued for the return of his property on the ground that an act of State could not be directed against a friendly alien resident in Great Britain; to which the government replied that, whatever rights a friendly alien might enjoy through residence in Great Britain, he had forfeited them by reason of his treasonable activities. The point was in fact never decided by the judges who tried it, obviously because they regarded the proceedings of the rebel Johnson and the civil servant who had confiscated his property as equally anarchic. But on the basis of the civil servant's defence Mr. Slade argued that whatever protection had been afforded to Joyce by his British passport he must have lost the moment he began to commit treason by aiding the Germans. However, he also argued that Joyce's passport could give him no protection, because he had acquired it by a false statement; yet it was hard to see how it could fail to protect him until the fraud was discovered and the passport was withdrawn. Supposing that William Joyce had fallen out with the Germans during 1940 and had become a civil internee, he could have called on the assistance of the Swiss Embassy in Berlin, as Switzerland was "the protective power" appointed to safeguard the interests of Britons in hostile territory during wartime.

All this filigree work delighted the little man in the dock, who watched his lawyers with a cynical brightness, as if he were interested in seeing whether they could get away with all this nonsense but had no warmer concern with the proceedings. He showed no special excitement, only a continuance of amused curiosity, when, on the third day of the trial, at the end of the morning, the judge announced that he would give his ruling on these legal submissions after the luncheon interval; and at two o'clock returned to the dock still with his usual eccentric excess

27

of military smartness and this sustained tight-lipped derisiveness. The judge announced that "beyond a shadow of doubt" William Joyce had owed allegiance to the Crown of this country when he applied for his passport, and that nothing had happened to put an end to that allegiance during the period when the passport was valid. In other words, he ruled that a person holding a British passport owed allegiance to the Crown even when he was outside the realm. This ruling made it quite certain that William Joyce was going to be sentenced to death; and if the sentence were carried out he would die the most completely unnecessary death that any criminal has ever died on the gallows. He was the victim of his own and his father's lifelong determination to lie about their nationality. For if he had not renewed his English passport, and had left England for Germany on the American passport which was rightfully his, no power on earth could have touched him. As he became a German citizen by naturalization before America came into the war, he could never have been the subject of prosecution under the American laws of treason.

Now it was certain that the little man was to be sentenced to death; and nobody in court felt any emotion whatsoever. That was what made this case more terrible than any other case that any of us could remember in which a death sentence was passed: it was not terrible at all. People wanted Joyce to pay the proper legal penalty for his treason, but not because they felt any personal hatred against him. They wanted to be sure that in any other war this peculiarly odious form of treachery, which climbed into the ears of frightened people, would be discouraged before it began, and that was about the limit of their interest in the matter. At no other such trial have the spectators, as soon as the jury went out to consider their verdict and the judge retired from the bench and the prisoner was taken down to the cells, got up from their seats and strolled about and chattered as if they were at a theatre between the acts. At no other such trial have the jury come back from considering their verdict looking as if they had been out for a cup of tea. At no other such trial has the judge assumed the black cap—which is not a cap at all but a piece of black cloth that an attendant lays across his wig—as if it were in fact just a piece of black cloth laid across his wig. He spoke the words of the sentence of death reverently, and they were awful, as they always must be: "William Joyce, the sentence of the Court upon you is, that you be taken from this place to a lawful prison, and thence to a place of execution, and that you be there hanged by the neck until you be dead; and that your body be afterwards buried within the precincts of the prison in which you shall have been confined before your execution. And may the Lord have mercy on your soul."

But the effect of these words was, on this uniquely shallow occasion, soon dispersed. It was indeed pitiful when Joyce was asked if he wanted to make a statement before sentence was passed on him, and he shook his head, the hungry and inordinate voice in him at last defeated. He had been even more pitiful earlier in the trial, when the judge had warned the jury to consider very carefully their verdict because a person found guilty must be sentenced to death, for he had put up his hand and touched his neck with a look of wonder. But that he deserved pity was noted by the intellect; pity was not felt. Nor was anybody in the court very much moved by the extreme courage with which he bore himself, though that was remarkable. He listened to the sentence with his head high, gave one of his absurd stiff bows, and ran down to the cells, smiling and waving to his brother and his friends, acting gaiety without a flaw. Such a performance would once have moved us, but not now. All has changed; and even a trial for a capital offence is quite different from what it was before the war. Then the spectators were living in a state of security, and the prisoner was an exceptionally unfortunate person who had strayed into a district not generally visited, perhaps for lack of boldness. But every man and woman who attended Joyce's trial had at some time during the past six years been in danger of undeserved death or pain, and had shown, or witnessed in others enduring such peril, great courage. These attributes in William Joyce made no claim on them, themselves pitiful and brave; and he could not arouse their interest by his exceptional destiny, since he was in the dock by reason of failure to acquit himself in their common destiny. So they turned away from him and left the court as if it had been a cinema or concert. But in the dark corridor a woman said: "I am glad his mother's dead. She lived near us in Dulwich. She was a sweet little lady, a tiny little woman.

I often used to stand with her in the fish queue. In fact, that's how I met her. One day after the blitz had been very bad, I said something about that blasted Lord Haw-Haw, and someone said, 'Hush, that's his mother right beside you', and I felt dreadful. But she only said—but she was ever so Irish, and I can't speak like she did—'Never mind, my dear, I'm sure you didn't mean it unkindly'." This story recalled the lilt of affection in the aged Mr. Holland's voice when he had spoken of Queenie.

The dark corridor passed to a twilit landing. Down a shadowed staircase the band of Fascists were descending, tears shining on their astonished faces. Joyce's brother walked slowly, his eyes that were soft and brown like a cow's now narrowed and wet, and the slight blond solicitor just behind him. There was a block, and for a minute the crowd all stood still. The solicitor plucked at Quentin Joyce's jacket and said kindly, "This is just what he expected, you know". "Yes," said his brother, "I know it's just what he expected." The crowd moved on, but after it had gone down a few steps the solicitor plucked at the young man's jacket again and said, "It's the appeal that matters, you know", and Quentin said, "Yes, I know. The appeal's everything."

At the counter where the spectators had to collect their umbrellas and coats, the charming jurywoman was saying good-bye to one of her colleagues. They were shaking hands warmly and expressing hopes that they would meet again. They might have been people parting after a cruise. Jostling them were the Fascists, waiting for their raincoats, garments which those of their guild affect in all weathers, in imitation of Hitler. The young man who looked like a gipsy held his head down. Heavy tears were hanging on his long black lashes. He and his friends still looked amazed. They had wanted people to die by violence, but they had not expected the lot to fall on any of their own number. Another dark and passionate young man was accosted by a reporter, and he cried out in rage that he had been four years in Brixton Jail under Security Regulation 18B, all for patriotism, and he had come out to see the persecution of the finest patriot of all. His black eyes rolled and blazed about him. They fell on another bystander, who was not the best person to receive his complaint, for her name had been on the Gestapo list, recently discovered in Berlin, of persons who were to be arrested immediately after the Germans conquered England, and it was doubtful, had this happened, if it would have led to anything so comfortable as four years in Brixton Jail. But the bystander did not blaze back at him. Not possibly could she have achieved this force. There was this new universality of horrible experience, these vast common martyrdoms, that made these unhappy egotists, insisting on their own particular revolts and heroisms, seem so pathetically obsolete. Not with any degree of picturesque intensity could the bystander have struck an attitude on the ground that she was on that Gestapo list, because about twenty-three hundred other people had also been on it.

The little band of Fascists gathered together in a knot by the door, and after they had wiped their faces and composed themselves, they went out into the street. In the open space in front of the building was a line of parked cars, and behind them stood a crowd of silent people. The Fascists walked away from this crowd, down a street that narrowed and lost itself in a network of alleys. Nobody followed them, but they began to hurry. By the time they got into the shelter of the alleys, they were almost running.

II

THE fight between the Crown and William Joyce over the continuance of the breath that shook his flimsy little body was waged throughout four months and all across London. It began in the golden warmth of September in the Old Bailey, and his case was reviewed during some bright November days by the Court of Appeal, in another damaged building, the Royal Courts of Justice, usually called the Law Courts. The Court of Appeal confirmed the sentence of death. Then Joyce took his last chance and appealed to the House of Lords, and there for a week stood his trial, in the precincts of Westminster Palace, which, still hugger-mugger within from bomb damage, looked across the river through the light December mists at one of the most moving memorials of the blitz, St. Thomas's Hospital, still operating but hideous in dilapidation.

The forms of the law, changing with each stage of the case, symbolized the increasing intensity of Joyce's ordeal. In the first trial, he faced one judge as he stood in the dock, with a wide court behind him, where numbers of his supporters formed groups expressing apostolic grief and loyalty. In the Court of Appeal, which is a simple, small, square library lined with law books, three judges faced him, and his supporters no longer were numerous enough, or distant enough, to be seen as a group of wild and unhappy young men in Hitler raincoats with a look of Irishry about them, but appeared as individuals. One could note the weak eye glaring in imitation of the two dictators, forgetful that they had both died in disgrace, and other features bespeaking the soul who, being nothing, passionately wanted to be something. Last of all, in the House of Lords, there were five judges to try the prisoner, and the most restricted and remote accommodation for spectators. Only his brother and his two best friends were present in court, and they were hidden from him. Nor would it have profited him if he could have seen them, for they were by this time neither a group nor individuals but personifications of anxiety. While the forms of the law changed round Joyce in the courts, the hatred against him in the world outside remained constant and severe. It was related to the ruin that had touched and surrounded every building in which he was tried. The people remembered that while they had fought fires and lost their kin and homes, a man who had lived all his life amongst them had mocked at their misery and rejoiced at the thought of their deliverance to their enemies. Those of us who attended the trials heard—if we mentioned to casual acquaintances, hairdressers and porters and shop-assistants, what we were doing—a monotonous, unimpassioned, but definite hope that he would not escape the gallows.

Joyce experienced a considerable change of architectural environment in the course of the trials. The Old Bailey is the standard official building that people liked putting up in the first twenty-five years of this century, whether in London or Paris or Berlin or Washington—unimaginative but well adapted to its purposes. What an advance that represented could be seen when the case went to our preposterous Law Courts. Erected in the full frenzy of the Victorian passion for the Gothic, the building is a swollen replica of a mediaeval monastery. The lofty but obscure hall, which is used for no purpose whatsoever except to exhibit a few small notices, is, as it were, an abbey church; and many of the officials have to work underneath it in a crypt. The Press Association is to be found down there, functioning in a monastic cell. Upstairs, curved and vaulted staircases lead to side chapels, which are the courts, and to other apartments that are all strictly loyal to the prevailing fantasy. Even the ladies' room preserves an ecclesiastical appearance, and is presided over by a woman with a dedicated air, whose costume blends the concepts of a wardress and a nun. She lingers in the memory because of her exceptional amiability. Many of the other officials and attendants have been infected by the oddity of their surroundings, and resemble the more resistant characters in Dickens. They were discouraging to the press, discouraging to Ministries which rang them up for seats for distinguished foreign journalists, discouraging to the general public who exercised their right to hear the case.

Down at the House of Lords it was very different. Corporeally the Houses of Parliament are a muddle of exquisite mediaeval architecture and capable but mediocre Victorian Gothic. They have been constructed according to the needs of the passing centuries, with occasional cancellations owing to fire and accident. Of the three places where Joyce was tried, it was the only one which was fully alive, alive like an old English or American house where sensible and pleasant people had lived for centuries, adapting it according to the knowledge of their generations. It was impossible to frequent the House of Lords without growing fond of it and being compelled to laugh aloud at it. Being alive, it presented the unpredictable quality of life. Yes, even at its threshold; for in the queue which waited every day at the entrance for admission to the public gallery were many African Negroes and Hindus, including some young women, very pretty and shapely in saris. Nothing seemed more unhappily clear than that these must be discontented members of the British Empire's subject races, sympathetically attending the trial of a fellow-rebel. But eavesdropping showed that they belonged to that large class of person, to be found in all races, which delights in the technicalities of Western Law for their own sake, and would exchange a native dance or the Taj Mahal any day for a good tort. They were interested in Joyce only as a golfer might be in a ball that has taken up an unusual position in the rough.

Each day of the third trial the spectators went up a stone

staircase to a lobby full of gossiping lawyers, outside the chamber where the Lords were meeting temporarily, because they had given their chamber over to the Commons whose home had been damaged by a bomb. They were then taken in hand by the attendants of the House of Lords, a body of spare and anonymous-looking men in ordinary white-tie evening dress, with the silver-gilt badge of the Royal Arms worn at the waistline. These men are a race apart, resembling the djinns in the *Arabian Nights*, though the magic never breaks down into malice. Their drill is perfect, their courtesy never cracks, and since they belong to a supernatural order, they see no difference between the children of men and are no respecters of persons. Nothing could have been more determined yet detached than their ejection of the wife of a judge, and a very important judge too, who had usurped the seat allotted to a not at all important young journalist. They owe their strongly individual character to the circumstance that they are employed by the Lord Chamberlain, one of the three great officers of the Royal Household. This is much more than it sounds. His office is a department of state, like the War Office or the Admiralty, and it administers all the royal palaces and the establishments, such as the Houses of Parliament, which pertain to the Crown not only in the person of the King but in its impersonal existence as the supreme authority of the state. This department is conducted with remarkable efficiency, owing to the very long shadow cast by the shortest of our English sovereigns. The Royal Household was pulled out of a state of squalid and spendthrift confusion by Queen Victoria; and ever since it has been run on decorous and economical lines which at once would be a credit to the state and avoid extravagance.

The attendants, who were under the supervision of a most elegant retired general, whose appearance and manners would have delighted Ouida, shepherded all the pressmen and the prisoner's friends into the Royal Gallery, a hall conceived and executed in the brownest style of Victorian architecture. There is the same feeling that everything rich, and not just plum cake, should be dark. On the walls, strips of mulberry-and-gold brocade divide vast blackish frescoes in which a welter of arms and legs set at every angle around a few war horses suggests military effort; about the doors are dingy gilded figures of kings and queens;

and in an alcove two toga-clad figures, quite black, though obviously they represent persons belonging to the white race, make expansive political gestures of a meliorist type. Here is demonstrated the unity of the English-speaking world. This is the matrix from which the brownstone houses of New York proceeded. But there is something newer and sadder. In one corner there is a glass-covered show table, in which there lies a book inscribed with the names of all the peers and their sons who were killed in the 1914-18 war. Each day a fresh page is turned. It has the heartrending quality, more unhappy than normal grief, which pertains to all memorials of the First World War.

Every morning, while we waited, a bishop in black robes and huge white lawn sleeves hovered at the door of the chamber in which the Lords sit, ready to go in and say the prayers which open the day's session, until an attendant cried, "Make way for the Mace!" and we were all ordered off the strip of oatmeal matting which runs across the ugly tiled floor. Then a procession came in, never quite at ease, it was so small and had never had enough start to get up the processional spirit. The Serjeant-at-Arms came first, carrying the great golden pepper-pot on a stalk, which is the Mace. Another attendant followed, carrying a purse embroidered with the Royal Arms, representing the Great Seal. Then came the Lord Chancellor, Lord Jowitt, one of the handsomest men in London, superb in his white full-bottomed wig, its curls lying in rows on his shoulders, and wearing a long black silk gown with a train carried by an attendant. He carried between the forefinger and thumb of each hand his black velvet cap. The ritual is not mere foolishness. The procession and the symbols are a mnemonic guide to the constitutional functions of the House of Lords, and are part of a complicated convention into which most of the legislative and judicial activities of Parliament fit conveniently enough, and which nobody would much care to rewrite, in view of the trickiness of procedure.

We had to stand a long time after that, for the opening prayers are lengthy. Around the room ran a shiny quilted red-leather bench—broken by ugly drab radiators—but nobody ever sat on it except Joyce's solicitor, that slight and reflective figure. He looked much older than he had at the first trial, and, indeed, was to die not long after; and it is not easy to estimate what it

35

must have cost him to have conducted for four months, with an efficiency which was remarked on by all the lawyers who followed the case, the difficult defence of one whose opinions cannot have been attractive to him and whom he had never chosen to defend. He did not seem quite so friendly as he had been with William Joyce's brother Quentin, who also looked much older. At the Old Bailey he had been a fresh-faced boy, seeming younger than his twenty-eight years. Now he might have been forty. Deep furrows had appeared in his forehead, and his eyes were small and sunken, and, in the morning, red with weeping. His face was bloated with grief and he had put on weight. With him were two friends: tall, gaunt Angus MacNab, ex-internee, who was plainly superior in education and social standing to his companions—the cranky gentleman so often, as Henry Adams complained, produced by the British people; and a young Fascist of Scottish origin, whose remote grey-blue eyes showed that he had escaped from the world into his dreams, which were not wider and kinder than the existence around us, as the dreams of most people are, but narrower and more troubled. All three were lifted to the heights of dignity by their grief for William Joyce, whom assuredly they were mourning as the early Christians might have mourned a brother about to go into the arena.

Some rumour of this cult had been spreading abroad since the trial began. The City of London greatly respected a certain aged stockbroker, belonging to a solid Scottish family, who conducted a large business with the strictest probity and was known to his friends as a collector of silver and glass and a connoisseur of wine. He had a beautiful house, which was kept for him by his sister, a tall and handsome maiden lady given to piety and good works, whose appearance was made remarkable by an immense knot of hair twisted on the nape of her neck in the mid-Victorian way. The old man's last years were afflicted by a depressing illness, during which he formed a panic dread of socialism, and for this reason he fell under the influence of Sir Oswald Mosley, to whom he gave a considerable amount of money and whose followers he often entertained. This is a repulsive thought when it is remembered that many of those followers were very ugly scoundrels; one was prosecuted for living on the earnings of a prostitute. The old man had a special fondness for William Joyce, who, being a lively, wisecracking, practical-joking little creature, as well as intelligent, was able to cheer up an invalid; and after his death his sister, who carried on all his enthusiasms, treated Joyce like a son. She let him use her country house as a meeting-place for the heads of his organization, and entertained him there so often that it was one of the first places searched by the police at the outbreak of war when they found that Joyce had left his home.

This woman, then over eighty and crippled by a painful disease, rose from her bed to travel up to London, an apocalyptic figure, tall and bowed, the immense knot of hair behind her head shining snow-white, and went to see William Joyce in prison. She returned weeping but uplifted by his courage and humility and his forgiveness of his enemies and his faith in the righteousness of his cause. To all those whom she especially loved she sat down and wrote letters describing her visit to this holy and persecuted man which truly might have wrung the heart, and she followed them with copies of the letters that he wrote to her from prison, in which he said that he knew well that the issue of his trial might be against him but was not dismayed, since he could think of no better death than dying for his faith. These pretensions on behalf of a man who worked to enable Hitler and Goering to set up Nazism in England were obviously fantastic, and there was only a minute and crazed fraction of the population which would accept them. Yet there was, as could be seen from day to day during these trials, some reference to reality in these pretensions, though the difficulty of seeing that, or anything else relating to the trial, in the House of Lords was very considerable.

While the Commons were sitting in the House of Lords, the Lords sat in the Robing Room used by the King and Queen at the Coronation and the opening of Parliament. This had been hastily converted into a copy of the old House of Lords, though it is no bigger than the big hall of an ordinary secondary school, and has no gallery for the press or the public. The improvisation had not been very successful. The spectators climbed a staircase steep as a ship's companion-way and found a small shelf with two tiers of seats for the press and a third for the press or the public, from which nothing whatever could be seen of the Joyce trial. Instead, they could see very clearly, were indeed forced into intimacy with, some of the most horrible

Edwardian frescoes imaginable. All that could be said for them was that they were appropriate to a chamber that was to be used as the House of Lords, in view of the notorious obsessional devotion of the British aristocracy to the horse. That had been traceable outside in the Royal Gallery, for in the blackish frescoes the horses had been the only living creatures which in a scene of catastrophe had remained the right way up. Within, the tribute was even more ardent. The fresco beside the gallery had the word "Hospitality" written underneath it, and showed a lot of people in old Covent Garden Wagnerian costumes on the set which the Covent Garden management always used when an abbey was needed, all of them welcoming a man who, oddly enough, was riding in on a horse. But that was not really hospitality. They were plainly glad to see him because he was riding a horse. Behind the gallery the word "Generosity" was written under a fresco showing a horseman refraining from killing a man lying on the ground, on the advice of his horse, who was turning an elder-statesman muzzle toward him. There was a horse in every fresco except one, in which there was a divine person instead.

As well as the frescoes, the spectators could see the two royal thrones at the end of the Chamber—the Queen's carefully built a little lower than the King's—raised on a dais with two steps. In front of the thrones, on the floor of the house, was the Wool-sack, a red, stuffed *pouf* on which the Mace was lying; during normal sessions of the House the Lord Chancellor sits on it. On the floor of the House there is also a table covered with very new and bright red leather, at which a clerk in wig and gown sat throughout the trial, cutting up paper with scissors as if he were preparing to amuse an infinite number of children. Running lengthwise on each side of the floor were the three rows of benches on which the peers sit, and there some were sitting. But they were no part of Joyce's trial, they were spectators like the rest of us. For though a prisoner appeals to the whole House of Lords for judgment on his case, the House refers the matter to a small committee of judges, drawn from a panel of law lords. In Joyce's case these judges numbered four, with the Lord Chancellor as a fifth. The counsel address this com-mittee not on the floor of the House but from the bar of the House, and the committee sits at a table close to the bar. The improvised gallery was over the bar of the House. To follow the case the spectators had to listen to a thin thread of sound emitted by invisible speakers under their feet. Quentin Joyce had to partake in this general inconvenience. Surely Hell could provide no greater torture than to follow thus a brother's destiny.

Yet there was something to be seen before one went up to one's seat. Pausing at the foot of the steep staircase and looking across the twilit space under the gallery, one saw the barristers, in wig and gown, silhouetted against the brightness of the lit chamber beyond, their faces turned towards that one of their number who stood speaking to the Lord Chancellor in his robes, sitting at his table with the four old judges who were dressed in lounge suits and swathed in steamer rugs against the bitter cold. In the furthest corner of the darkness under the gallery, with four warders to guard him, was William Joyce, his face altered by new wisdom and as yellow with prison pallor as if it were stamped on a gold coin. Time had acted on him during the trials as strongly as on his brother, but differently. Some of the change had been wrought by the eye of the beholder. At the Old Bailey he had seemed meanly and repulsively ugly. At the Law Courts, where he appeared before the Court of Appeal, he was not so. He was certainly puny and colourless, but his face had an amusing, pleasant, even prettyish, character. It was not good-looking, but it could be imagined that people who knew him well would find it easy to believe him far better-looking than he was, although he would probably make no such reciprocal generosity, for his own vice was plainly the icy coldness of the charmer. The alteration in effect was in part due to a considerable improvement in his health. He had arrived in England shabby and tousled and sickly, pulled down by the hardships of his months of homelessness between his last broadcast and his arrest and by the wound in his leg; but during his imprisonment he had eaten well and slept soundly, and was said to be the only prisoner who had ever consistently put on weight while under sentence of death. But the alteration in effect was also due in part to the circumstance that, while he had sat at the Old Bailey with the right side of his face towards most of the spectators, at the Law Courts he had turned the left side towards the court, and the left side was unscarred. The cut that had run from the lobe of his right ear to the right corner of his mouth had not only left a scar, it had destroyed the moulding and meaning of that side of his face.

He had received this wound during the years of adolescence, when pride and self-doubt fuse into anxious vanity. For he was full of pride in the sense of impatience with anything less than glory. That was written in his early letter to the secretary of the Committee for Military Education, and it was shown in the course of his education. His first bent was scientific, but when he sat for his Intermediate Science at the age of seventeen he failed in two subjects, and though this was natural enough, as his schooling had been interrupted by the family's hegira from Ireland to Lancashire and London, he turned his back on science and studied for a degree in arts. To cause him self-doubt, there was his tiny stature and his love of women. The scar, when it was new and red, must have been a terrifying disfigurement. It was another handicap which he had to overcome, for which he had to compensate. More fuel was given to his huge ambition, and he was committed to a certain career. It is not certain just how he received this wound. At the time he suffered the injury he was a student at Battersea Polytechnic, and it was then believed by his fellow-students and at least one of the staff that he had either been slashed with a razor or mauled with the leg of a chair by a Communist in a street-fight arising from a British Fascist meeting. It is also true that on one occasion he allowed it to be supposed, by a friend who had known him during the "troubles" in Galway, that he owed his scar to a wound inflicted by Sinn Feiners who had attacked him and his father in London.

Whoever followed William Joyce from the Old Bailey to the Law Courts found themselves thinking of him no longer as base and shabby, but as damaged and deformed. For, of course, it had not mattered how much he hungered for glory, how he cancelled the disadvantages of pygmyhood by courage and learning and the use of his prodigious voice. There was something there which would have been a bar between him and advancement, whatever he had made of himself. There was no harm in what he wanted to do; he wanted to help administer our complex social system for the benefit of the community; but few would not have felt panic at the idea of trusting William Joyce with such a task. It was obvious he could never have been trusted not to make a mistake, of such grossness as the mistake which led him, loving England, to plan her salvation through subjugation to the architects of Belsen and Buchenwald. There was at some point a partial blackness, as of a perforated ear-drum or a detached retina, and the consequence was barbarity. This was apparent even when the unscarred side of his face revealed his humour and acuteness, to a degree that was remarkable. Prisoners in the dock laugh more freely than is generally imagined; judicial jokes which so often annoy the newspaper reader are to them an opportunity for relaxation. But Joyce's amusement at his own appeal was more subtle than that. One of the judges on the bench was most picturesquely comic in appearance and might have come straight out of the *commedia dell' arte*. William Joyce watched him with delight; and he followed the legal arguments with an unusual detachment, once nodding in approval when a point was decided against him.

But here at the House of Lords he had endured a further change. He had still his humour and his love of glory. Every morning he was taken into the court while the public still waited for admission, and he never failed to express to his warders, laughing at himself but nevertheless making an honest confession, how much he enjoyed making this ceremonial entrance to the Mother of Parliaments. He still followed the legal argument with a bright eye. But the long contemplation of death had given him a dignity and refinement that he had lacked before. It could be recognized when he turned his eyes on the spectators who paused to look at him before they went up to their seats in the gallery. At the Old Bailey he had soon come to recognize those who were sitting through the whole trial, and it had entertained him to catch their eyes and stare them out. At the Court of Appeal he had more effectively, though involuntarily, disconcerted the gaze of the critical by the evident coincidence of his field of reference with what they could have claimed for their own. That he was a civilized man, however aberrant, was somehow clear before our eyes, and mournful. At the House of Lords he had gone past comparison, looking at us from a territory governed by another time than ours, and listening to the striking of an hour that had not yet struck for us.

The lawyers swung their argument back and forth for four

days. It was difficult to follow the unseen speakers, because what could be seen was often incongruous enough to be captivating. Mid-mornings, a stately attendant glided across the scene of baronial pomp bearing a very common little tea-tray for the comfort of the shivering judges. Peers dropped in to listen and sat about on the red rep benches, some of their eldest sons exercised their curious right to sit on the steps of the dais beneath the thrones. One peer lived through a most painful moment of his life during the trial. Following an intricate point, he ran his finger thoughtfully up and down behind the lapel of his coat, but suddenly stopped. A look of agony passed over his face, and he turned back the lapel. He had found a moth hole and for a long time was unable to think about William Joyce. But our attention was always drawn back by the unfolding story, which became more ironical each time it was restated in court, of a man who was being strangled by the sheer tortuousness of his family destiny. He was an American by birth who, by his father's wish, had pretended all his life to be British. Why? In the third trial, as in the first and the second, that question was never answered. It had become more perplexing as more knowledge about William Joyce had come into currency. He had stood as a candidate at a London County Council election and had at that time had to declare that he was a British subject; and that false declaration might have brought on him, had he been elected, a fine of £50 for every occasion on which he had sat on the council. Why did the father—who by all accounts loved his eldest son very dearly, and must have acquired a reasonable notion of the law's view of such ongoings in the course of his life as a close friend of the British Police government of Ireland —keep his own and his family's status as close a secret as if their lives depended on it? But perhaps they did. Such hooded figures live in a land not ruled by likelihood. This mysterious imposture, and this alone, brought Joyce to the gallows. The arguments of his counsel could not disguise the ineluctable process.

The legal content of each of the trials was slightly different; different as, say, three performances of the same piano concerto by the same conductor and the same soloist but by three separate orchestras. The thematic material and the harmonies were the same, but the interpretation varied; and the conditions of the

second and third trials permitted the polish that comes of prolonged rehearsal. At the Old Bailey the fantastic novelty of the
case and the disturbing excitement of the presence of the Judas
whose voice we knew so well, overwhelmed the court, and the
proceedings were disordered in their spontaneity. It was not
surprising that the shorthand notes of Mr. Justice Tucker's address
to the jury should have read as strangely as this:

Now as you have been very rightly told and reminded—you
have been told already once—William Joyce would play a very
small part in the world's history, and our demeanour, the way
we comport ourselves in the proceedings in this case, is of greater
importance to us than is William Joyce—observations that are
very true, but I only add this, that it is not only the way we out-
wardly comport ourselves in the proceedings in this court, but it
applies, and applies with even greater force, to the way you
comport yourselves when you retire to consider your verdict, to
be sure that you arrive at what you honestly believe to be a true
verdict according to the facts, regardless of opinion or anything
of that kind, and it applies to me in the very responsible decisions
of law that I have had to come to in this case.

The contentions on which Mr. Slade asked the Court of Appeal
to reverse the verdict returned at this initiatory trial were four,
and of these, three were repetitions of the legalistic ingenuities
which had been brought forward in Joyce's defence at the earlier
trial. The court, it was said, had wrongly assumed jurisdiction to
try an alien for an offence against British law committed in a
foreign country. Second, the learned judge was wrong in law in
holding, and misdirected the jury in directing them, that the appellant owed allegiance to His Majesty the King during the period
from the 18th of September 1939 to the 2nd of July 1940. (Because he had gone out of the country and had not left his family
and effects behind him.) Third, there was no evidence that the
renewal of the appellant's passport afforded him, or was capable
of affording him, any protection, or that the appellant ever availed
himself or had any intention of availing himself of such protection.
This third contention was argued on grounds which seemed to the
lay mind curiously frivolous. Contrary to vulgar opinion, it is
rare that what is said in a court of law runs directly counter to

common sense, although the manner of saying it may be excessively cautious or stuccoed and cockle-shelled with obsolescence. But this argument propounded something sillier than our human custom; we do not live our daily lives on the plane where it would be true that the protection which attracted allegiance was not protection *de facto* but protection *de jure*, not actual protection but the right to it, and that therefore a man who obtained a passport by fraud (as Joyce had done) would not owe allegiance in return for the protection he derived from it. According to this line of argument, a man who fraudulently obtained a British passport was in a better position than a man who obtained it legally, because he had to give nothing in return. The obvious way for the community to handle such a situation would be to prove that he had obtained the passport illegally and deprive him of it but make him discharge all the responsibilities he had incurred by possessing it up till the time when he forfeited it. Another submission made by Mr. Slade maintained that the moment the holder of a passport committed treason the power which granted the passport withdrew its protection, as the passport-holder had failed in his allegiance and therefore had no claim on the corresponding protection. This was obviously a catch, a Christmas-party riddle which had lost its way and could only have been made tolerable by mince pies and kissing under the mistletoe. The judge who looked like a character in the *commedia dell' arte* thought little of this point; he puffed out his cheeks and spouted out air through his leathery old lips as if he were a dolphin. William Joyce watched him with a lively delight.

The fourth contention related to the oddly incoherent summing-up of the judge at the Old Bailey. If there were any evidence that the renewal of William Joyce's passport had afforded him any protection, or was capable of doing so, and that he had ever availed himself of this protection, or had tried to do so, it was for the jury to decide whether this evidence was true, and the judge had failed to direct them on this issue. There was much more substance in this contention than in any of the others, or, rather, it seemed to be so; for its plausibility arose from the impotence of the written word to convey the significance of an occasion determined by speech. At the Old Bailey, Mr. Justice Tucker had said to the jury: "My duty is to tell you what I believe

44

to be the law on the subject, and that you have to accept from me, provided you believe the facts about the passport, going abroad, and so forth. If you do not believe that, you are entitled to reject it and say so, because you are not bound to believe everything, but if you accept the uncontradicted evidence that has been given, then, in my view, that shows that this man at the material time owed allegiance to the British Crown." None of us who had sat through the trial had the faintest doubt that he was directing the jury that they must decide whether they did believe or not that William Joyce had gone abroad with a British passport and had retained it for use. In the psychological situation built up by the arguments and personalities of the figures involved, those words had that meaning and none other. But when those words lay cold on the typewritten or printed page, they looked vague and perfunctory. Nevertheless, though the argument had that much in its favour, Mr. Slade dwelt on it only briefly, and the judges did hardly more than mention it in a judgment that was a workmanlike essay on the two sorts of allegiance.

There in the House of Lords there was being given a performance far finer than the highest level of the proceedings in the Court of Appeal: as far superior to that, as that had been superior to the Old Bailey. When these four old judges had a passage with counsel, it was as good as first-class tennis. They had been chosen for this work because they had supremely good minds, as well as the physiological luck that makes a man able to go on through the seventies into the eighties doing what he has done all his life better and better, even though he may not be able to address himself to new tasks or work continuously. The voice of each old man was characteristic enough to be easily identifiable, and often, in the quieter moments, recalled what was generally known about him. One amongst them had a small manor house set in a forest lying under the Wiltshire Downs. He lived there with a wife much younger than himself, who was perhaps the most celebrated professional horsewoman in England. At night he sat at his end of the table surrounded by his pupils, who had come to learn from him the subtlest mysteries of the law, and she sat at her end surrounded by her pupils, who had come to learn from her the subtlest mysteries of fox-hunting

45

and horse-breaking. The two groups were hardly able to communicate with each other, owing to the extreme specialization of each, but, as there is nothing so civilizing as scholarship and craftsmanship which have not lost touch with life, the judge and his wife lived together in the most agreeable amity. Again, as at all trials of Fascists, there was suddenly audible the discord of natural injustice which is ordinarily silenced by the artificial harmonies of civilization. These old men's lives were pressed down and running over with earned honours and sagely contrived pleasures; the young man sitting next to me, whose sports jacket was too brightly checked in crimson and emerald green and cream, whose head was held too cockily, whose face was too coldly fierce to permit confidence, was empty with an emptiness which would never be filled.

The third trial of William Joyce began on a Monday, and it looked as if the verdict would be given on Thursday afternoon. At one o'clock on Thursday counsel had finished their arguments, and the Lord Chancellor dismissed the court and bade it reassemble at three. Joyce's brother Quentin and his friend the Scottish Fascist rose miserably and went off to look for some lunch. This would be difficult to get, for in those days, just after the end of the war, people lunched early, and in few restaurants would there be tables free or much food left. Outside the Houses of Parliament everyone knew who they were and eyed them with wonder, aware of their peculiar grief, their terrifying sympathies. They crossed the street and passed into the crowds of Whitehall, and there they became two young men in raincoats among ten thousand such. Here lies the real terror in the international war of ideologies: that a city knows not whom it entertains.

When everyone had reassembled, the Lord Chancellor announced that the judges required more time to consider their verdict, and dismissed the court again until Tuesday morning. Tears stood in Quentin Joyce's eyes, and he and his friends pressed forward to get out of the hated place as soon as might be. But the attendants held all of us back, and we stood together at the head of the steep stairs, looking down on William Joyce as he was marched out among the four policemen on his way back to jail. The courage he had shown in the dock at the Old Bailey had not greatly impressed a court in which most of those present had some experience of facing danger and had found themselves able to acquit themselves creditably enough; but now he was doing something more difficult, being a prisoner who had lain four months under the threat of death and had not heard the sentence he had braced himself to hear, and was a little, ill-made man surrounded by four drilled giants. He held his chin high and picked his feet up, as the sergeant-majors say, and though he held his chin so very high that his face was where the top of his head ought to have been and though his feet flapped on his weak ankles, his dignity was not destroyed, but was made idiosyncratic, his very own. It appeared that there could be such a thing as undignified dignity. It also appeared that Joyce's body had the same resistance to culture as his mind. He was a graduate with honours of London University, but there was a quality about all his saying and doings which disguised his literacy; he was a good rider, he swam and dived to Polytechnic standard, he had tried hard as a featherweight boxer, he fenced, but his body looked as if he were fragile and unexercised.

The postponement of the verdict was to have a graver consequence for Joyce and his friends than mere anguish. England was anxious to see Joyce suffer the just penalties of the law, but it was very anxious, too, that no penalty should be inflicted which was not just. Both in London and in the villages people were asking themselves whether the trial was perfectly fair and whether we were being careful to be loyal to our tradition of impartial justice and to escape the Nazi contamination of our troubled times. In legal circles it had been remembered that the most conspicuous prisoner under a capital charge whose case had gone through the Court of Appeal to the House of Lords had been reprieved, though he was a most repulsive scoundrel. He was a night-watchman who had enticed a little girl into his hut with the intention of assaulting her and had suffocated her because she persisted in crying for help; his case had gone to the supreme tribunal because he was in a state of drunken delirium at the time and the law had not till then defined its view of the extent to which a man insane by reason of intoxication was to be held responsible for his actions. Ugly as the crime was, it had been felt that no civilized community should keep a man hanging over the abyss of death so long and then push him over, and he was not only reprieved but, it is said, was informed in advance that if he were found guilty he would be reprieved. Lawyers, remembering this, felt there was a considerable case for reprieving William Joyce.

Unhappily, during the postponement Sir Oswald Mosley had a rally of his followers at a London hotel. It was alleged that the owners of the hotel had not known the purpose for which their assembly room was taken. The attendance was a matter of hundreds; a typical enthusiast was Captain Gordon-Canning, the ex-Guards officer who had recently paid five hundred pounds for the bust of Hitler which was sold at the auction of the German Embassy: a man in his late fifties whose face was as unlined as if he were a young child. But the English public was disconcerted to find that even some hundreds of the anti-British and pro-Nazi people who had caused so much brawling and confusion before the war were gathering together with the plain intention of causing further brawling and confusion. It was reported that Quentin Joyce attended this rally.

On the last day of the trial the press and the Fascists no longer had the Royal Gallery to themselves. It was thronged with Members of Parliament, a comradely and self-assured crowd, happily gossiping on their own stamping-ground and much less respectful to the ceremonies of the place than the press and the Fascists had been. They had to be pushed off the carpet by the attendants when the Mace and the Lord Chancellor went by, so busy were they exchanging comments on Joyce which were not meant inhumanely but sounded so, because they themselves were in such good health and so unlikely, if things went on as they were going, to be hanged: "They say he isn't here today." "No, if he were acquitted, it would be awkward. They'd want to arrest him immediately on defence-regulation charges, and nobody can be arrested within the Palace of Westminster. They'd have to let him go down into the street, and he might get away." "Perhaps he's chosen not to come today. Shouldn't blame him." "He's very plucky. I saw him at the Old Bailey." "So did I. What a queer little fish!" Joyce's brother was standing beside the last speaker, but he seemed not to hear. Both the Fascists and the pressmen were all preoccupied with the need to dash up into the gallery the minute the signal was given, because the announcement of the verdict would take only a few seconds and might be over before they had climbed the stairs.

The Lord Chancellor and the four judges were sitting around the table at the bar of the House, as they had done every day, but now the red benches were fully occupied, the House was crowded with peers; there seemed so many it was remarkable that nobility had kept its distinction. As the press and the public took their seats in the gallery, the Lord Chancellor rose and stood in silent handsomeness till the place was still, and then said, "I have come to the conclusion that the appeal should be dismissed. In common with the rest of your Lordships, I should propose to deliver my reasons at a later date." Then the four old judges rose in turn and gave their opinions. While the first was saying "I agree", Joyce's brother and his friends got up from their seats beside mine in the second row of the gallery and clambered down to some seats in the front row which had been assigned to newspaper agencies and were not now occupied. Suddenly one of the suave attendants was standing behind them and was saying, in a tone of savagery the more terrifying because it was disciplined and was kept low so that the proceedings should not be disturbed, "You get out of there and go back to the seats where you belong". This seemed a most brutal way of behaving to men who were listening to a judgment that doomed one whom they loved; for all the judges except one were saying "I agree", and that meant that Joyce must hang. But on the face of the attendant, and of others who had joined him, there was real fear. However innocent Quentin Joyce and his friends might have been, at that moment or any other, they had become associated with the idea of violence, and from the front of the gallery a violent man could have thrown grenades into the court.

Meanwhile the ceremony went on, affecting in its beauty and its swiftness. The Lord Chancellor moved backward down the floor of the House, superb in his black robe and curled white wig, the only figure in a historic dress in the assembly, the symbol of the continuing rule of law. He halted at the Woolsack. He stretched out his hands to the peers on each side of the chamber and bade those vote who were content with the judgment. This was the last sad stage of the outnumbering of Joyce by the

49

law. Now scores of judges faced the dock, and he was gone from it. The peers nodded and murmured and raised their hands. At this point a young man with hollow eyes and pinched nose and a muffler round his scrawny neck, who was sitting on the public bench of the gallery among the Negroes and the Hindus, cried out some words which some among us could recognize as Scottish Gaelic, and then proclaimed in English but with a strong northern accent that William Joyce was innocent. Attendants formed a wall around him, but did no more, for fear of interrupting the proceedings. The Negroes beside him expressed horror with rolling eyes; the Hindus looked prim. Joyce's brother and his friends threw a glance at him which was at first startled and then snobbish. The interrupter was not one of their sort of Fascist. Meanwhile the Lord Chancellor bade those peers who were not content with the judgment to vote, and there was silence. He declared, "The contents have it," and strode from the chamber. The peers streamed after him. The place was empty in a moment.

Quentin Joyce and his friends ran down the stone staircase into the street. They did not look so upset as might have been expected. The man who had shouted made his way out of the gallery without being touched by the attendants, who looked away from him, having taken his measure. In the lobby outside, crowds of pressmen gathered round him and questioned him and took down his answers, which he delivered with the gasping haste of the evangelist who knows he never keeps his audience long. The elegant general who was in charge of the attendants murmured to the Superintendent of Police, "I say, do we want this sort of thing, or don't we?" The Superintendent said he thought that the man would probably go away of his own accord if he were left alone. So the eccentric held an audience in the House of Lords, the very considerable crowd that were coming in to take part in the debate on the American loan neatly dividing to avoid disturbing him and joining again, until the pressmen left him, having insufficiently appreciated the remarkable quality of his utterances. A young reporter asked him, "But don't you think it mattered that William Joyce betrayed his country?" and he answered, in the accents of Sir Harry Lauder, "William Joyce didna betray his country. Ye canna say a man betrays his country when he goes abroad to better himself. Millions of people have done that and nobody's accused them of betraying their countries, and that's what William Joyce did. He had a fine position waiting for him in Germany, and he just took it." Surely this was a mind as fresh as Shaw's.

Down in the street, Quentin Joyce and Angus MacNab and the Scottish Fascist were waiting, eager to speak to the press, eager to give praise to their martyr. That was why they had not looked so very greatly upset when the appeal was dismissed; they were like the people who, leaving a death-bed so painful to them that they could not have borne to contemplate it for another instant, find relief by flinging themselves into elaborate arrangements for the funeral. Angus MacNab, in his easy and gentlemanly but hollow and eccentric voice, was telling a reporter how calm William Joyce had been when he saw him in prison during the week-end. "He was in excellent spirits," he said, his eyes gleaming mystically behind his spectacles, "and he was discussing, quite objectively, and with all his old brilliance, the psychology of the four judges. He was wonderful. . . . But I must leave you now and go and tell my wife what has happened. My name? Angus MacNab, and please do not spell it M-c-N-a-b. The correct spelling is M-a-c-N-a-b." And Quentin Joyce was talking freely in his careful voice, which, without being mincing, was more gentlemanly and more English than any English gentleman's voice, because this ambitious and Anglophile family consciously ironed out the Irish brogue from their tongues. Some reporters were asking him to write an article or make some statement about his brother, which he was refusing to do, evidently out of loyalty to some code of family relationships. He seemed to me to be saying primly that it was for his sister-in-law to tell the story of Joyce when she was free, since a wife was nearer than a brother, and as such must have her rights. It was plain that he and all this group had felt themselves not less but more disciplined than the rest of the world, solid upholders of order. He went on to speak of some demonstration the Fascists would make against the sentence. "And believe me, there will be plenty of us," he kept on repeating, while the Scottish Fascist nodded. A year later this man was to insert in the *Daily Telegraph* an "In Memoriam" notice of William Joyce.

But there were not plenty of them. There were not anything like plenty of them—even outside Wandsworth Prison on the morning of January 3, when William Joyce was hanged.

Wandsworth Prison lies in a shabby district in South London, so old-fashioned that it begins to look picturesque to our eyes. It is a mid-Victorian building with a façade of dark stone, derived from a misunderstanding of Florentine architecture, and it is divided from the high-road by a piece of ground not belonging to the prison, consisting of some cabbage patches and a dispirited nursery garden, planned whimsically, with thin streams trickling under toy bridges and meandering between the blackened stems of frosted chrysanthemums. The prison looks across the high-road to a monster of a school—built in the style of a Burgundian château and set in the midst of a bald and sooty park—which during the war housed the institution ironically known as "the Patriotic School", where persons who escaped from the occupied countries were detained, often for dreary weeks, until they had satisfied the authorities that they had not been sent over by the Germans. An avenue runs between the cabbage patches and the nursery gardens to the prison's great doorway, which is of green panelled wood with a heavy iron grille at the top, set in a coarse stone archway. A small notice-board hangs on this door; and on it was pinned an announcement that the sentence of death passed on William Joyce was to be carried out that morning. On these occasions there is nothing whatsoever for a spectator to see except at one moment, when a warder comes out of a smaller door which is cut in the large one, takes down the notice-board, and replaces it after two other notices have been added to the first: one a sheriff's declaration that the prisoner has been hanged, the other a surgeon's declaration that he has examined the prisoner's body and found him to be dead. But about three hundred people gathered to see that minute shred of ceremony.

They gathered while it was still dark and the windows of the cells were yellow in the squat utilitarian buildings which stretched away from the Italian façade—and waited through the dawn till full daylight, stoically bearing the disappointment that the hour of the hanging was at the last moment postponed from eight to nine. Some of those who waited were pressmen, lamenting that there was no story here; straining figures on the roof of a yellow Movietone truck set up a tall camera to focus on the notice-board, certain that there would be nothing anywhere else in the scene worth recording. Others were people drawn by personal resentment. An old man told me that he was there because he had turned on the wireless one night during the V-1 blitz when he came back from seeing his grandchildren's bodies in the mortuary and had heard Haw-Haw's voice. "There he was, mocking me", he said. There were many soldiers who had strolled out for a little after-breakfast diversion from a nearby demobilization centre. As time went on, all these people danced to keep their feet warm on the frozen earth.

There were some who did not dance. Most of these, however, were not particularly interested in William Joyce. They were opponents of capital punishment, who would have stood and looked disapproving outside any prison where anybody was being hanged. The most conspicuous of these were two tall and oblong Scandinavian women dressed in black, who indulged in silent but truculent prayer. Quentin Joyce and his friends were not there; they were attending a requiem mass. It is possible that this particular spring of trouble may flow into the Church and there be lost, for during William Joyce's imprisonment he became reconciled to the faith in which he was born. But there must have been many Fascists who would not attend that service, either because they were not Christian or because they were not close enough to Joyce's family to hear of it; of these only a handful waited outside the prison, and of these only one grieved openly, standing bareheaded, with no effort to hide his tears at the moment of Joyce's hanging. Three others slipped through a gap in the trees of the avenue and stood in the nursery garden, where some rows of cabbage-stalks veiled with frost flanked a rubble rockery, naked with winter, and at that moment they practised a highly tentative reverence. Their bodies betrayed that they had had no military training, and they wore the queer and showy sports-clothes affected by Fascists, but they attempted the salute which looks plausible only performed by soldiers in uniform. It was the poorest send-off for a little man who had always loved a good show and done his best to give one; who, so the prison gossip went, halted on his way to the scaffold, looked down on the violent trembling of his knees, and calmly and cynically smiled.

III

DURING the trials there had flowed into the mind of the community a conviction that Joyce had not been guilty of any offence against the law. This was in part due to the inadequate reports of the proceedings, which were all that the press could find space to publish because it was starved of newsprint. This restriction had been obviously a necessity during the war, but it is a matter of historic interest that it was suspected that the Labour Government was prolonging it for political as well as economic reasons; for, as most newspaper owners are Tories, a check on the size of the paper amounts to a check on Tory propaganda. That the Labour Government as a whole nourished this intention cannot be believed, for it was of the opinion that its accession to power had been not only not hindered but actually helped by the election campaign of the Tory press.

The English public read almost nothing about the Joyce case which was not so disjointed as to be unintelligible. The news-editor had day by day to compress what could hardly be compressed at all until the trial was over and the legal arguments were grasped as a whole. The argument that was most easy to quote was the answer of the defence to the first indictment, which was the impossibility of convicting Joyce for the crime of being a British subject and adhering to the King's enemies, when in fact he was an American subject. The subsequent arguments, that Joyce had acquired a temporary allegiance to Great Britain, and had taken his obligation abroad with him to Germany by taking a British passport, were much more complicated to set down, and in any case were not sympathetic news material. In the course of Mr. Slade's defence he put forward certain simple negatives which were far more quotable than the complicated positives by which the prosecution established the existence of temporary allegiance to the Crown as a recognized conception, and the nature of a passport; and his own more complicated propositions were so complicated that they could not be quoted at all. He figures, therefore, in the news as a plain blunt man gallantly putting himself about in an attempt to save an underdog hunted down by the lawyer chaps. Though the press obeyed in the letter and in the spirit the rule which forbids comment on cases under trial, their selection of what to publish of the proceedings and what to suppress involuntarily supported a version of the story which the public had been ready to listen to long before the Joyce case got to the Lords. "Of course he can't be guilty of treason", it was said in all the London pubs. "He's a dirty little bastard, but we've no right to hang him, he's an American." And so it went on. "A miscarriage of justice," said the clerk in a government office, handing out a legal document concerning Joyce to an inquirer some months later, "that's what that verdict was. I hold no brief for the little man, though he was a wonderful speaker. I'm no Fascist, but I always used to listen to him when he spoke up our way by the Great Northern Hospital; but it stands to reason that giving an American a British passport can't change him into an Englishman. A miscarriage of justice, that's what that was." The illogicality of this point of view can be judged from the attitude of American law. Since 1940 the United States had declared that persons who owed the sort of allegiance to another country which William Joyce and his father had owed to Great Britain could not retain their American nationality. Michael Joyce's American naturalization would have been nullified had this act been in force earlier, because he had resided continuously for more than three years in the territory of the foreign state of which he had been a national before he was naturalized a citizen of the United States. William Joyce would have lost his American nationality under the same Act, had it been passed earlier, by his service in the Cadet Corps (after the age of eighteen) and by his participation in elections.

The legal profession also showed a discontent with the verdict which was startling to the laity. Of the nine judges who had considered the case only one, Lord Porter, dissented from the verdict of guilty; and he did not fundamentally disagree with his colleagues in their view of allegiance. His objection related to a passage in Mr. Justice Tucker's summing-up at the Old Bailey, which he regarded as a misdirection of the jury. But here the inadequate press reports had their effect. Treason is not a common offence, and cases involving nationality are rare, so many lawyers were quite willing to believe that a trial involving those two elements would bring to light a great deal of law which was new to them. They therefore accepted the reports without reservations, and were as much misled as anybody else. "I see", said such an one, "that Joyce's appeal in the House of Lords is going well for him." His reason for thinking thus was a remark addressed by the Lord Chancellor to Mr. Slade: "Surely the proposition is elementary that allegiance was only due from an alien while he was in this country." Heard, this sentence conveyed with brilliant crystalline peevishness that Mr. Slade was hammering home the obvious, and it was followed by the statement, "The question, surely, is whether there are any exceptions to this rule". Read out of its context, it sounded like an encouraging invitation to pass on after a point had been proved. But the lawyers' objection to the Joyce verdict had profounder roots than misapprehension. Like the press and the public, they felt a distaste for any attempt of the law to lay hands on Joyce which proceeded from the emotions and did not consult the intellect until it was asked to furnish an explanation for its own vehemence. They felt it more sharply and personally, because it was their mystery which was being profaned: and they, like all of us, are forced sometimes to doubt whether the mystery of the law is not itself a profanity, since we live in the New Testament world, and justice has been blown upon by mercy. This reluctance has now forgotten its cause, since we are no longer Christian. Hence it remains as a vague disquiet about inflicting punishment.

The disquiet which was shown by the man in the street was no sign of mercy or any other sweetness on the part of the age; rather was it a sign of its sourness. The people were saying, "William Joyce was a vile man but he should not have been hanged", and they smiled as they said it, calling themselves gentle and unrevengeful. But they were hypocrites, and were avoiding admission of the truth for a base reason. They should have admitted that William Joyce was not a vile man but should have been hanged, and they refused to make that admission for a base reason. They had cast their eyes on the conception of the law with a new and dishonourable intent. The law is a force which has never yet been finally analysed. To make laws is a human instinct that arises as soon as food and shelter have been ensured, among all peoples, everywhere. There have been yellow people who have flashed on horseback across continents, apparently too mobile to form customs, apparently preoccupied with slaughter and destruction; there have been black people who have squatted on their thin haunches unchangeably through the centuries, their customs drooling to superstition round them. These have been thought by men of other kinds to be without law, but that was an error. Both kinds of society had reached a general agreement as to how to order their lives, and ordained penalties against its violation. But neither they nor any other society could define exactly what they were doing when they were making that agreement and ordaining those penalties. Demosthenes said that every rule of law was a discovery and gift of the gods, and he added that it was also an opinion of sensible men. Nine hundred years later the great Justinian prefixed that same definition to his *Digest of Laws*, only changing "gods" to "God". This seems a paradox, for assuredly men are not gods, and the last thing a god or God could fairly be compared with is a sensible man. Yet Pagan and Christian alike realized that the law should be at once the recognition of an eternal truth and the solution by a community of one of its temporal problems; for both conceived that the divine will was mirrored in nature, which man could study by the use of his reason. This is the faith that has kept jurisprudence an honest and potent exercise throughout the ages, and still keeps it so, though the decline in religion has made many find other names for what is written in nature and has to be deciphered by such men as wish to be good: the service of humanity, the rights of the state, the sovereignty of intelligence or moral sense.

The Englishmen who thought that Joyce should not have been hanged had wholly lost this conception of the law. They do not believe in the divine will; nor do they believe in the service of humanity, the rights of the state, the sovereignty of intelligence or moral sense, to the extent of imposing penalties for treachery to the sought social end; which means they do not believe in it at all. They wish the law to be purely arbitrary: a transparent chessboard laid over life on which a game can be played, as an addition to its hazards, and even as a disguise for its real hazards. They want to procure this arbitrariness by exploiting the inevitable time-lag of the law. For the law, like art, is always vainly racing to catch up with experience. At every turn of history life presents the citizen with new obligations, and renders dangerous the exercise of his liberty in some sphere by suddenly rendering that exercise an affront to the liberty of others. It is the task of judges and legislators to alter the law that it may cope with these capers of time. By a gross inappropriateness judges and legislators are described always as sitting, the one on the bench, the other in the House of Commons or the House of Lords; for in fact they run, they run fast as the hands of the clock, reaching out to the present with one hand, that they may knot it to the past which they carry in their other hand. There are always lapses in time when the present and the past are not joined, and it is these which Englishmen such as wished Joyce to live love to exploit. They enjoy exaggerating this inability of the law to adapt itself immediately to the age; they attribute to it an absurdity actually found most frequently in regulations framed by the civil service and by local bodies, which have to deal with material objects with the aim not of defining them exactly but of prescribing action of a highly artificial nature in regard to them. It amuses them, in fact, to imagine a state of society in which it is possible to travel through life with a criminal purpose and yet never, because of this legal time-lag, pass outside the law; and they feel a laughing, winking admiration for the rogues that achieve this journey. A vast number of English people were ready to cheer the cold shark Horatio Bottomley, because he had exploited the unforeseen situation created by the existence of a gutter press, edited and owned by men who cared nothing for their repute among generally respected citizens, and read by a public which had a certain amount of investable capital and was ready to invest it without taking advice from any generally respected banker or stockbroker. It touched them neither in the heart nor the sense of self-preservation that most of Bottomley's victims were people like themselves, whose savings were their sole shield from actual want. Simply they derived pleasure from thinking of him as drinking three bottles of champagne a day and keeping a racing stable on the proceeds of crime which he managed to keep unimpugnably distinct from the illegal. It opened to all of them the prospect that one day they might find some such opportunity of gain easier than honest, and unpunishable, and it gave them an actual and immediate dispensation from a tedious duty. For if men are regarded as chessmen, who can but lose or win a game, they cannot be loved; they can only be assured of fair play within the rules of the game. The public who cried out that William Joyce should not have been hanged wanted the perverse satisfaction of seeing a man whose crime it knew by the testimony of its own ears go unpunished, thus being assured that life was moral nonsense. They hoped, too, to reward the impudence in him, which they had rightly judged to be as remarkable as Bottomley's; but they felt no interest in any other of his attributes. They would not love him. Yet there was certainly much to be loved in William Joyce.

IV

THERE is no sight more touching than a boy who intends to conquer the world, though born in all probability its slave. Young William Joyce was such a boy, and took the first step towards conquest; for he was brave. Perhaps he really lay deep in the heather that he might tell the Black and Tans whether the three men left the farmhouse in the fold of the hills; perhaps he only pressed in on the Black and Tans with childish information that was of no service to them. But such actions and such dreams depend for their origin on a resolution to die rather than live if death should prove nobler than life. That William Joyce was mistaken in his estimate of where nobility lay in his situation is not a great count against him since he was but fifteen. And behind William Joyce's political folly was a grain of wisdom, a degree of preference for the things that must be preferred if humanity is to survive. He liked the scarlet coats of the English garrisons; but it was Mozart himself who asked in one of his letters if there was anything in life finer than a good scarlet coat, and all scarlet coats take up a common argument. They dissent from the dark earth and the grey sky, they are for pride, they teach the bodies that wear them a good carriage, they are for dance and drill, for measure and discipline. It was not to be held against the boy that he preferred the straight-backed aliens in scarlet coats to his compatriots who slouched with hats crushed down on cowlicks and collars turned up round unshaven jaws on their performance of menial toil or inglorious assassination. His family —and he was loyal to his own blood—cultivated that preference. That the smart soldiers created the slouching assassins he could hardly have been expected to work out for himself at that age. He was indeed isolated from his age in a dream of astounding obsolescence, wholly alien from the society in which he believed himself to be at home. It was in a town in Lancashire, where rationalism is temperamental, in a period when the emotional attitude in which men stood easy was cynicism, that he wrote his letter to the University of London Committee for Military Education. From 86 Brompton Street, Oldham, in August 1922, he sent forth that message which was read in court: "I can obtain testimonials as to my loyalty to the Crown. I am in no way connected with the United States of America, against which, as against all other nations, I am prepared to draw the sword in British interests. As a young man of pure British descent, some of whose forefathers have held high positions in the British army, I have always been desirous of devoting what little capability and energy I may possess to the country which I love so dearly." No absurder letter can ever have been written from 86, or 85, or 87, or any other number in Brompton Street, Oldham; but the little creature was not quite absurd as he licked the stamp and the flap of the envelope and hurried with a swagger along the black street to the pillar-box, taking his first step towards the conquest of England. It was going to be of no consequence at all that he and his family had had to leave Ireland. He would conquer the larger island instead.

In October 1922 he sent in the completed enrolment form to the Officers' Training Corps from Number 10 Longbeach Road, S.W.2, where he was staying when he began his studies for his science degree at Battersea Polytechnic. Joyce's destiny drew him to South London; he crossed the Thames only to meet disaster. This is to say that his destiny led him away from London: from the London where England can be conquered. For South

London is not London. It even calls itself by a vague and elided locution that leaves out the name of the capital. "Where do you live?" "South the river." The people on the other bank never speak of their landscape as "north the river". They may go down east, or go up west, but they move within London, where the Houses of Parliament are, and the Abbey, and Buckingham Palace, and Trafalgar Square, and the Law Courts, and St. Paul's, and the Mansion House, and the Bank and the Mint, and the Tower, and the Docks. The house where William Joyce first took up his dwelling on the other side of the Thames stood in one of those streets which cover the hills round Clapham Junction like a shabby striped grey counterpane. Longbeach Road is a turning out of Lavender Hill, that drab highway which follows the crest of a ridge running from Clapham Junction towards Vauxhall, grimy but genial, so genial that passers-by, asked the way, cry, "First on the left, dear". Its humble heights look down steep northern side-streets to the railway tracks of the Southern Railway, streaked with metal as with water, the treetops of Battersea Park, and the spires and towers and embankments of the other London. The house itself was one in a line of those tiny houses which astonish by their lack of size, for their bow-windows suggest a sitting-room hardly large enough to permit an armchair on each side of the fire, and by the profusion of their artless ornament. There are panels of coloured glass in the front door, and the porch is lined with strips of tiles moulded in fat patterns, such as one sees in old-fashioned dairies; the roof of the porch is converted into an unusable balcony, and the front of the house is picked out with plaster incrustations, representing chains of leaves. Some builder had loved beauty, but had neither individual taste nor command over a tradition. It was a poorer and less pleasing house than any other ever inhabited by William Joyce, and indeed he was there only as a lodger. The boy had left Ireland alone in December 1921, his family staying there until 1922, and then making their home in Lancashire until 1923.

When Michael Joyce came south in the following year, he became, with superb adaptability, a grocer; and he took the step, unlooked-for in a dazed immigrant, of establishing his family in a house that was as delightfully situated as any in London.

Allison Grove is a short road of small houses which has been hacked out from the corner of the gardens of a white Regency villa in the greenest part of Dulwich, a queer cheap insertion in a line of stately properties. It has its own great sycamore tree and many syringas, and the most agreeable surroundings. Not far off is the Mill Pond, still a clear mirror of leaves and sky, and beyond it Dulwich College amidst its groves and playing fields. To the south a golf-course makes a wide circle of mock country, bounded by suburbs rising on round hills, which, cleansed by being seen through the unusual lens of smokeless air, shine bright as the villages in the background of Rowlandson water-colours. To the north, behind the line of mansions into which Allison Grove intrudes, lies the handsome Victorian formality of Dulwich Park, with its winding carriage drives and its large sheet of ornamental water. An Irish family that had to come to London could not have more cleverly found a part of London more spaciously and agreeably unlike itself, and their house was cleverly found too. One side of Allison Grove had been built in Victorian times; the harsh red brick had been piled up in shapes as graceless as outhouses and to heights obviously inconvenient for the housewife. But the houses were amply planned for their price; and one of them gave room enough for the Joyce parents and William and his two young brothers and his little sister. Nothing could have been handier. There was a railway station a few hundred yards away, and the spry little William used to run up the steps every morning on his way to the Battersea Polytechnic, leaving the house feeling empty, no matter how many of the family were left in it; and ran down them again in the evening, and filled the house again. The neighbours, who thought the Joyces out-landish but likeable, though curiously arrogant, all noted that William was the apple of the family's eye, and they could understand it, for the boy had certainly an air of exceptional spirit and promise. But, if William always left his home and returned to it like a conqueror, during the day at Battersea Poly-technic he must have suffered many defeats, being tiny, alien, and ineradicably odd. In 1923 he was to experience the crush-ing defeat of failure in two subjects in his Intermediate Science examination.

His reaction was characteristic. There was nothing disgraceful in his failure. He was only seventeen: his schooling had been much interrupted, first by his disposition to argue with his Jesuit teachers, since as the son of a Catholic father and a Protestant mother he never accepted Roman Catholicism easily. Later he was distracted from his books by civil war and change of country, and he could have tried again. But on this failure he immediately abandoned his intention of becoming a Bachelor of Science and turned his back on Battersea Polytechnic. It is interesting to speculate just what effect this step had on his destiny. His ambition was very strong; and it just might have happened that if he had become a Bachelor of Science he would have recognized the easy and brilliant future which this age offers to the Communist scientist, and would have ended as a colleague of Professor Haldane on the *Daily Worker* and Professor Bernal. As it was, he went to the Birkbeck College for Working Men, which is a part of the University of London, a physically sombre though intellectually vigorous institution, hidden in the dark streets between Holborn and the Law Courts, and studied the English language and literature and history. He made an excellent though odd student and passed with first-class honours, though for the first two years of his course he was subject to a new distracting influence. In 1923 he joined the British Fascists. This was an odd instance of his inability to get the hang of the world he meant to conquer. Mussolini had come to power in 1922, and warm admiration was felt for him by numerous persons of influence in England; and a young man might well have sincerely shared that mistaken admiration and at the same time have wished to use that admiration as a means of personal advancement, but joining the British Fascists was not the way to make that advance. This body was never numerous and had few links with the influential admirers of Mussolini, having been promoted by an elderly lady, member of a military family, who was overcome by panic when she read in the newspaper that the British Labour Party was sending a delegation to an International Conference in Hamburg. It was patronized by a certain number of retired army men and a back-bench M.P. and an obscure peer or two; but the great world mocked at it, and it had as aim the organization of amateur resistance to any revolution that might arise; it was a charade representing the word "barricade".

c*

If William Joyce wanted either to hold a commission in the Regular Army, or to teach, or to become a journalist, membership in this universally unfavoured movement was certain to be prejudicial to his hopes. It may be said that he was still young, but many a boy and girl of seventeen, determined to rise in the world, has cast a canny eye on such strategical pitfalls. But from first to last he had none of the adaptability normally given by ambition. The proof was later to be laid before the ears of all of us. Though William Joyce divested himself of almost every trace of Irishry, he never acquired anything that resembled any English accent, and, indeed, had only to open his mouth to betray that he was not a member of the traditional English governing class. It was partly this obtuseness which led to his membership in the British Fascists, but there were more positive factors at work. The party, as well as holding meetings of its own, made a practice of interrupting and breaking up the Communist meetings which were being held in London, especially in the East End, often with the aim of explaining and defending Bolshevik Russia. Joyce, according to a tutor who coached him at this time, took these affrays with extreme seriousness. He spoke of the Communists with real horror: as, in fact, Orangemen would speak of Sinn Feiners. There was working in him a nostalgia for the Irish situation. Later, in the air raids, we were all to learn that danger is a better stimulant than champagne until the fatigue is too great. William Joyce had experienced that gaiety when he was too young to know real fatigue. Hence he enjoyed, with a constant driving esurience, street fighting. No sport could be meaner. The thin boy wearing spectacles is cut off from his friends, he is hustled into an alley, his arms are twisted, his teeth are knocked in. But the sport was recommended to William Joyce by the memory of his courage in its springtime, and the excessive deaths in Russia gave him his excuse. He was led into temptation.

In 1925 he left the British Fascists. This may have been because he became involved in certain internal dissensions which appeared, inevitably enough, in the movement; dog of a certain sort is always eating dog. Or it may have been because he feared to fail in his arts course as he had failed in his science course, and sacrificed his hobbies. But before long he passed into a sphere of a much more urgent distraction. A week after his twenty-first birthday, on the 30th of April 1927, he married a girl of his own age, a chemist's assistant, the daughter of a dentist, who was remarkable for her pleasant good looks, and because she was a Protestant, he, the son of an Irish Roman Catholic father, the pupil of the Jesuits, married her at the Chelsea Register Office and set up a house in Chelsea. This registry office marriage was a fierce gesture of independence. He, the little man, who might well never have got a woman at all with all the tall men about, won a woman who was desirable; he stood up straight and struck the Pope of Rome across the face. It would be easy to pretend that all his subsequent errors and misfortunes followed from this rupture with his Church, but in truth his religious revolt was merely one link in a chain of dissents which it was his life work to forge. It is the weakness of imperialism that in a country occupied by a strange power no man can know the sweetness of conformity, can marry his will to the common will for happy ends. If he be at one with his fellow-countrymen he must be a rebel against the conquerors; if he be at one with the conquerors he must rebel against his fellow-countrymen. Whatever road Michael Joyce had taken, he was bound to be impaled on one horn or other of the dilemma, and his son, since his soul was of the stuff that can be stamped with ideas, was bound to be a perpetual rebel. That was what he was, and what he liked to be.

By 1933, when this phase of his life ended, he had as much reason for pride in his achievements as most young men of twenty-seven. He had no difficulty in supporting his wife and himself, for he had already, as a student, joined the staff of a tutorial college, which regarded him as one of its best teachers. He loved teaching. Many people remember him as a little man who, when he found that they lacked some knowledge, patiently and unselfishly instructed them in it. If he could teach them nothing else, he taught them chess. After he had taken his degree he continued his studies in a post-graduate course in philology, and later began a course in psychology at King's College. He also found time to pursue his political ambitions, and worked for the Conservative Party, not only practising his speaking but learning the technique of organization. It must be remarked that all these achievements brought him not an inch nearer any position of real power. He could never by any chance have been invited to join the staff of any school or college of conventional academic prestige because of this curious atmosphere of illiteracy which hung about him. Only uneducated people accepted easily that he was learned; educated people were always astonished to hear that he had been at a University. Even his handwriting, which was spiky and uneasy, suggested that he rarely took up his pen. (It casts a light on what being tried on a capital charge does to the most courageous of us that the notes William Joyce passed to his counsel from the dock were written in a script which, though clear and steady enough, differed in many respects from his normal handwriting.) It is inconceivable, too, that the Conservative Party, or, for that matter, the Liberal Party, or the Labour Party, should have admitted William Joyce to anywhere near the inner circle of operative power, even if that circle was drawn widely enough to dilute that power far below Cabinet strength. It was not only culture in the sense of book-learning which was inaccessible to him; it was also culture in the sense of the life of the people. A police officer who had known William Joyce for many years and had liked him said hesitantly, for he was speaking a few days before the execution, that sometimes Joyce had reminded him, even in the days before the war, of a real criminal, of the sort that make lags. It was not that he had then committed any crime, but because he, like the lags, "did not seem to fit in anywhere".

Between 1930 and 1933 his enthusiasm for the Conservative Party flagged, and during this time he renewed his connections with British fascism, which had now much more to offer him and his special case. A number of obscure people in London were at that time conscious that a disaster was overhanging Europe. Those who foresee the future and recognize it as tragic are often seized by a madness which forces them to commit the very acts which make it certain that what they fear shall happen; so it was natural that some of these should join with the young men who were gratifying a taste for street-fighting under the plea that they stood for order and fascism, while others joined with the young men who were gratifying a taste for street fighting under the plea that they stood for order and communism. Both were undermining the period of civilization which gave them

66

power to pursue these curious pleasures. Even so, the Fascists had destroyed order in Italy and enabled Mussolini to seize power, and the same process was then being extended to Germany. The Fascist wing of this movement would have existed without Sir Oswald Mosley. He was its follower rather than its leader. It had sprung up because people who, living in an established order, had no terror of disorder, had read too much in the newspapers about Mussolini and Hitler, and thought it would be exciting to create disorder on the same lines. If it had not arisen spontaneously it would have been fomented by foreign agents. It was a dynamic movement with roots that went deep and wide, and it did not impinge at any point on the world inhabited by the existing executive class. With the people that controlled politics, or commerce, or the professions, it had nothing to do. It grew beside them, formidable in its desire to displace them from that control, but separated from all contact with them as if a vast plate-glass window was between them. To no movement could William Joyce more appropriately have belonged.

It was Sir Oswald Mosley's peculiar function to give false hope to the British Fascists, to seem to lead them out of limbo and to introduce them into the magnetic field of national power. Ill-informed about all conspicuous persons, they did not know that he was one of themselves; he also had been born outside and not inside his environment. He had been born into the old governing class of the Tory aristocracy, but had brought his own plate-glass window into the world with him; and he had penetrated into the new governing class of the Labour Party to the extent of holding office in the first Labour Government, but had formed no tie of liking or trust which would prevent it from preferring any other of its members to him. It is probable that William Joyce, with his incapacity for drawing any social inference whatsoever, was as blind as the rank and file to the qualities of isolation and failure inherent in Sir Oswald.

Within two years after Sir Oswald had founded the British Union of Fascists, William Joyce became his Director of Propaganda and Deputy Leader of his party. He lived then in a home which, though cheap and unfashionable, possessed its picturesque distinction. He was staying in a flat in a road clinging to the lip of an escarpment in the strangest spot in the strangeness of

South London. It was far south of the river, where the tameness of town overspreads heights which, though insignificant in elevation, are wild in contour; and if it covers them with the tame shapes of houses it has to stack them in wild steepness. But above this urban precipice the buildings themselves were wild, with the wildness of eccentric architecture produced by a confident and transitory age. Outside the windows of his flat in Farquhar Road, two glaucous towers ran up into the sky and between them the torso of the Crystal Palace was at one and the same time a greenhouse and a Broad Church cathedral. In summer-time the night behind this didactic architectural fairy tale was often sprayed with the gold and silver and jewels of Messrs. Brock's fireworks, while a murmur of oh's and ah's and cheers rose from the crowds that walked in the gardens among the cement prehistoric animals which had been placed there in the mid-nineteenth century as illustrations to some argument about the inevitability of progress and the usefulness of knowledge. A little way up the road was the Crystal Palace railway station, the most fantastic in London, so allusive, particularly in its cast-iron ornamental work, to uplifting Victorian festivity that it would not be surprising to find its platforms thronged by a choir singing an oratorio by Parry or Stainer. The windows on the other side of the house where Joyce lived looked down on the whole of London, across the Thames, over the imperial city, up to the green hills of Hampstead and Highgate. The view reveals an astonishing number of parks, moderate in size, unvisited save by the people who live around them, ununified populations scattered over London, therefore easy to deceive, meet victims for Fascist propaganda. At night the lights of London make a spectacular theatre, and it is said that keen eyes can distinguish the light which burns above Big Ben to show that the House has not yet risen. It was from this flat, on the 4th of July 1933, that William Joyce addressed his application for the passport which cost him his life. He desired it for the purpose of travelling to France and Germany.

It was a consciously illegal act. Or was it not quite that? The statement he made after his arrest makes it appear that he had never been sure about his nationality—which is to say, that he never made sure about it, that he never paid the visit to a solicitor which would have told him everything. He took a gamble on it. He took yet another gamble on standing for the two-seat constituency of Shoreditch as a Fascist candidate in the municipal elections of 1937. But success was far away. 2564 people voted for him and 2492 voted for another Fascist, out of a total poll of 34,128.

He took another gamble when he gave rein to his passion for street-fighting in his new post and in cold deliberation and with burning appetite applied himself to the technical problems of creating disorders; for a conviction might mean deportation, if he were discovered. It was about this time that Michael Joyce, who had long been reconciled to his beloved first-born, tore up his American passport and all documents relating to his American citizenship before the round astonished eyes of his son Quentin, muttering his secret and commanding that it should be kept a secret, clairvoyant in his perception of the existence of the awful danger threatening his blood, but wrong, as clairvoyance nearly always is, concerning its precise nature and the point in time and space where that danger waited. He thought it was to be a common exile of his family across the sea, and must have seen it near at hand, about eighteen months after William Joyce took his first post with Mosley, when he and his chief, together with the Fascist officer for Sussex, Councillor Bentinck Budd, and a ranker named Mullan, appeared at Lewes Assizes on a charge of riotous assembly at Worthing. They were acquitted after a trial that lasted for two days, and disclosed the sickness that was rife among the obscure.

The incident at Worthing had followed a rhythm by which the normal course of life in provincial towns of England, and even in London itself, had been disturbed again and again during the past few years. First the local Fascists would announce well in advance that Sir Oswald Mosley was coming to hold a meeting in the largest local hall. Truculent advertisements and parades would prevent the town from forgetting it. The idea of violence would suddenly be present in the town. The proper course for those who were anti-Fascist was to abstain from all action on the day of the meeting, to stay in their houses and ignore it; but the idea of violence would enter into them also and they would feel under a compulsion to attend the meetings and interrupt and provoke the stewards to throw them out. Then relatives and friends would know what they were thinking, and would grow tense with dread. On the day of the meeting Sir Oswald Mosley and his party would arrive in a town already in the grip of hysteria, and there would come with them all the paraphernalia of competently conducted civil war: a complete counterfeit of all necessary preparations for battle, except the explosives. There were men in uniform carrying weapons, truncheons made of shot-loaded sections of hose-pipe sealed with lead; armoured cars; ambulances complete with doctors and nurses —making a picture that meant danger, that aroused fear, that provoked the aggression which is fear's defence. The anti-Fascists, who had at first expelled the idea of violence from their minds and then reluctantly readmitted it, gathered, unstrung by their abhorred mental guest, round the hall in which the Fascist intruders were holding their meeting, spinning out words to cover the emptiness of a programme that contained nothing but anti-Semitism and an intention to establish dictatorship against the general will. When the Fascists came out they paraded in front of the crowd, bearing themselves insolently, until they provoked hostile demonstrations. Having provoked these, they assaulted the demonstrators, who struck back. So the civil order which generation after generation of Englishmen had insisted on creating in despite of tyranny and the lawlessness of their own flesh, lay dead in the street.

At Lewes this foolish and horrible story was told once more. The meeting had been over at ten. A hostile but inactive crowd had been waiting outside the hall. Mosley's lieutenants came into the street, bearing themselves in the jack-booted way, with elbows bent and clenched fists swinging. They began to speak in offensive tones to the people standing by. One paused in front of a boy of seventeen, a post-office messenger, and said something to him. The boy did not answer, and the Fascist asked, "Don't you understand English?" The boy, looking at the Fascist's black shirt, said, "I don't understand Italian", and the Fascist hit him. At Lewes Assizes, Sir Patrick Hastings, while cross-examining this boy, asked him, "Can you think of anything more insulting than what you did say?" It is of course a barrister's duty to get his clients out of the dock, and Sir Patrick was defending the four Fascists; and he had the right to ask any question he thought proper. But it is interesting to remember that Mosley had visited Fascist Rome not long before and had taken the salute with Mussolini at a review. Sir Patrick was no doubt encouraged by the atmosphere of the court. There were sound reasons why this should not be wholly unfavourable to the defendants. It was obvious that the Fascists could not be regarded as solely responsible for the riot. That the anti-Fascists had sinned as well as being sinned against was shown by the number of tomatoes they had thrown at Mosley and his lieutenants; these could hardly have been found lying about the streets of Worthing at ten o'clock at night. There was, moreover, a witness for the prosecution who, though an interesting personality, provocative to the imagination of the novelist, raised certain misgivings. He was a Red butler. This might be the name of a species of butterfly, and indeed he appeared to be highly peripatetic, for since he had retired from the service of the rich he had joined the New Fellowship, an anti-Fascist body considered by many to be Communist, and had travelled round the country selling anti-Mosley pamphlets outside Fascist meetings. Sir Patrick, cross-examining this witness on the contents of these pamphlets, asked him, "Do you believe a word of this rubbish?" though he had quoted at least one sentence from them which was unimpugnable in its accuracy: "Mosley is receiving money from nobody knows where and open support from Mussolini and Hitler". Mosley did not publish a balance-sheet, and he had been the guest of both the dictators. But the pamphlets certainly contained a great deal of nonsense. They implied that Mosley had promised Malta to Mussolini and parts of the British Empire to Hitler, and, as it would have been impossible for either dictator to give Mosley effective help to seize power in England, and as once he was the dictator of England he would have been their superior in resources, it is hard to see why he should have made any such commitment. The evidence of this witness made it appear possible that some of the anti-Fascist organizations were providing an opposition hardly less irresponsible and professional and dangerously itinerant than the Fascists.

During the trial the judge made certain interventions. A witness for the prosecution affirmed, when questioned about an incident in a certain street, that "the whole affair seemed to be a joke on the part of the crowd". This statement made Mr. Justice Branson request: "Tell us one of the jokes. I am always interested in good jokes." The witness replied, "They were singing 'Mosley's got the wind up' and that sort of thing." Mr. Justice Branson majestically inquired, "Do you call that a joke?" He also had passages with the police witnesses. It appeared that the defendant Budd and his wife, who lived in Worthing, had sent several passionately apprehensive telephone messages to the police station before and during the meeting. One was sent from the hall where the meeting was being held. "Tell Superintendent B—— to send some men down to restore order. If it is not done I shall go out and take the law into my own hands." The constable who received this message took no action, because his superior officers were already on the spot outside the meeting. Mr. Justice Branson commented severely on his failure to act. Later a sergeant was examined who gave a picture of the debauch of savagery with which the police force of this seaside town had had to deal that night. In a typical passage the witness described how he had seen Fascists rush to the doorway of a chemist's shop, had followed them and when they had run away had found a person lying on the pavement unconscious, and then had turned round and seen another person, who was one of the witnesses in the trial, lying in the road, also unconscious. Mr. Justice Branson interrupted this witness to say: "I understood you to use the phrase, 'The crowd which first chased down South Street'. Was there a crowd which chased down South Street?" The sergeant answered, "There was a large number of people." Mr. Justice Branson asked, "Why do you change your language? One expects in these cases that police will give their evidence fairly and frankly. Just bear that in mind in answering the rest of the questions."

It was not surprising that William Joyce was acquitted at Lewes. There was no evidence to connect him with the riot that had taken place, and it was said by Sir Patrick Hastings that his name did not appear in any of the depositions. The other three defendants were also acquitted. At the close of the case for the prosecution the judge said he must take the responsibility of telling the jury that it should find a verdict of not guilty. As the jury expressed its full concurrence with this direction, and announced that it had been its intention to request that the evidence for the defence should not be heard, since the prosecution had failed to make out its case, and as the cases of assault which had been brought against some of the defendants in the local courts had been dismissed, the effect of the trial on William Joyce must have been intoxicating. It is of course certain that the judge conducted the trial with perfect propriety; and the jury obviously carried out its duties as conscientiously. Nevertheless, the Lewes trial may well have exercised a powerful influence on William Joyce's determination to travel the road that led to the gallows. Indeed, the courts of law, civil as well as criminal, provided considerable encouragement for the ambitious Fascist at that time. But in the civil courts it was hardly the lawyers who could be held responsible. Virtue has its peculiar temptations, particularly when it is practised as a profession. The good are often so well acquainted with the evil intentions of the wicked that they report their speeches as if these candidly expressed their intentions instead of, as is customary, veiling them in hypocritical dissimulations. This has on many occasions led to the award of heavy damages against the good in cases brought under the laws of libel and slander by the wicked. The anti-Fascist press were not mindful enough of this danger when they dealt with Mosley, whom they considered to be wicked. In one libel action Sir Oswald Mosley won, and rightly won, a verdict entitling him to five thousand pounds damages, and his costs. It must have seemed to William Joyce that society had gone a long way towards certifying that fascism was not incompatible with its institutions, and it must have seemed to him that the opposition was unscrupulous and antisocial.

The daily routine of his work must have encouraged him in this delusion that he and his kind enjoyed the acquiescence, even the fondness, of society. It was unfortunate that the police liked him. They did not show him this favour because they shared his faith. It is a mistake to think that the police favoured the Fascists over the Communists—as they certainly did—on political grounds. There were, of course, policemen, as there were generals and admirals, who were deceived by the Fascists' use of the Union Jack and slogans about Britain into thinking them conservative patriots instead of international revolutionaries. There were others who regarded the Communists as bloodstained

Bolsheviks, and admired the Fascists as their enemies. But there were many who thought, and both common sense and wisdom was with them, that if the Communists had ignored the Fascist meetings and refrained from interrupting them, the Fascists would have been checkmated, since they would not then have been able to exercise violence and plead that they were defending the right of free speech. They would then have had to attack Communist meetings or make unprovoked assaults on Jews in order to get their street-fighting; and in that case policemen who arrested Fascists would have been able to get them convicted. As it was, they were constantly forced by the Communists' actions into arresting Fascists who were discharged by magistrates because they pleaded that they acted under provocation; and there is nothing a policeman likes less than seeing the charge against a man he has arrested being dismissed. This is partly, though not entirely, a matter of pride. It also concerns his promotion. If there is any blame to be attached to the men involved in these proceedings, it should not fall on the police but on the magistrates, who were so very often satisfied that the Fascists had been provoked. But for magistrates and police alike, the situation was exasperating. If a citizen went to a meeting held by a party which advertised its loyalty to King and country through every material and spiritual loudspeaker, and which was notorious for its easy resort to violence, and the citizen remained seated during the singing of the national anthem, police and magistrates alike felt a disinclination to concern themselves with what subsequently befell that citizen. They were of course wrong. Their business was to suppress violence, however it had been provoked. But such citizens, and all those who played the Fascist game by accepting their challenge, were either irritating masochists or troublemakers obeying Communist instruction.

If the police liked Joyce it was because he persuaded them he was alleviating this ugly situation. He was a fine disciplinarian. His men were truly his. On them he now could play all the tricks of charm that take in young hero-worshippers; the recollections of a previous encounter, stated with a suggestion that an ineffaceable impression had been made, a permanent liking engendered; the sternness broken by a sudden smile. He had also learned the trick of turning his puniness into an asset of terror; a little man can be terrible when he outstares a taller and stronger subordinate who has been insolent to him, and coldly orders another subordinate, still taller and stronger, to inflict a brutal punishment on him. "Joyce really had his men under control," said a member of the police force, "and he was always fair to us. We could never come to an understanding with the Communists; if we saw the leaders it was hard to get on terms with them, and if we did persuade them to alter a plan they didn't seem able to make their men carry out the alteration. But if I went to Joyce and told him that his men were doing something that wasn't fair on the police, trying us too hard or interfering with our time off, he'd have his men right off that job in half an hour, and there'd be no grumbling. And he always kept his word, we found him very straight." This officer— and he spoke for many of his colleagues — thought Joyce a far abler man than Mosley. It is possible that William Joyce was, at that time, a person of real and potent charm offering the world what Blake said pleased it most, "the lineaments of gratified desire". He saw his path to greatness clear before him. He experienced the sharp joys of public speaking and street-fighting nearly every night, and every month or so the more prolonged orgy of the great London or provincial meetings. Moreover, the routine of fascism freshened and liberated the child in its followers. Mosley had taken a black old building in King's Road, Chelsea, formerly a Teachers' Training College, where he housed his private army of whole-time members of the British Union of Fascists; and there life was a boy's dream. Uniforms were worn that were not really uniforms, that at once claimed and flouted authority, as adolescence does; there was discipline, savage (and therefore sadistically sweet) while it lasted, but perfectly eluctable, not clamped down on a definite period of time by the King's Regulations; corridors were patrolled by sentries beetling their brows at nothing, executive officers sat at desks laden with papers alluding to mischief as yet too unimportant to justify authority in taking steps to check it; dead-end kids that could call what was dead alive and the end the beginning only because they knew no better, innocently and villainously filled rubber truncheons with lead. There is nothing like infantilism for keeping the eyes bright and the skin smooth.

At this time, too, Joyce must have been intoxicated by new experiences of several kinds. His family now deny that he ever went to Germany before 1939. But others believed that he made the journey more than once and shared in the long, sterile orgasm of the Nuremberg Rally, held on the great barren place which once had been rich farmland, where crowds, drunken with the great heat, entered into union with a man who was pure nihilism, who offered militarism and defeat, regulation and anarchy, power and ruin, the cancellation of all. That was a deep pleasure, surrounded by shallower ones: the drives through the entrancing country, scored with the great works which German Joyces had ordained by a wave of the hand, the visits to the fine villas which German Joyces had made their own and stuffed with works of art, the eating and drinking from the Gothic and Renaissance tables of German Joyces where the heavy goblets stood on Genoese velvet. In his own country he frequented the homes of the wealthy Mosleyite supporters, and there perhaps knew less than the absolute enjoyment Germany could have given or did give him. Few of the upper-class supporters of Mosley were intellectually distinguished in any way that induced the relinquishment of social prejudice. Only an eccentric, equally distinguished as a physicist and a steeplechaser, and a peer whose enthusiasm for fascism was part of his passion for the grotesque and wholly conditional upon its failure to realize its objects, come to mind as probably unbiased by class feeling in their response to charm; and of what they would have considered charm William Joyce had none. It would be impossible to exaggerate his lack of any attractive distinction. He had his wit; everybody who met him in England or Germany agrees that he never talked for long without putting a twist on a sentence that surprised the hearer into laughter. He had also the same pleasantness that was remarked on so often by the officials who had charge of him during his last days. But he was not, as they say, a gentleman. The other upper-class supporters of Mosley were for the most part professional soldiers and sailors, usually in their fifties; and of these some asked William Joyce to their houses out of a sense that they should recognize his services to the movement. He was to them, nevertheless, like an officer risen from the ranks. Awkwardnesses occurred. One week-end he was a guest at the country house of an army man who kept a large stable; and on Sunday morning the host let his guests try some of his less valuable horses. William Joyce, who had learned to ride as a boy in Mayo and Galway, handled his horse so well that he was allowed to try another one, a fine and difficult thoroughbred. The host's father, an old gentleman so deaf that he could not tell whether he was shouting or whispering, stood among the other guests and watched. "How marvellously Mr. Joyce rides!" a lady bawled into his ear. "Yes!" he bawled back. "But not like a gentleman." Nobody was sure whether Mrs. Joyce had heard.

When a man's social horizon widens, his sexual horizon rarely stays where it was. There was a rackety recruit to fascism, a wealthy young man who had suffered the initial handicap of being expelled from an ancient school, not for perversity but for precocity induced by the enterprise of an American actress, who took a cottage for the summer term near the school. He invited Joyce to a shooting-party, where he met the sister of an Irish peer and was profoundly impressed by her. She felt no corresponding emotion and probably never knew of his. It may have been such disturbing encounters which first suggested to William Joyce what might not have occurred to him if he had stayed where he was born, that he need not always stay married to the same woman. From the beginning, it is said, his life with the girl he had married when they were both twenty-one had been a cycle of romantic ecstasy and quarrels and impassioned reconciliations; he would turn anything into a fight. He took it for granted, too, that he should spend an amount of time with men friends, which must have made home life exiguous. During his time of service with Mosley his relations with his wife grew more and more purely quarrelsome, and in 1936, although they had by then two little daughters, this marriage was dissolved.

On a visit to Lancashire, where he was always at home, since he had known it as a child, and where he had had some of his greatest successes as a speaker outside London, he met the woman who was to be his second wife, a pretty and spirited girl, the daughter of a textile warehouse manager and an enthusiastic member of the B.U.F. She was a trained dancer, who often performed at cabaret shows given at festive gatherings of North

Country Fascists; she was slender and graceful and took her art seriously, but threw her ambitions away to serve her husband and his ambitions. Though outsiders thought that Joyce's second marriage followed the same pattern of ecstasy and dissension and reconciliation as his first, there was apparently a deep and true love between him and his wife which was to endure to his death. There is indeed to be recognized in the conventional prettiness of her face a certain not conventional solemnity and submissiveness, as if she knew she should bow to a great force when it visited her; and it appears certain that she believed William Joyce to be that great force.

He left South London, that had been with the exception of a few periods his home since he was a boy and used it as his base for his first steps toward conquering the world; that was still the home of his father Michael Joyce, who had bequeathed him a certain mystery, and Queenie, Joyce's mother, and his two brothers and sister; that was his appropriate home. Where the drab rows and the complacent villas shamed their builders by losing their drabness and their commonplace quality because of the hills on which they were set, which, under bricks and mortar, retained the wild shapes of nature—there should always have lived this puny and undistinguished little man, who was the theatre for the desire of glory and an irresistible impulse to death. He moved to the north side of the river, but not to imperial London. Till he left for Germany, he lived on the flat lands in the south-west, inland from Chelsea, at the foot of the slope that falls from Hyde Park and Kensington Gardens, and they house the underlings of imperial London. When he married his second wife he was living in one of the dreariest spots in the dreary district on the east side of Brompton Cemetery: a place where the cats limp and have mange, and the leaves bud brown in the spring. It was the first of his London homes that was dull and characterless; he might have chosen it when he had ceased to care whether the routine of life was pleasant because he was so preoccupied with the crisis of the future. The ceremony to which he went forth from this grey home was at the Kensington Register Office. He could have been married by a priest if he had wanted; since his first marriage had been civil, neither it nor the subsequent divorce existed, in the eyes of the Church. But he was still at war with the traditions of his father; and none of his family was among the witnesses. But one witness came later to know Joyce's family very well: Angus MacNab, then and for ever after a worshipper of Joyce, who was to sit with Quentin through all three trials.

V

WILLIAM JOYCE'S second marriage brought him north of the river. Perhaps it had a direct effect on what he was ultimately to do there; on his decision to desert Mosley and become an agent of Nazi Germany. It is true that a number of factors unconnected with Joyce's private life were driving him towards that decision. Chief among these was his relationship with Mosley. Joyce was nobody's fool, and never weak in self-esteem. If he had ever looked up to Mosley, which is doubtful, he very soon came to look down on him, and that at the very same time that he was satisfying himself as to his own unusual powers as a speaker and organizer and leader of men. It can be taken as certain that, if the police thought him more able than Mosley, he held the same opinion with some intensity. Moreover, it is impossible that Joyce was blind to the gulf that yawned between one part of the Fascist Movement and another. The wife of one of the few Fascist leaders who were in the inner ring with Mosley was asked, "Did you and your husband ever ask Joyce to your house?" She answered in horror, "Oh, no, never. That was the great thing that worried us all, about what we were to do after Tom"—as Mosley was known to his familiars—"had become dictator. We didn't know how we were going to get rid of all these dreadful common people we had had to use to get power." It is unlikely that the sentiments behind the remarks would have remained hidden from the cold eyes of William Joyce, and that he would have missed the political implication behind them. He may have recognized that the purge of June 1934 was inherent in all Fascist movements; and he may have asked himself just why Mosley had chosen him as Deputy Leader of the Party. It would have seemed more natural that the position should be filled by one of the army or naval high-ranking officers who supported the movement, rather than by an insignificant little man with no social influence, for whom Mosley had no personal liking. William Joyce was tough enough to put the question in that form, and shrewd enough to answer it by admitting that his charm for Mosley was the obvious unlikelihood that he would set up as a rival for leadership of the movement.

There was also a difference between their outlook on policy, which became more marked as time went on, and in which the advantage lay with Joyce so far as simplicity was concerned. Mosley had started his movement before Hitler came to power; Mussolini had been his inspiration. But very shortly after 1933 the emotional interest of the British Fascist movement shifted to Germany. This was in every sense natural, for what makes every Fascist movement go round is the pickings for the boys; and the boys in Italy had never had anything like the swollen and novel pickings that came to the boys in Germany. Moreover, many of Mosley's followers were seduced in a way not at all dishonourable to them, by the innocent face of the world's enemy; pine-woods on little hills, small grey-green glossy lakes, fields striped with the different stitches of cultivation neat as embroidery, russet-roofed villages with headlong gables and church steeples that have swallowed pumpkins—all the setting for fairy stories about millers' sons that make fortunes and buy the world. There was also the refreshment of meeting other young men and swimming with them in a bath of infantilism, of showing off and being shown off to, of boasting and believing boasts and boasting again, of making vows to meet next year and bathe again in these waters that are fresher and wash off the dust better than the waters of adult life, which are themselves dusty.

Mosley would feel such influences less than his followers, for he was travelled, was used to luxury, had some taste, and had had the full dose of infantilist indulgence which is permitted and even required from a young man of means. But he seems, like many people, to have believed that Hitler was a man of supreme ability, and perhaps felt some personal liking for him. That he married his second wife in Hitler's presence may have signified either real affection for Hitler or a desire to build up an alliance by intimacy. While William Joyce was cold but naïve, Mosley was hot-headed but sophisticated; he could argue with his own passions in defence, not of the truth, but of his own ends. Hence Mosley could bear to proclaim the Nazi doctrine of a totalitarian and anti-Semitic state without overt propaganda for Hitler. His line was to admit admiration for Hitler and Mussolini, but to deprecate any excessive interest in Continental affairs and profess belief in isolationism. "Mind Britain's Business" was his slogan; and he assured the public that if Hitler were given a free hand in Europe and were returned his mandated colonies, and we at home suppressed the Jews, the peace of the world would be guaranteed, and the British Empire would be immune from attack. But he was careful to say that if Hitler should ever attack the British Empire, its peoples would of course defend themselves, and would be victorious. William Joyce wanted to preach acclamation of Hitler as the saviour of the world on such unconditional terms that by implication it must be the duty of every good Briton to resist any British government which took up arms against him.

Both these policies would work out to the same result. If Great Britain pursued an isolationist policy and let Hitler conquer Europe, he would have no reason to refrain from crossing the Channel and setting up what government he pleased; and there the matter would remain, for it would be extremely difficult for America to come to the aid of an invaded Great Britain which had acquiesced in the invasion of all the rest of Europe. In these circumstances it would certainly have been the Fascists from whom Hitler would draw his quisling government. On the other hand, if the Fascists devoted their cause to the pro-clamation of the greatness of Hitler, and preached collaboration freely and frankly up to the declaration of the war and afterwards (within the limits set down in the law of treason), then again it would seem certain that the Fascists would furnish the quislings when they were needed. Of the two policies Joyce's frankly admitted the international character of fascism, which makes a man ready to be traitor to his country, his county, his town, his street, his family, himself, and loses its dynamic power if it does not act by and through this readiness for treachery. More-over, it was designed on the plane of heroism, and for that reason, had England been defeated in 1940, might have been more corrupting, for there would have been less shame in going over to the quislings if they had shown themselves brave men.

But policy was not the only subject of disagreement between Mosley and Joyce at this moment. Joyce was, for the first time in his life, troubled about money. He had been brought up in a household where there had always been enough to maintain the simple satisfaction of all needs. He had supported himself and his first wife adequately on his earnings as a tutor, which he had been able to stretch by taking on extra classes. For his chief pleasures, which were public speaking and street-fighting, he did not pay but was paid. For his lesser pleasures he could afford to pay. For example, he had a fine radiogram and a large library of records, chiefly operatic. Now, however, he had to make a home for himself and his second wife and support his first wife's children, and Mosley was paying him a small and inelastic salary. He needed an increase in pay just at the very time when Mosley was least likely to give it. Mosley must have been in genuine financial difficulties. It is said that he was spending nine-tenths of his income on the cause, but that went nowhere in maintaining a private army of anything from twelve hundred to two thousand, together with a greater number of subsidized hangers-on. It is true that he was financed by some industrialists, and by some City firms, even including one or two who by reason of their origin should have been most careful not to compromise themselves in this direction. But these industrialists were not the great magnates who were persistently rumoured to be contributing to Mosley's funds; they were for the most part old gentlemen at the head of minor firms who had only moderate means at their disposal. If the City firms were sometimes more generous they were also more canny, and both alike were beginning to be less forthcoming. They had contributed because they had believed Mosley to be a stabilizing force in society. But do what he could, he could not prevent his movement from looking what it was, revolutionary. The increasing brutality of the brawls with Jews and Communists was betraying the nature of its inspiration.

Also, time was to reveal that the right sort of recruits were not coming in. The only distinguished men that ever joined the B.U.F. were Major-General John Frederick Charles Fuller, the most brilliant writer of our time on the art of war, and Sir Arnold Wilson, an extremely able colonial administrator. Another writer of some standing and much charm supported the party, but it was too generally recognized that he had not been sober for thirty years for his political opinions to carry much weight. There should have been some appeal to the Kipling tradition in an officer who was the author of a best-seller about army life in the East, but he was unnegotiable by reason of his devotion to Oriental mysticism in its quainter manifestations. About this time a Fascist leader was driving a banker who was regarded as a possible convert back from a week-end which had seemed very profitably spent, when he realized that they were passing the home of this officer-author and suggested that they should stop and call on him. The banker was delighted. But the butler repelled them. The major was in, and the butler would take a message to him, but he could not possibly be seen. The Fascist persisted, and finally the butler, who was a traditional butler, for this was a traditional home, broke down and said, "It's no use, this is the day he spends sitting on the roof with his Yogi having his perpetual enema". British fascism did hardly better with its aristocratic supporters. One of these bore a title founded by a historic personage of the first order. If any-body alluded in his hearing to his great ancestor "the great Duke of——" his brows would contract and he would say huffily, "The *first* Duke of——". Later he was to give his life nobly in the war against fascism, and this anecdote relates to a superficial oddity and not to the sum of him. It is worth while recalling only to explain the difficulties that Mosley was having in creating an impression of normality. Even with his numerous service members he had his difficulties. He had to handle these with care, lest possibly an officer of personal attractions and gifts for oratory and administration should dispute his leadership. But all the same, it was a pity that his most active service supporter should be stone-deaf, although it is true that deafness has more than once played a decisive part in our great island story; our pro-Bulgarian policy, which has so disastrously endured for generations, was largely the work of a *Times* correspondent who travelled through the Balkans ceaselessly but without being able to hear a word that anyone said to him. Worst disappointment of all, however, was a wealthy and aristocratic young man who created a most favourable impression at the Nuremberg Rally, but was a Communist deputed to infiltrate the Mosley Movement.

Naturally enough the movement was short of subscriptions and Joyce was paid no advance on salary commensurate with his ability; and he was therefore left in a state of insecurity and with a feeling that Mosley had failed to fulfil the promise he had seemed to make to his obscure followers, the promise that those outside should find themselves at last inside, that the powerless should find themselves as equals among the powerful. Some time in the beginning of 1937 a police officer who knew Joyce found himself alone with him in a compartment in a late train from the midlands which had a break-down. For a time they talked of impersonal matters, then, as the delay lengthened, fell into silence, which the police officer suddenly found himself breaking with the question: "Joyce, what do you really think of Mosley?" He had no idea why he asked that question; he had heard nothing of any breach between the two. The little figure, which had been huddled in fatigue, now fixed the police officer with eyes cold as ice. Joyce was famous among the British Fascists for his power to curse, and for the next ten minutes, quietly and steadily, he used it, then sank back into apparent slumber. The police officer paid him the classic compliment of saying that he never once repeated himself, and added that "there was nothing ordinary in it," and he summed up its content as an opinion that "Mosley was letting them down by doing his job so badly". A few weeks later it was announced that Mosley had dismissed Joyce from his post as the Director of Propaganda and Deputy Leader of the Party, for the reason that he was under a necessity to cut down on his salaried staff.

There were certainly two interacting forces leading to this breach: Joyce's need for money and his determination to preach supernational instead of national fascism. Very soon it was being said that Joyce's need for money was the real cause of the dismissal, and that because it had pushed him to an extreme step. He had been detected, it was said, in embezzling the funds of the Union. This does not seem probable. Many people, not Fascists, who had dealings with Joyce, declare that they found him honest, and it would seem likely that he would be. The

Joyces were a very respectable family, "the sort of people", as a neighbour said, "who went to evening classes"; nourished in the night of revolution though they were, there was that in them which carried some daylight with it. He must have had a bias towards honesty which was unlikely to stop functioning when he, an ambitious man, still saw every possibility of realizing his ambition, and when he must have had a very good notion of where he could get money for the asking. Joyce himself told a version of the story which is quite credible, though not a complete explanation of the breach. He said that he had told Mosley that he must have more money, and was going to raise his own salary and take the increase from certain funds which were Mosley's own property; that he had believed that Mosley had realized that he was speaking seriously; and that after he had made this adjustment for some time Mosley had sent for him and, having completely forgotten their earlier discussion, had raged at him as an embezzler. Apparently the administration of the B.U.F. was so informal that this story may well have been true. Yet it does not cover all the facts of this breach. If Mosley was startled at the notion of dishonesty in a follower, the British Fascist Movement must have differed strangely from its foreign counterparts. The violent are often thieves as well. If dishonesty had been the complaint against Joyce, one would have expected him to leave the Union quietly, as others had done before him. On the contrary, the breach was ostentatiously public and clear-cut. It seems more likely that Mosley had discovered that Joyce was making affiliations of the very sort he was particularly anxious to avoid.

When Joyce left the B.U.F. he took with him another conspicuous member, John Beckett. This was a man much older than himself, one of those pathetic casualties of the Labour Party whose failures have been due not so much to their own demerits as to the difficulties besetting Members of Parliament belonging to a political party long in opposition. He had started life as a shop assistant, was disabled in the First World War, and had emerged in the first years of peace as a popular speaker on Labour problems, largely owing to his attractive physique and his abundant vitality. In 1924 he was elected to Parliament and shortly afterwards made a spectacular protest against the government's neglect of the problem of unemployment, seizing the Mace and threatening to throw it down on the floor. It was one of those gestures made by bad actors, which they imagine fraught with complex significance but which the audience sees simply as their farewell to good fortune. It was right to cry out against unemployment, and doubtless this man's heart was in his cry, but all the same it was the wrong cry. He was in Parliament for six years, then he passed over to the Independent Labour Party, organized Mosley's New Party, followed him into the British Union of Fascists. He married a beautiful actress, the widow of a well-known actor, and was later divorced; he went bankrupt; he had other troubles connected with the courts. In 1937 he was the editor of the B.U.F. official organs *Action* and *The Blackshirt,* being an able technical journalist. It must have been inconvenient for Mosley to lose both Joyce and this man at one and the same time, but he, like Joyce, received a very definite and final note of dismissal.

Within three weeks of leaving the B.U.F., Joyce had founded his British National Socialist League; and very soon afterwards he had an office in London and an official organ, *The Helmsman.* This was quick work; it also cost money. It is true that it did not cost much money, but then Joyce had almost none. He had gone back to his work as a tutor, and was doing well, but not so well that he could earn much more than would support himself and his wife and meet other obligations. The British National Socialist League could never boast a membership that was more than a fraction of the strength of the B.U.F., and never pretended to live on its subscriptions. The only sub-scriber to British National Socialist League funds who has been identified with any certainty was the old Scottish stockbroker whose sister was later to visit Joyce in prison, and he gave generously, but nothing that went into thousands. Joyce himself declared that he was financed by certain industrialists, but it seems most unlikely that any industrialist shrewd enough to have maintained his business would have thought it worth while to subsidize this lone little man who, however great his gift for organization, had now only a handful of followers to organize. There was, on the other hand, a great deal of German money lying about in England at that time, to be picked up by anybody who chose to take a certain amount of trouble.

How little that trouble needed to be, how that money could petition to be picked up can be illustrated by the case of the two young women with strong right-wing views who thought it would be amusing to write and publish a news-letter. After a couple of numbers appeared they were approached by a man holding a teaching position in a certain University, who told them that he would finance their news-letter to the extent of two or three thousand pounds, provided only that they published a certain amount of approving reference to Hitler. If William Joyce accepted money from such sources, he was breaking no law. In the United States it is a crime to take money from the representative of a foreign power without registering as a foreign agent, but in England such an act can be performed with impunity, and it would be easy to name a number of English persons on the right and the left who have benefited by transactions with Continental governments anxious to have friends in England. The United States law is, however, rendered nugatory by the power of bribery to take forms other than cash payments. There, as in England, publishing houses specially founded for the purpose can commission propagandist works, the management of societies for friendship towards specific countries offer well-paid jobs, a Continental government can buy whole editions of books or subscribe for thousands of issues of a journal. We might judge that Joyce was accepting such benefit from certain recorded actions of his which seem to show him trying, in his scrubby, spirited, awkward way, to be honest and give good value for his bribe, to be logical and not shrink from committing an act of treason in time of war, which he rightly believed to be no worse than an act of treason committed in time of peace in the hope of provoking war. But this is speculation, and it must be realized that though it is not impossible that Joyce accepted money from those with whom he conspired, it is quite certain that he did not commit treason for the sake of gain.

Some time after Joyce had left the British Union of Fascists and set up his own movement, he and his wife had moved to a very pleasant home, the most expensive home he occupied in his whole life: the top flat of a doctor's house in a soberly agreeable square in South Kensington. It would never have been let to him had he presented himself as the prospective tenant. But it

D

was taken by Angus MacNab, whose obvious good breeding and gentleness impressed the doctor and his wife very favourably. He explained to them that he was setting up in business as a coach in partnership with a friend named William Joyce, and at a second interview brought with him Mrs. Joyce, whom they thought not so well bred as he was, but pretty and agreeable. On these samples of the household they concluded the transaction, and were disconcerted when its third person arrived with the removal van, which contained a prodigious amount of books and some poor sticks of furniture, and proved to be a queer little Irish peasant who had gone to some pains to make the worst of himself. The wearing of uniforms by private persons was by then illegal; so he and MacNab always wore black sweaters of a shape calculated to recall the Fascist black shirt. His suit and trench-coat were deliberately kept dirty and shabby in imitation of Hitler's turn-out; he cropped his hair in the Prussian style and never wore a hat; he always carried a very thick stick; and he bore himself with a deliberate aggressiveness. The doctor and his wife instantly took a dislike to him, which they were to find not unjustified when they saw more of the household. They liked his wife and thought he treated her tyrannously, overworking her and giving her no thanks, in the peasant way. He was tiresomely exigent about his meals; and not only had she to cook them, but had to wash up afterwards, and then run off to help at the League office in the day-time, in the evening, at meetings. But the doctor and his wife had to admit that she adored him and that he evidently made her very happy.

They had other complaints against him. Their new tenants were indubitably noisy. Joyce had always loved noise. A young man who knew him during his first marriage tells how he learned chess from him in a tiny room just big enough to hold two chairs, a table and a radiogram which blared continually at full blast. It was torture for the pupil; Joyce took it as natural. Here the household banged doors and stamped about when they came in excited from their meetings, and sometimes gave rowdy parties. To one of them they invited the doctor's wife, who happened to be alone that evening. She was not reassured. Some of the guests were wild Irishmen—the same that attended his trial. These were for the most part from families with the same roots as the Joyces, who had been supporters of the British occupation of Ireland and who had had to leave the country for safety's sake when Home Rule was granted. One among these was the son of a man who had performed an act of charity towards a man he found dying of gunshot wounds beside the road without inquiring into his political affiliations, was consequently victimized by his neighbours till he was obliged to take refuge in England, and there died in poverty, leaving his family aggrieved because they had received no adequate compensation from the British government. The doctor's wife was unaware of the pathetic antecedents of these merrymakers, but she was disconcerted by the vehement quality of the merriment they made, and she came to her own conclusions when she met a gentleman with long hair who was wearing a scarlet cloak and a pectoral cross, and who introduced himself as the monarch of an Eastern European nation; it was not revealed to her that he had once been sentenced to a term of imprisonment for the publication of obscene poetry, but she felt there was something a little odd about him.

Nevertheless the doctor and his wife did not attempt to terminate the lease. They were moved to this forbearance partly by their kindly feeling towards Mrs. Joyce, who, they foresaw, would suffer greatly in one way or another through her marriage. They also liked MacNab, who was amiable and fantastical. Once when Joyce had gone off with the key to the flat and a pipe had burst inside it, MacNab, explaining that he had been a leading member of the Oxford Alpine Club, swarmed up the back of the Kensington house, by pipes and window ledges and gutters, till he found a window open on the fifth story. But the doctor and his wife developed more serious reasons than these for tolerance. One of their sons was taken ill and had to miss a term or two at his boarding-school, and during this period MacNab and William Joyce coached him, the one in Greek and mathematics, the other in Latin and French. The parents found the boy was getting better teaching than he had ever had in his life, as they discovered that these two strange men really cared for the things of the mind, really possessed unusual intellectual capacity. After that they sometimes asked their tenants down to their sherry parties; and they found to their surprise that though William Joyce was so obviously odious in so many ways, so vulgar, so pushing, so lacking in sweetness, many of their guests found his conversation interesting and amusing and even charming. They were baffled. They did not know what they themselves wanted to do; but if they had known, the doing of it might not have been easy. The rent of the flat was paid with perfect regularity. It would have been difficult to break the lease except on very contestable grounds, and contest was certainly not out of Joyce's line.

So it seemed as if this exile was to lose his rootlessness in a place that asks roots to grow, and promises the grown plant pleasantness. Joyce's flat looked down on a communal garden of the sort that make South Kensington so pleasantly green; the houses which back on them have their dining-rooms built out into this garden. In summer-time the ladies of these houses often sit with their friends among tubs of flowers on the flat roofs of these dining-rooms, taking tea and looking down on their well-schooled children, who play on the lawns below. In late summer-time, in the year 1938, William Joyce sat in his pleasant home and applied for the renewal of his passport. It might be assumed that he had been sent for by someone who wished him to go abroad. It might also be assumed that he had not expected this summons, for he had let his passport expire without applying for its renewal. It had run out on the 6th of July. This was September the 24th: five days before the Munich Agreement was signed. Nothing is gained by the postponement of an application for the renewal of a passport. At whatever date the application is made, it is renewed from the date of its expiry. It is possible that William Joyce felt no exultation at all while he was filling in his application form. He had said that he had faced danger as a boy, but that was nearly twenty years ago. Ever since then he had lived cradled in the safety of the civil order of England which he and his Fascist friends and Communist enemies were vowed to destroy, and safety becomes a habit. He must have liked the green dignity of this garden part of Kensington; he would not have chosen to lodge there if some part of him had not remembered the home of his boyhood, that was also green, that was also London, in Allison Grove. He must have liked the setting of his life, and its core. He liked teaching; he had his meetings; and he was still deeply and romantically in love with

90

his wife. If he had given an undertaking to leave that home when a certain voice called him, then he must daily have known a real anguish.

That time Joyce did not have to give value for his bribe. The hot wind of danger blew and fell again; and immediately after Munich, Joyce lost his colleague Beckett, the former editor of *Action* and *The Blackshirt,* who severed all connections with him and started a pacifist organization of his own, which followed an ineffectual course and landed him safely in internment in 1940. It was as if he had caught some intimations of the end to which Joyce's policy was to lead him, and recoiled. At that time, too, Joyce began to lose the friendship of his landlords; and the German radio sounded too loud through the house, the hiccoughing piano achieved the Horst Wessel song too often. The breach widened when Hitler walked into Czechoslovakia; the doctor and his wife were standing in the hall aghast at the news when Joyce came in, and asked him, "Now what do you think of Hitler?" Joyce said, unsmiling, "I think him a very fine fellow", and went on his way up to his flat. MacNab came in a little later. The doctor and his wife pressed him for his opinion; and he too approved. The curious friendship between the two households, so unequal in social background and in character, faded from that moment, though the doctor and his wife still showed kindliness to Mrs. Joyce. Joyce, working alone, worked frantically. He spoke to every society that would let him inside its doors, in the warmer weather he had an open-air meeting every day, and sometimes several in one day. It was as if he were trying to leave an impression on the public mind that could be counted upon to endure; and indeed he partially succeeded in this aim. An enormous number of people in the low-income groups heard him speak, some during the years when he was with Mosley, and even more during the period when he was his own master.

Many people in the higher-income groups had also their contact with Joyce, but they did not know it. Anybody who was advertised as a speaker at a meeting appealing for funds or humane treatment for refugees from Nazi persecution would receive by every post, for many days before the meeting, threatening messages, couched always in the same words, and those words always so vague that the writers of them could not have been touched by the law. They were apt to come by the last post, and the returning householder, switching on the light, would see them piled up on the hall table, splinters from a mass of stupidity that might not, after all, be finite and destructible, but infinite and conterminous with life. Their postmarks showed they came from Manchester, Bristol, Bournemouth, Bethnal Green, Glasgow, Colchester. All over the country there were those who wished that the stranger, being hungry, should not be fed, being naked should not be clothed. Goats and monkeys, as Othello said, goats and monkeys; and the still house would seem like a frail and besieged fortress. This device was the invention of William Joyce. The people who heard him in the streets sometimes saw this alliance with crime displayed. A number of his meetings were provocative of the violence he loved; he was twice tried for assault at London police courts during the year preceding the outbreak of war, though each time the wind that sat in so favourable a quarter for Fascists blew him out with an acquittal. But at many others of his meetings he used all his powers, his harsh, sneering, cajoling, denatured, desperate voice, his quick and twisting humour, his ability to hammer a point home on a crowd's mind, to persuade the men and women he saw before him of the advantages of dictatorship, the dangers of Jewish competition and high finance, the inefficiency of democracy, the greatness and goodness of Hitler, and his own seriousness. His audiences were not much interested in his arguments and were shrewd enough in their judgment of him. Many remembered him seven years afterwards. Only a very few said, "I liked him." Most said, "He has the most peculiar views, but he really was an extraordinary chap", or some such words. "Extraordinary" was what they called him, nearly all of them. This impression might not have served Joyce so ill had the days brought forth what he expected. If the Germans had brought him with them when they invaded England and had made him their spokesman, many Londoners might have listened to him with some confidence because he was a familiar element in a scene which conquest would have made terrifying in its unfamiliarity; and they might have felt awe, and perhaps, still more, confidence, because there was something of the wizard in the little creature.

William Joyce's secret masters issued their second summons to him eleven months after the first. During that time his circumstances changed. In July he had left his agreeable home in South Kensington, at his own instance. In June he had suddenly written to the doctor saying that, with much regret, he must confess himself unable to carry out his three years' lease, which had still another year to run; the number of his pupils had, he explained, suddenly showed a sharp decline. The doctor answered, possibly not without some feeling of relief, that Joyce was at full liberty to sublet the flat, and this Joyce undertook to do. One day, before they left, the doctor's wife met Mrs. Joyce on the stairs and, with the extreme sweetness and generosity this couple always showed their strange tenants, paused to tell her how sorry she was that their connection must end for so sad a reason. She said, "All our fortunes vary, you know. One goes up and one comes down and then one comes up again, so you mustn't worry if things are bad." To her astonishment Mrs. Joyce burst into tears, flung her arms round her neck, and sobbed out, "You do not know how bad they are, you have no idea how bad they are." About this time a strange visitor appeared. A man who, like so many of the British National Socialist League, was Irish, rang the bell marked "Joyce" that was beside the doctor's bell at the front door. Joyce came down, opened the door, looked at the visitor, slammed it, and went upstairs again. The visitor went on ringing, and began to pound on the knocker. MacNab came down, white-faced, and opened the door, parleyed with the visitor, but, like Joyce, retreated. Out on the porch the visitor rang the bell and hammered on the door and began to shout. The doctor's manservant went out and tried to send him away; he cried out that he must see William Joyce, no one else would do. The door was shut, he remained outside, crying out in accusation, in imploration, in panic, as one who knew a great shame was to be committed and could not stop it. The police would have been fetched, but at that moment the doctor arrived, a tall, authoritative man, and took him by the arm, and turned him round towards South Kensington Station, and told him to follow the road to it. He went off, mumbling about a catastrophe. What is significant is that Joyce, for all his volubility, could not find an explanation for this incident.

Paying their rent up to the last minute, leaving no tradesmen's bills unsettled, the Joyces moved to a lodging as poor as any he had known since he had left Longbeach Road as a boy. It was a basement flat in a short street of dreary and discoloured houses, mean in size, which lies on the Warwick Road side of Earl's Court Station. Over their roofs, making them more dwarfish, looms the stadium, in formless height, more senseless than anything sculptured by unsentient forces, morbid with the sick pallor of concrete; and at the end of the street is the wall of Brompton Cemetery, panelled with openings covered by wire netting, which disclose the sparse tombs among the rank long grasses on the cemetery's edge, and the distant white crowd of stout Victorian dead round the central avenues. This was not only a melancholy home for Joyce, it was minute, no broader than a henhouse. It might have been chosen by a man who believed himself about to start life again at the beginning, without a penny behind him; if William Joyce had had to go back to tutoring he would have found it hard to re-establish himself. Or it might have been chosen by a man who believed himself about to go on a long journey and to need no more than a place to keep his clothes and his baggage till the time came to pack the one inside the other. It was probably chosen by a man who held both these views of his future. Human beings are mercifully so constituted as to be able to conceal from themselves what they intend to do until they are well into the doing of it. William Joyce must have been sure, in the summer of 1939, that there was going to be war, for we were all sure of that. And with half of his mind he knew what part he was going to play in it, but with only half; for again he let his passport expire. He did not apply for its renewal until the 24th of August; and that date destroys William Joyce's last claim on our sympathies. For it is one day after Hitler signed his pact with Stalin. Then this man who all his adult life had hated Communists must have known that his leader was an opportunist and not a prophet; that he himself was apostle of a policy and not a religion; that there was nothing in the cause to which he had devoted his life that was equal in worth to the ancient loyalties, which will not kiss their enemies upon the lips. Now he should have seen what was on the underside of the banners stamped on the overside with the swastika that hung between the sky and the stadium at Nuremberg. Now he should have recognized that the words he had been saying since 1927 were "Evil, be thou my good". But he would not open his eyes or unstop his ears, and in that darkness full of colour and in that silence full of cries and cheers he stood fast and chose damnation. It is here his happy marriage helped to contrive his doom. He had made his decision to go over to Germany with the knowledge of his wife. To have gone back on it would have been a confession that he had been unwise when he made it; and he may have feared that such a reversal might have looked like a failure in courage. There are risks the most loving will not take with the beloved.

This damnation was not simply sought. For William Joyce did not go to Germany on the eve of the war on an off-chance, and offer his services, and find that they were accepted. That there was a long and complicated and illicit series of events behind his appearance in Berlin in September 1939 is proven by the recollection of one who, in that year of doom, was a school-girl. One summer evening she was walking in the Fulham Road with her uncle, a young man who was a member of the British National Socialist League, when they met William Joyce, who was well known to both of them. He seemed strangely excited, and he told them, laughing extravagantly, that when he had been driving his car on the previous day he had been pulled in by the police for a trifling breach of the traffic regulations. The schoolgirl and her uncle were puzzled by his emotion. The uncle said, "But this is nothing. All sorts of people get run in for motoring offences." Joyce answered, waving his hat and clapping it back on his head, "Do you call this a motoring offence? I would call it a holding offence!" and went on his way. A "holding offence" is a device often and properly used by the police. When the police suspect a man of a serious crime but cannot prove him guilty of it, perhaps for the very good reason that he has not yet committed it, they watch him to see if he does not commit some minor offence, such as a breach of the traffic regulations. If they are lucky and he acts according to their expectation, then they can serve him with a summons, and until he has faced his trial can exercise a certain amount of control over him. During this time they can prevent him from leaving the country. Late in August 1939, in a street near Queen Anne's Gate, William Joyce met an acquaintance who had long ago been his neighbour in East Dulwich, and they halted and had a chat. When they parted, Joyce's acquaintance noted that he turned into the building beside which they had halted, and realized that this was the Passport Office. Even before that the name of William Joyce must have been posted at every port; and as soon as he fetched and had in his possession a renewed passport the warning signal should have been repeated. But a few days afterwards the police were searching for him all over the country; the old lady in Sussex was questioned, and her house was watched. William Joyce had found a port at which there was either a break-down of routine fantastically fortunate for him, or another traitor, working with him on the same pattern of treachery.

VI

IN Germany autumn is not as it is in England, a sweet time of sleep and mellowness. It is not as autumn is in America, a cold forest fire, that fills the eyes with flames, and the veins with a gay ice; all seasons in that continent bring unrest, but that is the happiest restlessness of the four. In Germany it is as if a beautiful burgess matron, it being no longer lawful that she should remain flesh, were turned to gold, before she turns to marble. For there autumn stands still like a statue, and is not grand, but is magical, and hard as metal. On the lakes the images of the dark pines and the yellow birches lie bright as themselves, and the morning mists have sharp edges. Virginia creeper clothes the little villas with redness like the glow from an elfin foundry. On the paved terraces above the swelling and darkened rivers, where the townsfolk walk on Sunday afternoons, the horse-chestnut trees shed those leaves like spread hands of a substance just sallower than gold. The air is like iron; those who sail up the waterways which run all the way from the Wannsee to the Baltic find their lips seared, though they may not feel very cold, by the air which has also come by water, and further, from the cap of the Arctic.

Into this season, which is one of Germany's particular graces, William Joyce was brought directly by his treachery. One day his little feet twinkled up the area steps of his basement flat; and at the top, no doubt, he paused to put his arm round his wife's waist and give her a hug. His eyes must have been dancing. No matter what his misgivings might have been, the risks of the adventure must have enchanted him. It must, indeed, have been intoxicating for him to go through London, where he had never been of any importance, where he was at best a street-corner speaker better known than most, and know that, if he won his gamble, he would return to it as the right hand of its conquerors. There would be then no building he would not have the right to enter, bearing with him the power to frustrate its existing function and constitute another. There would be no man or woman of power whom he would not see humiliated, even to the point of imprisonment and death. The first should be last, and the last should be first, and many would be called and few would be chosen, and he would be among those that were chosen. He left the damp and the fog which would soon close in on London, and the obscurity which had closed in on him ever since he was born, and he went out to the perfect autumn of Germany and the promise of mastery. Very soon he was established in a home in that most delightful suburb of Berlin, Charlottenburg, where there are broad streets and wide-windowed flats and little avenues of villas in flowery gardens. He lived in the Kastanien Allee — Chestnut Avenue — where the trees shed their yellow hands in great numbers down a picturesque vista.

William Joyce must have been happy during the first weeks of the war. He had reason to feel proud of his escape from England to Germany, as an achievement in the *Scarlet Pimpernel* vein, and as the result of a firm act of the will, which, as month passed month of "the phony war", seemed justified. It must have certainly appeared to him that England, decadent in its democracy, was going to fall into Hitler's hand so soon as he chose to try it on its stalk. He must also have enjoyed the amenities of Berlin, the opportunity to practise every sport; he was still only thirty-three, and he had never had enough time to play. His career is not encouraging to those who say that Satan

97

finds work for idle hands to do; from his middle teens he seems to have worked nearly all his waking hours, and to have slept little. He must also have enjoyed speaking German, a language which he had studied with a great deal of pleasure. And he enjoyed the fellowship of the Nazis, whom he believed to be about to inherit the earth because they were not meek. On the 18th of September 1939, exactly fifteen days after the outbreak of war, he joined the German radio as an announcer of the news on the English service, and had very soon become a reader of the news.

His voice was very soon recognized by the doctor and his wife in South Kensington, who had already begun to wonder about their former tenants. When an officer of the National Fire Service had come to examine their attics for combustibility they had found an inexplicable addition to their home. In a cistern loft, accessible only from the flat the Joyces had occupied, a bed had been put up and was there with its bedding. There was plenty of room to put up a bed in the ordinary rooms of the flat; the loft could be entered only by a very small trap-door, and it must have been very difficult to get the bed up through it; there was almost no space to spare round the bed. It must have been put up there during William Joyce's tenancy, for somebody who had to be sheltered without the knowledge of the doctor and his wife. Now William Joyce had lost a friend-ship which he had found it hard to win, and of which he had been proud. He cannot have fulfilled his duties very long without wondering just how competent his new friends the Nazis were. They underrated his remarkable powers as a broadcaster, and gave him nothing to do but read news bulletins. But he was used to being thought little of by people when he first met them. That the news he was broadcasting was often fatuously untrue, and rendered all German propaganda suspect by its untruth, was probably unknown to him. When he told England that in September or October 1939—long before any bombs had fallen on the British mainland—Dover and Folkestone had been destroyed, he may well have believed it. It is worth while noting that this period of Joyce's service to the Nazis was given an interest in England which it lacked for him. The local details by which Joyce was supposed to show that he had a direct channel of communication with England, such as allusions to stopped town-hall clocks and road repairs, are not in fact found in the records of his broadcasts. They were invented as part of a whispering campaign designed to weaken public confidence, which was carried on by Fascists, some of whom, if not all, belonged to organizations other than Joyce's British National Socialist League. Ignorant of the inaccuracy of his broadcasts, and the use that was being made of them, Joyce may have been bored with his work; but he cannot have felt such a passive emotion about the conditions in which he worked.

He must very soon have looked round the office of the English section of the Rundfunk in panic. It is said that the Duke of Wellington, on seeing some troops for the first time, exclaimed, "I don't know if these fellows frighten the enemy, but, by God, they frighten me!" So might William Joyce have exclaimed when he first saw the colleagues who had been artlessly assembled by Dr. Goebbels's propaganda machine. The only one of any definite personality was Norman Baillie-Stewart, who had been tried for selling military secrets to Germany in 1933 and had then been sentenced to five years' penal servitude. But the Germans made use of Baillie-Stewart only with extreme caution. The rest were inglorious odd-come-shorts. The most sympathetic among them was an elderly lady called Miss Margaret Frances Bothamley, who before the war had helped to found a body called the Imperial Fascist League and run it from her flat in the Cromwell Road. She was in a state of extreme confusion. She had brought with her to Germany photographs of the King and Queen and the Princesses, with which she ornamented her flat; and she believed that in her youth she had made a secret marriage with a German music-master named Adolf, whom she appeared to identify with Hitler. During the first months of the war Joyce was forced to recruit a member of Miss Bothamley's organization, who had been spending the summer in Germany: a colonel's daughter who was a member of one of the most famous literary families in England on her father's side and was related to a most exalted peer on her mother's side, but who had, through a series of unhappy accidents, found herself in her late forties lost in less distinguished worlds. She began by being an enthusiastic pro-Nazi, but, being fundamentally not without

99

honesty and decency, turned against the regime, and annoyed Joyce by sitting about in the office and doing knitting with an air of silent criticism.

There was also Mr. Leonard Black, who must have been a disappointing colleague for William Joyce. He was under thirty, and he had a long history behind him of inextricably confused idealistic effort and paid political adventure. He had at one time been a member of the B.U.F., but had left it and had later been a paid organizer in the service of the Conservative Party, while at the same time—which was odd—carrying on pacifist agitation. Then he went abroad and taught English at various branches of the Berlitz School of Languages, and was so doing in September 1939. It was his story later that the day before war was declared he went down to the station and tried to buy a ticket to England, and found they would not sell him one for German money, and, as he had no foreign currency, went home. Few of us do not know the mechanism employed. He had wanted to stay in Germany. He said, "I ought to go and see about that today. But tomorrow will do just as well. I have a lot to do now. I will go tomorrow." He did that until one day when somehow it became possible to put aside all engagements and take the necessary steps; and on that day it happened that those necessary steps could no longer be taken. Then he returned home saying, "Well, I have done all I could. Nobody could have told that today it would be too late. It is not my fault." And at the back of his mind a voice must have said with cold cunning, "Yes, I will be able to tell them that, if things go wrong and I am called to account", while another voice said, "Look, you Nazis, I have stayed with you". Few of us—except the people who are in fact intolerable nuisances by reason of their incapacity for compromise—but have at some time or other behaved according to this formula. William Joyce, having just abandoned this formula at the great crisis of his life, was unlikely to feel sympathy with Leonard Black or other recruits of his type.

He owed the presence of Black in his office to the activities of a certain Herr Albrecht, whose business it was to see what Englishmen stranded in Germany would do for their hosts. He sent for Mr. Black and a friend of his called Mr. Smith and questioned them as to their readiness for co-operation. Mr. Black went home and wrote Herr Albrecht a typically ambiguous letter. "Dear Herr Albrecht," he wrote, "I write to make it perfectly clear that I have not offered to work for the Gestapo. I would never think of doing that, and I absolutely refuse to sell my country. There is a certain price I will not pay. The most I would do is radio propaganda." And he ended with a postscript which bears a significance beyond his intention. "Mr. Smith", he wrote, "will not even do radio propaganda." Mr. Smith, using that term in its generic sense, did not even do radio propaganda. Only a small proportion of the civilian internees or prisoners of war turned traitor; and of those that did, many found themselves too noble to be the instrument of their own ignobility and went back to their camps, where some of them were punished till they died, and all suffered grave torment. They were not many, the men who could split their minds in two and pretend that while they were serving Germany they were making contact with anti-Nazi elements and sabotaging Nazi activity, which was the defence that nearly all of them kept at the back of their minds and produced at their trials. All such men hated William Joyce, who did not split his mind, who desired to make England Fascist, and, to procure that end, was ready to help Germany to conquer England, and never denied that desire or that readiness, either during the war or after it.

He sat among the hatred of these poor silly creatures, and knew a more humiliating hatred from some others who worked in his office. A certain number of Germans had been drafted into the office, men who had a special knowledge of the English language and English life. As such men had usually acquired their knowledge through having English relatives or having been educated in England, many were anti-Nazi. They despised Joyce as a traitor to his own country and an enemy to their own country, the true Germany; and they were gentlemen, and cruelly knew he was not a gentleman. But there was another painful element in the office, which must have cut William Joyce far deeper. The Nazis were prone, in all sorts of circumstances, to make a peculiar error. When one of their enemies became their friend, they went on treating him as an enemy. However ready he might be to serve their interests, however much they might need his help, they continued to savage him. The great historic example of this curious trick is their treatment of the Russian soldiers and civilians who, by tens of thousands, gladly surrendered to them as they invaded Russian territory in 1941 and 1942. These people who might have been their most valuable aids then and for ever after, they packed into cattle trucks and sent off to camps where they were starved and tortured. Later they were fetched out and invited to fight alongside the Germans, but by that time their enthusiasm was not what it had been, and the treatment they received in training and at the front failed to revive it. The Germans acted on the same perverse principle towards the British broadcasters, who were all favourably disposed towards them to start with, and, having burned their boats, had every reason to remain firm in the faith. But at the head of the British section, which they had as if in mockery called the Concordia Bureau, they placed a certain Dr. Hetzler, who was so much of a brute as to seem to many of them a maniac. Throughout the war he exercised every sort of ferocity on his wretched staff, English and German.

Two Germans were to tell a British court what Dr. Hetzler had been, in evidence that was disinterested and, indeed, unaware of its own portent. When Mr. Black was tried at the Old Bailey early in 1946, the prosecution called as a witness one of the German technicians who had recorded his talks. He was an S.S. man, a lank and hollow-cheeked young man, who might have been carved in wood in the thirteenth century, and he spoke a peculiar wooden German which might come to be natural in a man who had been drilled all his youth by tyranny and then marched along a straight road for many years in the direction of defeat. He was called Krumpiegel; surely one might as well be called Rumpelstiltskin. As he gave evidence, there stood beside him the interpreter who is one of the chief glories of the Old Bailey, that slender and distinguished old gentleman of Spanish Jewish descent, Mr. Salzedo. He was very courteous to the defeated barbarian but plainly savoured a certain satisfaction as, in his silvery voice, he translated the comic expressions used by barbarity. "Did Black look happy when he was at the Concordia Bureau?" asked the defending counsel. Mr. Salzedo translated: "He says that he does not consider happy (*glücklich*) an appropriate word to use in connection with Black's personality, but for the greater part of the war he could fairly be described as contented (*zufrieden*)." The defending counsel continued: "But did Black seem to be contented in his relations with the head of the Bureau, Dr. Hetzler?" Krumpiegel looked more wooden than ever; he folded his arms behind him, said some words, and looked blank as an ill-treated child that has told the truth about its tormentors and does not believe that it will not be punished for it, whatever the grown-ups say. Mr. Salzedo translated: "He says Dr. Hetzler's relations with his employees were never a source of gratification." There came later to give evidence for Mr. Black one of the anti-Nazi Germans who had worked in the Concordia Bureau. This young man wore an air of desolation more usually presented by places than by persons. There used to be a derelict factory on the New Jersey marshes which had the same air of not having, anywhere in all eternity, a possible use. His evidence gave Mr. Black little help in proving his innocence, but absolved him from mockery. A question made allusion to Dr. Hetzler. The anti-Nazi paused before answering. In accomplished, springless, exhausted, pedantic English, he said, "Dr. Hetzler was . . . the *prototype* . . . of the Nazis." Both Black and this young German had been battered by huge irrational waves, tides obeying the moon of Hell.

It would be interesting to know whether these waves ever battered William Joyce. At no trial did any evidence emerge that threw any light on his relations with his employers; and on the American correspondents who alone of the outside world saw him during this period he left only an impression of laughing, cursing, story-telling garrulity. The little creature was, as we were to see later, so tight-lipped that we cannot construe this as evidence that he was not savaged like his colleagues. But whether he suffered this violence himself or not, he must have observed its infliction upon others; and that would be his first experience of the real suspension of civilization, the real reversion to barbarism. If a rebellious Fascist was beaten up in the cells in the barracks of King's Road, Chelsea, if a Jew was chased up an alley in Bethnal Green, this violence might be valued by persons with peculiar tastes, as a pearl; but a pearl has to be formed within a shell, and civil order was the shell in which an act of violence could preserve its exciting quality. A world where violence was the shell as well as the pearl was new to William Joyce, and it cannot have been an easy conception to accept. But there must have seemed, as 1940 went on, not much need to worry about what were obviously only temporary conditions. When there were gathered in as Nazi harvest first Norway, then Denmark, then the Low Countries, then France, there was nothing on earth to prevent the fall of England; and all the poor misfits in the Concordia Bureau must have had their heads stuffed with infantilist dreams. In these dreams a fast car, long as a bus, would be sent down to Dulwich to pick up the family and bring them to Joyce's office: which would have been in Buckingham Palace, or in the War Office, or Downing Street. . . .

It would, in fact, have been in none of these places. Inexorably the law that to him that hath it shall be given would have come into operation again; there would certainly have come forward as quislings after the first few days of the German occupation this popular historian and that expert in foreign affairs, this civil servant and that leading Communist, and these would have been given precedence over William Joyce, who would have found himself fulfilling just the same subordinate role in the new dispensation as in the old. But that he would not have suspected. He must have imagined himself saying to his father and mother, smiling, "Well, this is my room. Do you like it? And the next one is mine, too, that's where my three secretaries work." He would have talked his young brothers and his sister into taking good jobs, and would have found admiring Angus MacNab, whom he had released at once from internment, a post that would keep him close to him. In the evening his wife would have worn fine new dresses, like the wives of Goering and Goebbels, in a home he had no doubt long since chosen as he passed it in his little car, on the way back from a meeting. Mr. Black had friends at Brighton, and, in his daydreams, would have extended his protection to them, for he was generous. They were afterwards to put up bail for him. Miss Bothamley, no doubt, would have explained the beneficent intentions of the

104

invaders to Queen Elizabeth and the Princesses; and the colonel's daughter, who was a kindly creature, would have looked after the interests of her former husbands. No expert has ever been able to explain just why the situation in which these dreams might know a partial realization did not materialize. It must have been a sickening blow to the inhabitants of the Concordia Bureau when weeks and months passed, and the Nazis still did not invade Britain.

There came the air raids, and the apotheosis of William Joyce. He was a revolutionary, and a revolutionary blows both hot and cold: he hates order and he loves it. He wants to overthrow the order which exists and which may be the only order capable of existing. But he risks the annihilation of all order only because he believes he can evade it and can substitute for the existing order another which he believes to be superior. This may be an absence of order which, by a mystical logic, he has proved to be more orderly than the presence of order. It may be an order which subconsciously he knows to be uniquely inefficient, which alone can restore nothingness to a world so obstinately created, so irretrievably stuffed with things. All the available energy of the will is poured out into the destruction of a system which, however, has come into existence not at the behest of that finite force, the human will, or any number of human wills, but as the result of the interaction of innumerable forces, some invested in man, some diffused through earth and air and fire and water. Not in the short space of a catastrophe will the nature of man be modified; so the human interests which profited by the system survive after it has crashed. So when the will and earth and fire and water set about to make a new system, it is bound to be like the old. In revolution there is a vast explosion of the creative powers, and nothing is created; nothing is even altered. The appetite for death that is in us all is immensely gratified, and that is all.

The French Revolution has given pleasure to all subsequent generations because it was an outstanding event which afterwards proved never to have happened. A number of revolutionaries arose and overturned the monarchy of France because of its tyranny and its financial and economic inefficiency, in order that they might substitute a republic which should give its people liberty, make them equal, and join them in fraternity. When the dust settled, France was ruled by a self-crowned emperor who wielded power more absolute than any French king had ever been given by the priests who crowned him; and the society which reconstituted itself after his fall conferred on its people increases of liberty and equality and fraternity no greater than were won by other nations untouched by revolution. The Russian Revolution, which is plainly going to be a source of still greater satisfaction, achieves a more perfect balance; for, with an enormously greater expenditure of blood than France ever saw, it slowly reconstituted the Tsardom it destroyed, identical in spirit, and reinforced in matter; so that the waste of the revolutionaries' creative effort is manifestly more extravagant. William Joyce was among those who were setting their hands to the Nazi Revolution, which, with an infinitely greater expenditure of blood than either France or Russia had seen, was to tear down Europe and leave it in ruins, as it is today and shall be until our souls and earth and air and fire and water make it again.

Therefore he must have known delight as the German planes went out to destroy England, and anguish too. For though the revolutionary's love of death finds joy in what he does, his love of life knows it to be criminal. That is why he contrives that the drama of the revolution shall develop so that in the end he shall pay for his crime with his life. The scaffolds of Paris took, in the end, all those that set them up; and of the actual engineers of the Russian Revolution, all but a handful were hoist by their own petard. So when the German planes went out against England, William Joyce, the sublime example of this extreme type, stood in Berlin at the microphone, conspiring to replace the complex social organization of Western civilization by a system which was not a system, which had not an idea in its head but to set people who needed work to do some work, it did not matter what, and to shut up people whom it did not like in concentration camps, and which was now to press home its negativism by making a useless war. He sent out to his own country, where his parents and his children were still living, threats against their safety, speaking of the planes that were being sent out against them so that they should be burned to death, of the hundreds of thousands of "gross registered tons" (a phrase the traitors always enjoyed reading) of their country's shipping that were being sunk so that they should starve, and very early in the battle of Britain a bomb fell on Michael Francis Joyce's house in Allison Grove. Nothing remains of it now save a hole in the ground beside the remains of a neighbour's basement; a fine tree, long grasses, and lilacs and syringas grown wild-branched for lack of pruning give the scene a certain elegiac beauty. The family lost all their possessions except a trunk full of old papers and a few pieces of furniture, and they went to live at a rest centre until they were found another house. To strangers they seemed arrogant and unmoved by the shame of being kin to Joyce, who by now had been identified by many people, particularly in this district, as the news reader on the German service known all over England as "Lord Haw-Haw". But when a worker in the centre came to Mr. and Mrs. Joyce and told them that she was a friend of the doctor and his wife who had been Joyce's landlords in South Kensington, and that she herself had met Joyce, the old man and his wife broke down. William had always been the difficult one of the family, they said, but they had never thought he would be led away into doing anything so terrible as this, for he had always been a good boy at heart. It was perhaps his trouble, they pleaded, that he was too brilliant. They were ultimately found a house, a characterless little modern villa in an uninteresting part of Dulwich, which must have been too small to hold a family of such numbers and such strong individualities. It is not easy to understand why Michael Francis Joyce, who was by then over seventy, and his wife, who was growing very frail, did not go to the country under the evacuation scheme. But there was no real reason why Lear should have wandered on the stormy heath instead of taking shelter from the storm. Men sometimes feel, however, that if a certain hammer falls it is their part to act as anvil. Michael Francis Joyce lived among the amazement of the news and the bombs until he died five months later, on the 19th of February 1941.

It is not known whether Joyce heard of the destruction of his family's home and the death of his father at the time of these events; but it is not impossible that he did, however loyally his relatives kept their obligation not to communicate with him, for the Joyces had connections and friends in both Eire and the United States. In any case the tide of his joy was on the turn. It had risen to its height in that same time when the house in Allison Grove was bombed, when his father and mother were dependent on strangers for a hearth; when he, for no discernible reason but to curse the true facts of his birth, became a German citizen; when he sneered over the radio because the planes England sent against the Nazi revolution dropped their bombs on sham cities, *doppelgänger* Berlins and Hamburgs and Essens, laid out on fields with lights, where mock fires were started to make the raiders believe they had hit their targets. But destiny knew tricks worth three of that. In time the Berlin night above William Joyce's head was sprayed with such gold and silver and precious stones as he had seen when he had stood with his young wife at the windows of his flat by the Crystal Palace, watching the fireworks displays. But these bore real fire; and after the flames came worse: the sound of doom. An American correspondent who broadcast from Berlin up to the time of Pearl Harbour has described how one night he could not leave the Rundfunk building because of a fierce R.A.F. raid, and took shelter in the company of William Joyce and his wife, and how Joyce served out a stream of amusing and inventive oaths against the raiders. He smiled as he blasphemed; but his was true blasphemy, a railing against life, the way things grow, the way things happen, reality itself. Now he tried to break the one link his egotism had maintained with any real object outside himself. That he and his wife loved each other deeply cannot be doubted, but as the war went on his treatment of her became noticeably unkind. When a child is moved to hatred by some action of its parents and screams at them and beats them with its little hands, and its rage wears out, it feels guilty, it sobs, it devises means of punishing itself, it goes and stands in the corner of its own accord. William Joyce, aware of the offence he had committed against the intimates whom he had addressed over the air to tell them that they were less than strangers to him, aware that the strangers whom he preferred to these intimates had destroyed the hearth of his father and driven him out to die under an unloved roof, felt guilty, and tried to punish himself by making a stranger of his wife, the one intimate left to him. The reality of the love between them would not permit him to make the sacrifice, but his sense of sin egged him on to it during those years when the city he had chosen as his, because it promised to be his accomplice in violence, altered and assumed the character of an accuser: when every morning more and more of the huge houses where brutal people lived in the pride of their unkind flesh showed themselves blackened by fire and hollow as skulls, and told Joyce to remember death.

During these years his work in the Rundfunk became more degrading in nature. From the beginning he had been engaged in the unhandsome business of recruiting announcers and speakers in the camps of British civilian internees; but a gloss could be put on its unhandsomeness. If among the internees there were many like the sturdy Mr. Smith who were Britons in fact and sympathy and conveyed to the Gestapo that they would "not even do radio propaganda", there were others like his friend Mr. Leonard Black, who had come to work in Germany because of a deep affection for the country, and the colonel's daughter, who was a member of a British Fascist society and had been caught by the war when she was paying her annual visit to renew her ecstasy of catching sight of Hitler. There were other internees who were British only from a legal standpoint, such as people who had been brought up in Germany since childhood or who were the children of mixed marriages; and of these a number were sincerely glad to have an opportunity to perform any service asked of them by what they considered as their real fatherland. But as the war went on William Joyce was obliged to do more and more of his recruiting among prisoners of war, first drawn from the mercantile marine, then from the regular services, the army, the navy, and the air force. In only a very few cases could Joyce have the slightest reason to suppose that the men he was approaching would have any ideological bias towards fascism. What he was doing was to seek out men who as prisoners of war were undergoing an extreme physical and mental ordeal, and to bribe them by promises of freedom and food and drink and the society of women into sacrificing their honour: which was no empty phrase in this connection. When they went to the microphone with William Joyce, they broke their oath of allegiance to the head of their state and cut themselves off from their comrades for reasons that were apparent and contemptible, and they committed in little such an act of cruelty to their kin as Joyce had committed to his, on his own grand scale; they transferred their loyalty to the people who were dropping bombs on their parents and wives and children. It was an ugly business and it grew uglier in the handling.

At first very few prisoners yielded to temptation. The British authorities had foreseen the situation and had made provision for it. Members of all services were warned before they left England that the Germans would ask them to broadcast, putting it to them first that they would thus be able to reassure their families regarding their safety, and they were ordered to refuse in any and all circumstances. The British officers who were put in charge of prisoner-of-war camps under the German staff constantly warned all ranks of the attempts that would be made to seduce them, and kept an eye on those who seemed likely to succumb to seduction. Moreover, certain men, mostly non-commissioned officers, were put through a course of training before they went abroad which prepared them for the ordeal of fooling the Germans and serving as spies. One of them, a quartermaster-sergeant of the Gunners named John Henry Owen Brown, who has since retired to a villa called The Wee House in a Thames-side suburb, resembled a Homeric hero in his courage and his cunning. Few of these Pimpernels came into action at once; so that all the Germans got for some time was an odd prisoner or two who, dazed by shock or by natural imbecility, consented to be interviewed before the microphone regarding the circumstances of his capture. They did not take serious steps to improve their position till 1942, and the big drive they made did not show its results until 1943 and 1944. There were never many traitors, but there were some, and this was inevitable, because the number of prisoners of war was so large that it was bound to include a few representatives of the Fascist minority in Great Britain, and rather more than a few rogues and madmen. Moreover, some sane men were losing their balance under the pressure of the terrible conditions peculiar to the life of a prisoner of war, the worst of which is the uncertainty concerning the duration of his imprisonment.

The most interesting example of the sincere Fascist traitor was a pilot officer in the R.A.F., a man of forty, who joined the S.S. and wrote broadcasting scripts for Joyce. He uttered a revealing remark when a court-martial sentenced him to ten years' imprisonment for an extreme act of treason which might well have cost him his life. He said indignantly to his lawyer, "This just shows how rotten this democratic country is. The Germans would have had the honesty to shoot me." The Nazis made curiously little use of this honest and lettered fanatic or any of his kind. They seemed more at ease with the rogues and the madmen and the sane men off their balance, whom they took great trouble to procure, almost more trouble than one could think would have been necessary. They established holiday camps, at which the conditions were comfortable and even, to the eyes of many privates and ratings, luxurious; and the German welfare officers in the ordinary prisoner-of-war camp approached men whom they had marked down as likely prospects and told them that, as they had of late been working specially hard or seemed to be in poor health, it had been decided they should go for a month to one of these special camps. It would very often be true that these men were overworked and ill, and therefore the invitation seemed to them a welcome sign of humanity in their captors, and when their own officers told them not to accept it, the advice seemed a sign of their inhumanity. Most of the men thus tempted kept their heads, but some did not. These were exposed during their sojourn in the holiday camp to gentle propaganda, and at the end of the month were returned to the normal discomfort of their original camp. After they had had a few days on which to brood on the change, Joyce or one of his agents paid them a visit and suggested that a permanent return to comfort might be arranged if only they would read some scripts before the microphone. It would be explained that these broadcasts would be extremely pro-British and would simply aim at the affirmation of German good-will towards Great Britain, and this was often true, for this was the early radio policy of Dr. Goebbels.

This was a cleverly designed procedure, because it gave the men a pretext to get out of the prisoner-of-war camp and retain a show of self-respect, but most of the men on whom the promise of comfort reacted were not greatly interested in their self-respect. As a typical broadcasting traitor there may be taken Francis Dale, a New Zealand Commando, the son of an Irishman in business as an undertaker in an English provincial town. He was captured in Crete in 1941 and in a couple of years fell into the Nazi net, for reasons he disclosed with pathetic candour in his statement. "After coming out of the various prison camps in Germany, where we had, to say the least, lived a rather rough life, coming into this villa, furnished as it was with every luxury, completely shattered us. We did not know what to think of it. The food was nothing special, but the place was so comfortable." In 1946 this man appeared at the Old Bailey, in the course of a curious exploration of the possibilities inherent in the criminal law of England. He had been court-martialled under the Army Act and sentenced to ten years' imprisonment, and he had been out of jail to give evidence against one of the four traitors charged with high treason; and now he was emerging to give evidence against six merchant-seamen traitors, which he offered quite without malice and indeed attempted to cancel by several artless efforts to convince the court that he and they, united in a common state of nobility, had all committed acts of sabotage against the Germans. But his appearance alone prejudiced his claim. His breadth of shoulder was more than human, and every now and then he sucked his teeth or sniffed as a pig grunts, just to register the continuity of consciousness. Everything about him spoke of simplification on the scale indicated by a sentence in a well-known American book on the care of dogs: "After a dog has had a love affair, it puts on its hat, goes away, and doesn't write". The seduction of such a person would not have been difficult; and it was hard to understand why the Germans took such pains over it, or why, when their aim was accomplished, they made such a fatuous use of him. For he was employed to deliver such stuff as this:

"Once more I say, people of Great Britain, just think for a moment and you will realize how much we are losing, individually and as a nation, as a whole. The sooner we stop this senseless slaughter and come to our right senses and furthermore kick the Jews out of our country, the sooner we shall be able to secure peace for ourselves and for the rest of the world and, above all, shall we secure a return to the high British standards of living that are so dear to us all. Let them remain, and we shall find ourselves sold to everlasting Jewish bondage and our children will only be able to turn round and say that we delivered the Empire to the Jews."

The only words in this broadcast which might have riveted the attention of English listeners were its last sentence, which was, remarkably enough, "United we fall". By this time the English, who had for ten years housed a large Jewish population which had had to flee for its bare life before persecution, were unlikely to believe in the international power of the Jews, and were even less likely to believe, after having suffered the blitz and passed through the severest phase of the food shortage, and had their hearts jerked out of their breasts again and again by the North African campaign, that they had more to fear from the Jews than from the Germans. It is not easy to believe that William Joyce, who was no fool and had a long experience in propaganda, could have believed that the broadcasting of such stuff was politic. He was certainly a passionate and sincere anti-Semite. Every time he spoke of those whom he called, in a drawled, sneering dissyllable, "The Jeeoos", his acquired accent cracked and fell away and his strong native Irish had its own way. But it was the line of his cunning to suppress his immediate passions for the sake of the ultimate victory; and it might have been expected that he would at this particular juncture have broad-cast messages that pretended a German passion for tolerance, and readiness to let bygones be bygones and race be race. But though he was sometimes represented as directing the policy of the Concordia Bureau, it seems certain that the direction was entirely in the hands of the German Foreign Office, and that he had no say in it at all. It is to be noted that people who were accustomed to hear Joyce speak in public and talk in private in England declare that they could not recognize the substance of his broadcasts as characteristic until late in the war; some say that he was not his true, vehement, salty self until as late as D-day.

In 1943 he was still obeying orders; and the man whose efficiency was respected by the metropolitan police must have thought those orders fairly silly. He must have marvelled over the fuss that his masters made over Mr. Walter Purdy. This young man, the son of a widow living in Barking, was twenty-two when he was captured at Narvik, where he was serving as a junior engineer in H.M.S. *Vandyke*, and he suffered from a psychological form of St. Vitus' Dance. He had always to be committing some action, whether it bore any relation to any he had committed before or was to commit afterwards, and his reasoning self spent most of its time trying to pull these unrelated actions into some sort of coherence. His entry into the Nazi service began when he had been a prisoner of war for three years and had got into a certain amount of trouble, having been sentenced by the German authorities to ten days' imprisonment for having struck a superior officer of the camp. At this point he bought from one of the German officers a copy of Joyce's book called *Twilight over England* and got him to send it up to Berlin with a request that he should autograph it. His excuse for doing this was that he intended to take the book home and sell it, and that Joyce's signature would raise its value. But he had a link with Joyce, for he had met him nine years before when for a brief period he had been a member of the Ilford branch of the B.U.F.; and three weeks after he sent Joyce's book to Berlin he left for one of the holiday camps. Before he went he gave a fellow-prisoner a letter addressed to the Senior British Officer, with directions that it should not be given to him until the camp was broken up at the end of the war. This letter contained a statement that he intended to disregard the instructions forbidding co-operation with the Germans which had been issued by the authorities, if any opportunity arose to persuade the Germans to repatriate him to England or a neutral country.

This letter was plainly a form of insurance policy. If the Germans won the war, then he would be on the right side, and his friend would never have the opportunity to give up the letter. If the Allies won, then he had this letter to prove that he had disobeyed orders and broadcast for Joyce only because he hoped to get back to England. It must be noted that practically all the traitors defended themselves on the ground that they had gone over to German service in order to get opportunities to escape and to do what they could to sabotage the German war effort. This defence was so invariably raised, and by men of such different types, that it seems probable that it was suggested to them by the agents who recruited them. "After all, you can always say that you thought you would have a better chance to escape once you were out of the camp, and that you meant to send messages home over the air, or put sugar into the petrol tanks of our vehicles, and so on. Nobody will be able to say you did not."

The first part of this suggestion Walter Purdy had dealt with by his letter; on the second part he brought to bear his peculiar proliferating ingenuity persistently during the remaining two years of the war. He worked well for Joyce, broadcasting violent anti-Semitic propaganda. At the same time he conducted an immense and animated correspondence with his family in London, suggesting in veiled terms that he was incorporating in his broadcasts information to the Royal Air Force about the weather. In those letters he used the term "Eric's boss" for the R.A.F., because he had a nephew called Eric who was a sergeant in that force; at one time he wrote that "the instructions I gave were concerning weather or not my cash to them had been received, and weather they have been able to invest it in the securities I previously mentioned in my letters", and he summed up his instructions in a little poem:

When it is just good night,
There's not a flight of birds who'll take the sky,
But when the moon is bright,
On a good good night,
There's many a man will try.
A good night all is just the call,
For brave men good and true,
But a good good night to everyone
Is the best good night of all.

This, of course, alleged a special significance in the ending of his broadcasts. The originals of these letters were destroyed by a flying bomb during the last months of the war, but there is no doubt that they existed, for his family, highly respectable and well-meaning people, gave them to an official of the Red Cross, who forwarded them to the proper quarters. Walter Purdy stuck to the story he told in these letters right to the very end. Only when he was under cross-examination in the dock of the Old Bailey did he realize that the British authorities knew that his broadcasts were not direct but recorded, and that the recordings were not always used the same day they were made, and that in consequence his warnings must always have been valueless, and that he must have been well aware of this. For all the intelligence and crazy creativeness of his scheme, he lacked the something in his brain which would have warned him that, once the war was over, the British authorities would have no difficulty in acquainting themselves with the routine of the Rundfunk.

While Walter Purdy was carrying on this deception, which must have taken up a great deal of his time, and put him to much trouble, he was living through adventures of a cast peculiar to his experience. At one point he was taken away to a British prisoner-of-war camp at a place called Colditz; and he claimed that this was because the Germans had discovered various deeds of daring which he had committed, including two attempts to murder William Joyce. It is to be noted that the trial at which he told this story began on the same day that the House of Lords was disallowing William Joyce's last appeal against his conviction for treason. A very good reason for doubting this story is the fact that at Colditz there was working the superb British agent, John Henry Owen Brown, fulfilling his function as an Intelligence agent in communication with England from within a German camp; and about this time the Germans had become suspicious of him. When Purdy got to Colditz he met an officer with whom he had been imprisoned in another camp, a dentist who had apparently become distraught through prolonged separation from his drill; for though Purdy arrived at the camp alone, which was always considered a suspicious circumstance, he engaged Purdy in an extended and unreserved conversation ending with inquiries as to what he thought of John Henry Owen Brown, and when Purdy disingenuously replied that Brown was quite a nice fellow but too friendly with the Germans, he assured him that he was mistaken and that Brown was "doing very good work, and he has to appear to be friendly with them". They then went to look for the postal officer, and the fate which was presiding over the occasion led them to the entrance of an escape tunnel, the existence of which was not known to the dentist. Later Purdy was present at a reading of B.B.C. news, which, of course, revealed that there was a wireless hidden in the camp. As soon as he arrived at the camp he had to submit to interrogation by several of the senior British officers, who had to collect information which might be helpful to prisoners intending to escape, and to these he told a not implausible story of having escaped from a holiday camp, of having been sheltered in Berlin ever since by a woman, and of having been recaptured because he had lost his fake papers in an air raid. But suddenly he told them the truth, accusing himself in terms of complete self-abasement, crying out that he had behaved like a rat and a traitor. He expressed himself with a fantastic honesty which carried a double threat for himself. His confession was couched in terms that would have cost him his life if the Germans had heard him; but when he was asked by the Senior British Officer, "Suppose the Germans allowed you to go back to this woman who I understand you are living with in Berlin, would you then give away what was going on in the camp?" he answered, "I am afraid I would". He explained that he was very much in love with the German woman who had befriended him; this was the manageress of a pastrycook's shop, called Margarethe. He wanted to marry her, and for that reason he would have to give the information if the Germans promised him his freedom in exchange for it.

The Senior British Officer then said, "In that case there is nothing I can do except to try to get rid of you", and he ordered him to be put under close arrest, which is to say, that two English officers were continually with him, and requested the German Camp Commandant to take him out of the camp. This was done very shortly afterwards. It was a morally mysterious incident. For not only would the Germans have shot him if the British officers had repeated in detail what he had said to them, ill might have befallen him in the camp once he had refused to give a pledge of secrecy. Discipline did not prevent some very unpleasant things happening to prisoners of war whose comrades believed them to be informers. But we do not know how long that Dostoievsky mood lasted. Within a very few days the Germans entered the camp and went straight to the tunnel to which the unfortunate dentist had unwittingly led Mr. Purdy, and also searched for the secret wireless set and found it; and the British agent, Quartermaster-sergeant Brown, was interrogated by a number of German officers, and by a Major Hempel, a Counter-Intelligence officer, and Dr. Ziegfeld, a Foreign Office official, with both of whom Purdy was in frequent contact. Brown was then regarded with such suspicion that he had to lie low for the time being. It was, however, the opinion of the Old Bailey jury that these events were unconnected with Purdy's sojourn in the camp, and he was acquitted on the charge arising out of them.

It is pleasant to learn that the British agent, Quartermaster-sergeant Brown, returned to work not very long after Purdy brought this trouble on him, having convinced the Germans of his lack of integrity, and in November 1944 carried out a characteristic operation. He sent four prisoners of war who were working under his orders to do a job of house-cleaning in a villa in Berlin belonging to the German Foreign Office, which was now shared by Purdy and another traitor. Untroubled by German supervision, they searched the house and found in the wastepaper basket, that ancient focus of international interest, some correspondence deeply compromising to Purdy. But the net was to do nothing so simple in Purdy's case as to close in on him. When Germany crumbled into defeat there began for him the nightmare that all the traitors knew at that time. They were treated like unloved children whose parents are doing a moonlight flitting: stuffed into the van and told to hold their noise or else. On April 7, when the Americans were nearing Hanover, he was in Berlin; two S.S. men in plain clothes called and told him to pack a bag and come with them. They put him on a train for Italy with a mixed bag of traitors, and there they were taken from place to place until he and a Dutch broadcaster stole a motor-cycle and rode towards the German front lines. Finally they were captured by Italian partisans, who handed them over to the American army, where they were interrogated. Just after the end of the war he was repatriated to England, and there he was interrogated, four days later, by Inspector Davis and Inspector Edwards, two Scotland Yard men who had been lent to the War Office and had done distinguished Intelligence work. They took an immensely long statement from him, in which he told the whole story of all he had done for the Germans, claiming that he had been moved at times by a desire to serve Great Britain, and sometimes by the fear of death. And no proceedings were taken against him.

This was natural enough. No evidence had then come in from the officers of the camp at Colditz; and most people who met Purdy thought him insane, an impression which was confirmed by the extraordinary nature of his statement. At that time the authorities had too much on their hands to bother overmuch about a lunatic who had certainly strayed into the Rundfunk but who had been more trouble to the Germans than he was worth. The matter might have rested there had not Purdy continued to be himself, to create his unique and suicidal experience. He remained closely associated with his Margarethe till the break-up of his life in Berlin. Very soon after he arrived in London, however, he fell deeply in love with a young typist; and his emotion had the curious effect of making him write a complete account of everything he had done in Germany. It is interesting that this account, which was many thousands of words long, was almost the same, sentence by sentence, as the statement he had given to Inspectors Davis and Edwards, weeks before. He put this in an envelope and gave it to the typist, telling her she was to send this to a solicitor if he was arrested.

He was not sure himself why he did this. Sometimes he said it was because he was afraid that if the police arrested him after all, he would not be allowed to consult his solicitor and supply him with the true facts of his activity in Germany; and sometimes he said that he wanted people to read the statement after he had been hanged and understand what sort of man he had been. His next step was one that many much less intelligent men than Purdy would have recognized as unwise. He abandoned his sweetheart before he had recovered the envelope. She opened it and read its contents, which were a complete surprise to her. From motives not so much of greed as of anger, she told him that she would take the letter to the police if he did not give her a sum of money large enough for him to find it hard to raise. This threat, as the letter was practically a replica of the statement Purdy had made to the police, need have amounted to very little. But Purdy thought it right and proper to go into the nearest police station and, in a dramatic monologue delivered with great force and brilliance, appeal to the law to protect him against this attempt to blackmail him. He told his full story without the slightest reserve; and when the dazed constabulary appealed for guidance to headquarters, the result was positive. By now the reports from the officers who had been at Colditz had come in, and if Purdy was well enough to be going about London in an active state he was well enough to stand judgment for his crimes.

So it happened that he was arrested and charged with high treason, not with the milder crime of an offence against the Defence Regulations, for the reason that such acts as the betrayal of the secrets of the camp at Colditz, of which he was then believed guilty, were precisely those which the authorities wanted to see punished. He was prosecuted on three counts; and on the two counts arising out of his broadcasting and the preparation of leaflets for a propaganda branch of the S.S. he was found guilty, but on the third indictment, arising out of his activities in Colditz, he was found not guilty. He was sentenced to death, and returned to Wandsworth Jail, where William Joyce was awaiting his execution, and was put in another condemned cell; but hardly noticed it, being rapt in a new interest. The police like no crime less than blackmail, which indeed is the iciest sin, far further from love than murder. As soon as they had Purdy's case well under way they prosecuted the typist who had betrayed him for demanding money from him with threats. Immediately Purdy became inflamed with a desire to give evidence in her favour. It seemed mean of the girl to deny him his last opportunity for an exhibitionist display by pleading guilty; but that she did, at a trial where a kindly judge, realizing that she was a satellite caught in the extraordinary orbit of a fated person, gave her a sermon and bound her over. It is probable that this frustration clouded Purdy's satisfaction when, after his appeal had been rejected, he was reprieved. There were two considerations which made this reprieve inevitable. He had been acquitted of the one charge out of the three which was really serious enough to merit death; and everybody who had been able to form any impression of him, including the lawyers, who had been fascinated by the bright, darting ability he had shown throughout his trial, was of the opinion that if he could not be certified insane, as he certainly could not have been, it was only because his brand of eccentricity was peculiar to himself and therefore could not be related to the recognized categories of madness. It is distressing to think of this unhappy creature, whose only law was activity, who was an existentialist without knowing it, condemned to the numbness of life imprisonment.

One of the most curious features of this curious case was the enormous number of Germans with whom this odd but unimportant person was in contact. It had taken an elaborate machine and a welfare officer and a Foreign Office official (*Gruppenführer*) and William Joyce to recruit him. Once he was inside the system he received the attention of an army of men, often with titles that indicated the holder of a University degree —Dr. Springbern, Dr. Kurt Eggers, Dr. Menzel, Dr. Ziegfeld, Dr. Adams, Dr. Hafferkorn, Dr. Minzel, Dr. Wansche, Major Hempel. These persons, who were presumably highly trained and maintained by the German government at considerable expense, spent a great amount of time and energy on interviews and correspondence with this uneducated and ill-balanced person, and at least two S.S. agents (including one bearing the delightful name of Herr Wockenfuss—Mr. Distaff-foot) seem to have followed him about for long periods. The net return for this expenditure was some unimportant information about a tunnel in a prisoner-of-war camp, a wireless set, and some information about the British agent, John Henry Owen Brown, which would have been important if they had not disbelieved it; and a number of broadcasts of the familiar and ill-advised type: "Next time you travel by train or bus and one of your companions is obviously a Jew, I want you to observe his actions. You can hardly mistake their dominant characteristics—their coarse, greasy hair, their greasy foreheads, their negroid lips—but their actions betray their race more than their appearance", and so on. It is, moreover, more than likely that Purdy did not even compose these broadcasts, but received them from Joyce and read them.

It is hard to avoid suspecting that the organization of British treachery had become a racket, and that a number of Germans were exploiting it to find themselves easy and remunerative jobs at a safe distance from the front. It is hard to avoid suspecting also that German administration was not highly efficient. With all this wealth of personnel it was discreditable that a villa used by the German Foreign Office for its agents should have been searched, not by one English spy, but by four English spies, who sat on the floor round the wastepaper basket and read its contents at leisure. This state of affairs must have disgusted William Joyce, with his pride in his brisk competence. He must have found his office abhorrent to his sense of order and his hope of victory. It is significant that the colonel's daughter, whom he had always disliked, had, after sitting about the Concordia Bureau for some years knitting in a sullen manner, made her departure. She had gathered her tattered integrity about her, sold all she could lay her hands on to pay back to the Germans every mark they had ever paid her, and had swept off into a concentration camp, from which she was to emerge, at the end of the war, into twelve months of prison and such subsequent exclusion from the society of her kind, such bleakness and hopelessness, that one may count her as having paid her bill and more.

It was true, too, that William Joyce probably had at this time a bit of his own sort of fun. The Concordia Bureau was responsible for providing broadcasters for what was known as the New British Broadcasting Station: a station which pretended to its listeners that it was operating on British soil. One broadcaster, with a duplicity which would never have been suspected in one of his idealist demeanour, frequently tried to convince British listeners of this by assuming a Cockney accent and a wheeze in which he breathed, "You'll probably 'ear us to-morrow night at the same hour, but it's getting 'ard, the police are always on our 'eels nowadyes". It is unfortunately not open to us British to laugh at this ridiculous enterprise, since the Allies engaged in similar follies. They are objectionable in principle, if only for their effect on the nationals of the power which broadcasts. Either they detect the fraud and distrust their own government, particularly in its handling of the radio; or they do not detect the fraud, and believe that there are sympathetic and constructive parties in the country they are fighting which in fact do not exist. These enterprises are objectionable also in practice: the broadcasters who have been told to disregard our common obligation to tell the truth are apt to feel that this implies the disregard of all other moral obligations, and hence it happened that there was sent over the air such nasty fantasies as broadcasts purporting to come from microphones secretly installed in the bedroom of an enemy leader who is raping a girl. The proceedings of the New British Broadcasting Station were for the most part merely pitiful. But it presented one feature which was highly offensive on religious grounds, though not so offensive as the broadcasts which were simultaneously being emitted from the Irish station in Berlin. On that service educated men, some of them writers of standing, simpered pietistic sentiments combined with carneying praises of the regime which was murdering and torturing millions of their fellow-Catholics in Poland. Still the New British Broadcasting Station gave its own invitations to nausea. It was fairly offensive that a speaker who called himself "Father Donovan", but who was obviously not a priest, since his chorus-boy falsetto would have led to his rejection by the broadest-minded seminary, delivered mock sermons in which he spooned out sanctimonious references to the mysteries of the Roman Catholic faith. "Father Donovan" was in fact a seaman in his late twenties, who was a prisoner of war; and the dirty, sniggering joy he took in his impersonation made him one of the most unpleasant yet one of the most infantile of the traitors. But those who listened to him often soon became conscious of something in his broadcasts which was apart from him and less crudely unlikeable. The substance of his talks was quite different in spirit from their delivery. They might have been written by someone who had suffered in childhood from having to listen to a great many bad sermons by Irish priests of inferior type, and was now privately getting his own back on them by seeing just how far he could go in reproducing the sickly nonsense at its worst without crossing the line into obvious parody. In view of Joyce's attitude to the religion of his father it is very probable that the talks of "Father Donovan" represent the only real fling his harsh sense of humour was allowed to enjoy during these dolorous years.

There was no end to those dolours. The staff he was given became more and more terrible. It was bound to be poorer than the staff of Germans whom the B.B.C. employed to broadcast on its German service, for we could draw on an army of refugees who were many of them noteworthy in both character and intellect, fully conversant with the case against fascism; but the Germans need not have given Joyce the really extraordinary subordinates with whom he was burdened. Purdy was only an extreme example of their general undesirability. A fair sample were the two broadcasters who were sent him from the Channel Islands. One was an eccentric and passionate Salvation Army officer who, knowing either less or more about Eva Braun than we do, believed that the personal purity of Hitler was about to redeem the sinful world. The other was a young and beautiful school-teacher whose philosophy was very different. This unhappy girl, a stepchild who had never got on with her family, had fallen in love with a German officer during the occupation of Jersey. For three years she had worked for German contractors who were erecting military and naval establishments on the island, and when her lover was ordered to Germany in 1943 she accepted his offer to take her with him. When she got to Berlin her lover, who seems to have been as thrifty as he was libidinous, found her a post in the Rundfunk. As she had discovered that he was on excellent terms with his wife, from whom she had expected him to get a divorce, with the view of marrying her, she started work in no cheerful state of mind, and as the shadows deepened over Germany she became more and more lugubrious.

So too did Mr. Black. His life had not been without some causes for brightness. He had written a novel with a Fascist-cum-pacifist message, representing the Nazis as comely young men devoted to athletics who would never have thought of fighting if the uncomely and unathletic democracies had not forced war on them. This novel was published by the Nazis, who distributed it widely in prisoner-of-war camps and in neutral countries. Mr. Black was actually possessed of a quite remarkable gift for writing light fiction, but it is doubtful whether that particular work would have easily found a publisher in any other circumstance than this convulsion of history. Mr. Black might have said, like Peer Gynt when God marooned him on a desert shore because his yacht was going to be blown up,

"God is thoughtful—but economical, that he isn't". He had also formed a beautiful friendship with an American cabaret dancer named Frances who had been caught in Germany with a troupe at the time of Pearl Harbour: a lustrous creature on the turn of twenty, with chestnut-gold hair, and a complexion like an advertiser's allegation, and legs that surprised because they were still better than perfect, and an air of slight (and not unlovable) disorder about her appearance which revealed that she was the girl, to be found in every travelling show, whose stage clothes (and hers alone) get left behind in St. Louis. They met while attending the American Church in Berlin, and after some time he helped her to get back to America under an exchange scheme. But these two sources of satisfaction cannot have outweighed the factors in the situation which must have distressed Mr. Black.

He was having a worse and worse time at the hands of the Nazi head of the Bureau, Dr. Hetzler, the inflamed and frantic bully. At his trials he tried to make capital out of these attacks, and to represent them as disputes in which he defied Dr. Hetzler as a representative of the Nazi tyranny and defended the interests of the Allies. But it was not successful. Mr. Black's lawyer questioned the exhausted and hopeless anti-Nazi who had come to give evidence for his client on this point. "Did you ever see Black showing signs of disagreement when he was talking with Dr. Hetzler?" he asked. "Yes," said the anti-Nazi, "I saw sometimes that while he was talking to Dr. Hetzler he was tapping on the desk." "You mean, don't you," said Mr. Black's lawyer hopefully, "that he was beating the desk—hitting it?" "No," said the anti-Nazi, thoughtfully, "he was tapping on the desk with a pencil." From this appalling answer Mr. Black's lawyer rushed on to his next question: "And when did this happen?" The anti-Nazi replied with the same deadly thoughtfulness and conscientiousness, "In the autumn of 1944 and the spring of 1945". That was too late.

The other German witness who appeared for Mr. Black was of a very different type, but did him no more good. He had originally been a journalist. He was not an anti-Nazi, and he had served in the German Foreign Office since the year after Hitler's accession to power. He was not an attractive person, and, indeed, though he cannot have been a Jew, possessed all the features mentioned in Mr. Purdy's broadcast on the physical characteristics of Jews. Yet he recalled that well-known Gentile figure, the Vicar of Bray. He had worked for the Nazis; doubtless he had worked for the Weimar Republic; now he was working for the Allied Control Commission; if and when the next atomic bomb bursts over Europe, he will be found standing a safe distance behind the people who let it off. But with all this adaptability there was a failure to understand what one would have thought so obvious that it would have to be grasped as part of the *prolegomena* to adaptability. Mr. Black had claimed that he had broadcast a great deal of pro-British propaganda over the German radio, and the prosecuting counsel had thrown some doubt on the probability of this. So Mr. Black's lawyer asked this German Foreign Office official whether he thought this contention could be true. With a broad explanatory smile, as of one who is only to show the ignorant how the works go round, he answered that of course what Mr. Black had said was true, for it had at first been Dr. Goebbels's policy to send out propaganda that would please and conciliate the British. It did not occur to him that an English court would like Mr. Black no better for having been an instrument of Dr. Goebbels. But if he did nothing for the defence he opened a peephole on history.

The troubles of the Concordia Bureau were not merely internal. Though Baillie-Stewart and a small staff worked for the German Foreign Office, the Concordia Bureau was a part of Goebbels's Propaganda Office, which was the hated rival of the German Foreign Office. The primary cause of the rivalry between these Ministries was the fact that the Propaganda Office was a Nazi creation and the German Foreign Office was full of Junker stuff whose roots had not been torn up during the Weimar Republic because they had been so deeply planted in the soil of Germany under the Hohenzollerns. The rivalry had deteriorated, as all else in German life, and had become something very like a struggle between two gangs to get the bigger share of loot in a "protected" area. Perhaps because of simple departmental jealousy, and perhaps because of the large number of jobs connected with the Concordia Bureau, the Foreign Office took more and more interest in the Bureau as the war went on; and hence Mr. Black was able in 1944 and 1945 to appeal to the German Foreign Office for protection. When Dr. Hetzler threatened to send him to a concentration camp he made such an appeal, and the people who intervened and saved his life— for it appears that Dr. Hetzler was by then so maniacal that he designed the extremest persecution of this insignificant little man —were the same people who were concerned in the attempt on Hitler's life in July 1944. This was apparently the group that struggled to take control of the Concordia Bureau out of Goebbels's hands. The Foreign Office official who gave evidence for Black stated with considerable emphasis that he knew him to be personally acquainted with the Foreign Office members of this group. Plainly he spoke from within the orbit of this conspiracy; his words built up the event before his hearers and reminded them that it had really happened—it had not merely been something printed in a newspaper—and gave it the maculate quality of reality. Some of the conspirators, of course, had been earnestly desirous of killing Hitler because they were sickened by his evil life, and they, poor souls, had certainly had their heads chopped off. But there were others. Some had had no time to waste on moral judgments but had been anxious to go on living and had struck at the hands that were dragging them down to death, and no doubt they too, careless through urgency, had not been lucky with their necks. Others again were simply rats that intended to leave the sinking ship. They, having all their wits about them, could save their lives, and could use their length of days to claim what crowns of glory are the portion of their departed fellows.

VII

PEOPLE repeat their actions over and over again. William Joyce had accepted Sir Oswald Mosley and had come to despise him and had parted from him. The presumption is that he would accept Hitler and come to despise him and part from him. That second alienation must have been hastened by the blows he received during the year following October 1942, when John

Amery came to Berlin. That arrival must have assaulted Joyce in the areas of his greatest sensitivity: in his race feelings, in his class feelings, in his family feelings, in his intellectual pride, in his ambition—which must now have been asking itself if it was ever to mount the throne it had been promised—in his instinct for self-preservation.

John Amery had packed into his thirty years every kind of folly and recklessness, and in 1936, when he was twenty-four, he had been declared bankrupt. He left England and became a supporter of Franco, for whom he smuggled arms over the Spanish border with the connivance of the French ex-Communists Doriot and Déat, who, like many of their kind at that date, had become Fascists. When the war broke out he remained on the Continent, still travelling between Paris and Madrid, and it is believed that the traffic which he carried on then took a reverse direction and that his Cagoulard friends now received support from certain Spanish elements. It is useless conceiving him as either a mercenary trafficker or a dogmatic Fascist. He was another Purdy, but was at once more intellectual and more confused, and had a good many years of addling dissipation behind him. At the fall of France he fled to the south of France; but the Vichy government, which was trying to preserve its credit with the French people by dissociating itself so far as possible from the frankly pro-German Cagoulards, and which was irritated on its prudish side by his revelry, treated him as an unwelcome guest. Its distaste for him increased, and at the end of 1941 it put him in prison for eighteen days and released him on condition he lived in the mountainous district round Grenoble. He was at the time, so those that saw him say, very addled, very bored with the provincial life to which he was thus restricted, and in need of money. It is not surprising, therefore, that he offered his services to the Italians, who never answered his letter, and then to the Finns—then engaged in their anti-Soviet war— who declined them. But the local German armistice chief, Graf Ceschi, took him under his protection. Amery said that this association was not of his seeking, that the overtures came from the Graf, and in view of what happened this is not incredible. In the autumn of 1942, a German officer took him and a French woman who was perhaps his wife to Berlin. There they were received by a Dr. Hesse, who belonged neither to the German Foreign Office nor to the Propaganda Office, but to Hitler's personal staff. Thereafter, for a period of several months, John Amery was the most petted and best advertised English propagandist that had ever been put on the German radio. Immense trouble was taken to draw the world's attention to his broadcasts, which were repeated several times in an evening on one particular night in the week. He was given luxurious hotel accommodation, with a heavy expense account. He was sent all over Europe to address camps and give interviews to the local press and was photographed and filmed as if he were a Hollywood star.

In many ways Amery must have got Joyce on the raw. Amery was an Englishman, and the conflict between England and Ireland had never quite resolved itself in Joyce's mind. He adored the English, he had fought for them as a boy, or had at least performed some services which he thought of as fighting for them, and he genuinely believed that as a Fascist he was labouring to confer benefits on England. All the same it was to England that he had come as a boy and had been sniggered at as a queer little bog-trotter with a brogue; it was in England that he had been denied the power and position which he felt to be his right by virtue of his intellect; and ancient hatreds, however much they may be adulterated, often return under stress to their first purity. When William Joyce cursed the raiders who were bombing Berlin, he cursed them as an Irishman cursing the English. Now here an Englishman had come, late in the day, and was put ahead of those who had been drudging in exile for years. Amery was a gentleman. He had been born on the imperial side of the river Thames, heir to every advantage for which William Joyce had craved, and he had thrown away all of them that were not physically ingrained; and his retention of these must have constantly galled Joyce. His voice was charming, it told of a secure home built on a tradition of ease, of the right school. Any listener would accept it as a certificate that this man belonged of right to the places of power, though the life he had lived had annulled that certificate again and again. To Joyce, who could not open his mouth without betraying that he had been born of the people and reared amongst them and had tried frantically to annul that destiny, Amery's voice must have been a soft, pleasant taunt. It is an indication of Joyce's sensitivity on this point that when he was granted a German military passport in 1944 he described his father, who had been first a contractor and builder and then a grocer, as an architect.

Amery's life, too, was a double cause for uneasiness in Joyce. Few could meet Amery without wishing that their own lives had kept closer to the pattern prescribed by society, so obvious was it that his departures from it had brought on himself a soft oddity and on those who loved him deep and humiliating pain. William Joyce had had trouble, but it was not this; and it is the way of a guilty conscience to insist on the gulf that yawns between the offence which burdens it and other people's offences, which are always far more gross. And, indeed, he had the right to despise Amery, for, though he liked a glass of whisky at a party as much as the next man, he kept himself hard as nails for his work, and paid his debts. As for his intellectual superiority to Amery, that must have stung him. He had, as the broadcasts he composed towards the end of the war disclosed, a limited and avid mind of great ability, which he had cultivated to the satisfaction of London University. Words flowed from Amery's mouth in the conventional groupings of English culture, but he had no intelligence, only a vacancy round which there rolled a snowball of Fascist chatter picked up from Doriot and Déat. Yet here he was installed in a suite at the Kaiserhof, while Joyce had only a flat in the suburbs, with an unlimited expense account which meant opulence compared to Joyce's unimpressive salary; and here was the German radio cupping its hands round its mouth and shouting to the whole world that it must listen to Amery's broadcasts, though they could have no propaganda value whatsoever. That Amery was an excellent broadcaster, that the radio, which is one of the greatest liars in the world, transformed him into a pure and eager boy, burning with sincere indignation at the moral evils of Bolshevism, was beside the point. He was known to every newspaper reader in England as the problem child of distinguished parents, who had made countless appearances in the police courts, and the sole result of putting him on the air would be to make English listeners feel sympathy with his family and a reiterated conviction that the Germans were terrible cads. Worse still as propaganda was Amery's project, known at first as the Legion of St. George. This was a body to be drawn from British prisoners of war who were to fight alongside the Germans against the Russians to save Europe from Bolshevism. This was enough to make the former director of Mosley's propaganda squirm in his seat. None knew better than he did what chance there was of raising such a legion. He knew that only a sprinkling would join and that these would be mad or bad. He knew also that a recruiting campaign conducted by John Amery, accompanied by a female companion whose appearance would be interpreted by the ordinary soldier as a call to the joys of peace rather than to the tasks of war, would make English treachery a laughing-stock; and traitors have their pride like other people. He must have perceived that the Germans were in some ways very stupid, and perhaps he doubted whether they were going to gain the victory which was necessary if he were ever to realize his ambitions, or even save his life.

Yet German propaganda was perhaps never less stupid than in the exploitation of John Amery. For propaganda has many uses beyond persuasion. Sometimes it aims at throwing up a smoke-screen. What it aimed at in this case can be deduced from the character of Amery's gospel, considered in conjunction with the date. Though Amery's speeches held a few drops of anti-Semitic poison, his real preoccupation was hatred of Russia and communism. He made it a condition that the Legion of St. George should be regarded as an exclusively anti-Bolshevist force, and should be used only on the Russian front; and there exists a leaflet, issued after his concern with the body had ceased, but expressing his views, which runs:

We are fighting with the best of Europe's youth to preserve our European civilization and our common cultural heritage from the menace of Jewish Communism. MAKE NO MISTAKE ABOUT IT! Europe includes England. Should Soviet Russia ever overcome Germany and the other European countries fighting with her, nothing on this earth would save the Continent from Communism, and our own country would inevitably sooner or later succumb. We are British. We love England and all it stands for.

Most of us have fought on the battlefields of France, of Libya, Greece, in Italy, and many of our best comrades in arms are lying there—sacrificed in this war of Jewish revenge. We felt then we were being lied to and betrayed. Now we know it for certain. This conflict between England and Germany is racial SUICIDE. We must UNITE and take up arms against the common enemy. We ask you to come into our ranks and fight shoulder to shoulder with us for Europe and for England.

Now, in the autumn of 1942 the Germans were beginning to feel nervous. It had appeared from the end of August that the situation in North Africa might not end their way, for Rommel's great offensive had been halted, and that because of his lack of aircraft. The Allies' air attacks on Germany were becoming more and more formidable. The Japanese were not doing so well as had been hoped. Germany was not certain that it was beaten, but then again it was not certain that it was going to win; so it formed the idea that it had better sacrifice some of its ambitions and get rid of some of its liabilities. If it could stop the war with Russia which it had so rashly initiated in 1941 it would have its energies free to fight Great Britain and the United States. But if it was to start peace negotiations with Russia these must be kept secret, for two reasons. One was that if Great Britain and the United States heard of them they might use argument and force to dissuade their ally from the proposed desertion; and the other that, even if they failed, they would surely cut off the stream of supplies which they were sending out to their ally, and which would form a useful addition to Germany's armaments if they went on to the last moment and were taken over by her when she again joined forces with Russia. It might throw dust in the eyes of Great Britain and the United States if, just at the time when these secret negotiations were opened, the Germans started a new anti-Bolshevik campaign. They made their first overtures to Moscow; and John Amery was fetched out of his retreat in Savoy in October 1942, and broadcast during the first part of 1943 and began his recruiting tour of the camps. Nobody else could have drawn such widespread attention to an anti-Bolshevik campaign. If William Joyce or Baillie-Stewart had made these broadcasts and gone on that recruiting tour, not a soul would have taken the slightest notice. It was the unique and fatal distinction of John Amery to be the one person out of the earth's population who could serve the German purpose; and the Nazis did not mind looking fools so long as they could create the impression that they were still actively anti-Bolshevik.

It is to be remarked that from the middle of 1943 the fortunes of John Amery suffered a marked decline. The negotiations between Germany and Russia had broken down. He was no longer welcome in Berlin; and when he lost most of his personal belongings in one of the famous raids which, on every night between the 22nd and the 26th of November 1943, assailed Berlin, he was awarded a decoration for exceptional bravery and packed off to Paris. From there he was sometimes sent to the occupied countries, such as Norway, Belgium, Czechoslovakia and Yugoslavia, out of sheer nastiness: to prove that the British were degenerate, that a leading British statesman could have a son who betrayed his country and hiccoughed as he did it. Soon they stopped letting him do even that, and in September 1944, with savage and indecent irony, they sent him down next to act as confidant to Mussolini, now at liberty and a poor figure of fun after his undignified rescue from Allied hands. "Enter Tilburina, stark mad in white satin, and her confidant, stark mad in white linen." What is the sin against the Holy Ghost? It is perhaps to deal with people as if they were things: to pick them up and set them down, without respect for their uniqueness, for their own wills.

In Germany, William Joyce sat and waited for the end. He moved about; most often he was in Berlin, but sometimes he was in Eupen and at Luxembourg, at the end he was in Hamburg; but always there was over him the same sky, the *mitteleuropäische* sky, which is clearer than the English sky and is not loaded with its dreary fogs, but has its own nocuments, which are madness and defeat. He was involved for the last year or so in the aftermath of the unfortunate harvest of Amery's brain, the Legion of St. George, known as the British Free Corps. After Amery had been ejected from Berlin, having served the Nazi purpose, the Legion had been handed over to the S.S., and its name had been changed to the British Free Corps, and its recruits either were drawn from Joyce's broadcasters or broadcast for him afterwards. Fifty years ago or so Rudyard Kipling wrote a poem about the "gentlemen rankers", the men of the upper and middle classes who, after having disgraced themselves in private life, hid themselves from their class by enlisting in the British army as private soldiers, and he commemorated this tragedy of a vanished world in a stanza which ran:

> We have done with Hope and Honour, we are lost to Love
> and Truth,
> We are dropping down the ladder rung by rung;
> And the measure of our torment is the measure of our youth,
> God help us, for we knew the worst too young.

These lines give a fair enough account of the British Free Corps. They had done with hope and honour. They had all left their camps after being warned by their senior officers that they were taking a step which would cut them off from the society of their own kind, and passed into a state of degradation which made it inevitable that society would carry out its threat, not from nursed intention but as a result of the natural recoil from something that stinks. The Germans had, of course, far too much sense to keep on with the Legion because they thought they could raise enough men to form a fighting unit for use on the Russian front, or anywhere else. They wanted them for quite another purpose. They put these men in villas in various pleasant parts of Germany, and dressed them in German uniforms with flashes with the letters B.F.C. and the Union Jack to show that the wearers were British soldiers, and let them go rotten with idleness and indiscipline and debauchery. They did a little drill and learned German, and, as one of them said, "otherwise did nothing except lay around, and go into the town, where we drank and associated with women". There were never many of them. It appears that of the hundreds of thousands of prisoners of war in Germany only thirty-odd volunteered for the corps. But even so small a number, split into groups and sent into the German towns, drunken and with prostitutes on their arms, did something to raise national morale in 1944 and 1945 and persuade the Germans that it was all true, what they had been told, and that they could not possibly be conquered by those degenerate people the British.

It was unsentimental truth that most of the British Free Corps had known the worst too young. One had been a prisoner for two and a half years since, as a boy of fourteen, he had been taken off a torpedoed British ship by a German submarine. Another had given a false age when he volunteered for the army in 1941, and was just seventeen when he was captured in Italy. The one believed that John Amery was Foreign Minister of Great Britain and had somehow been ejected from his country and was being kindly assisted to regain his rights by the Germans; the other accepted an assurance that the British Free Corps was six divisions strong. Some were young and, moreover, had been troubled even before the war had begun. Such was Ronald David, a black-browed young gipsy who faced life with the mask of the romantic rebel: his sullen darkness at once defied society and confessed unassuageable sorrow because it had rebuffed him. He had been born in New South Wales, was left an orphan at three weeks old, and was then adopted by an unmarried woman too elderly for the task of rearing a boy into adolescence. When he got into his teens he made more than one appearance in the juvenile courts; and when he was seventeen he went to sea. Six months later his ship was captured by the German raider *Admiral Scheer*, and for a long time he travelled in her under hatches, from ocean to ocean, in heat and hunger. Eventually he was landed at Bordeaux and went from camp to camp, not settling down anywhere till he was about nineteen. Then he stayed in one camp for some time and was seduced by a German girl named Annaliese, who worked in the camp censorship office and who was greatly loved by him. It was his story that the German Security officers discovered them sleeping together and threatened to have them sent to concentration camps unless he joined the British Free Corps. This is probably true. The Germans certainly arranged for such seductions as a basis for blackmail; the girls were usually privy to their intentions, but the men very rarely suspected this. But they did not apply this form of blackmail except to men they thought good subjects for corruption, by reason of lechery or rare compulsive thirst or sourness of disposition. It was characteristic of this prisoner that

135

he made an open avowal of his intention of joining the British Free Corps to his fellow-prisoners, quite unnecessarily, and had to be shut up in a cell for his own protection.

Some there were who were in such deep trouble before the war that they had stayed young when they were not. There was poor Herbert George, who, though of medium height, had the look of a Disney dwarf. His deeply lined skin was puckered into thin folds in the apprehensive expression of a chimpanzee, and his features so far departed from the normal that those who met him found themselves looking back again and again to see if they could be as they were remembered, though the total impression was by no means monstrous, merely animal and odd. He was thirty-five, but his life had passed like a flash, too full of trouble to allow maturity to come to him. Thames-side police courts had been the theatre of his woes. Once a chicken had been stolen; then a gas-meter slot had been opened and emptied; once someone had missed a shirt and scarf. It was too much, it was really too much, flesh and blood couldn't stand the worry. On an astonishing occasion he attempted to defy the canon which Hamlet erroneously believed the Everlasting had fixed against self-slaughter. When he had served the mild punishment inflicted on him for that offence, he enlisted in the army, but was discharged as daft. This was, however, only the beginning of a military career which was to be, in the strictest sense of the word, unique. For he had always been interested in politics, and when the Spanish Civil War broke out, he volunteered to serve in the International Brigade and actually fought in Spain. He soon deserted; but the incident was purged of the sordid by the candour with which, having crossed the Pyrenees and reached the Channel on foot, he sought the London offices of the International Brigade and reported as a deserter. He then went to sea, as he had done at intervals all his life, and continued as a sailor after the war broke out. In 1940 he was an oiler on a steamer that was torpedoed off Narvik, and was in one camp and another until 1944, when he received a letter from his mother saying that his wife had just gone to hospital to have a baby. After thinking over this for a long time he decided that it could not be his baby, and was deeply distressed, and when, at about the same time, two merchant seamen who had joined the British

Free Corps came to enrol recruits, he enlisted, just as a sad little dog, finding himself far from home in streets where they throw things, with rain falling and the dusk thickening, will follow any passer-by.

Such poor silly souls were easy to soak in liquor; and they all, even Herbert George, who was not sexually attractive, found obliging German girls. In that they did not differ from those among them who were not so young and who knew quite well what they were doing. Six of these, who were known as the Big Six, definitely professed some enthusiasm for the aims of the British Free Corps; and of these, some were well educated. One, the son of a Lithuanian merchant settled in England, had been at an English public school. It was surprising that he should have been in the British Free Corps, for he was a Jew, certainly on his father's side. He may not have known this, for he had been brought up out of contact with his father's family and had early gone to the Colonies; but the Germans must have known it if any intelligent officer had examined his papers. It is possible, however, that by this time the Germans were handling the British Free Corps in a spirit of such profound cynicism that they were willing to overlook their racial theories. In this group, though it had some intellectual pretences, there are few traces of the waking of the ideological forces that might have been expected. The Lithuanian had joined because he was distraught and activist at the same time that he was pessimistic and melancholy, and he wanted to find himself a niche in the international society which he thought would be erected after the inevitable defeat of the Allies. One of the Big Six, Francis McLardy, a qualified pharmacist, had been a member of the B.U.F. from 1934 to 1938, but this could not be regarded as the sole factor which had brought him into the British Free Corps, though it might have been the determining one. He had been a sergeant in the R.A.M.C. and, being captured at Dunkirk, was sent to work in a prisoner-of-war hospital in Poland. There he was caught breaking a rule and was told that he was to be sent to the worst camp in Poland, which was famous for its abominations. Rumour had it that there the starved prisoners fell on the bodies of their comrades that dropped dead and tore out their livers, their kidneys, and the soft part of the thigh, and ate them.

An American prisoner who was found in the camp when it was liberated has testified that this happened, though not many people could bring themselves to do it because the bodies were so lousy. To avoid being sent to this camp, McLardy wrote to the authorities and expressed that he wanted to join the Waffen S.S. and fight the Russians. That he was moved by the desire to save himself from this hell cannot be regarded as a valid excuse, for thousands of men, finding themselves in the same position, chose to suffer the pains of that hell rather than serve the men who made it.

It is possible that McLardy's failure to reach their standard was due to the sympathy with the architects of such hells which he had been taught by the B.U.F. If that is so, it was the most direct influence exerted by Mosley on the proceedings of the traitors in Germany. Impotent in everything, he was impotent in this. The other adherents of the B.U.F. who appeared among them had lapsed from membership some time before the beginning of the war, and their cases prove nothing except that silly young men were apt to join the B.U.F. in some circumstances and in others were apt to become traitors. Neither here nor in any other theatre of war was there proof that the B.U.F. had issued instructions to any member of the armed forces. A private in the R.A.S.C. named Theodore John William Schurch, of Swiss origin, who was hanged two days after Joyce for treachery committed after he had been captured by the Italians at Tobruk, alleged that he had joined the British Army in 1936 under instructions from a Fascist organization, but if this was true, which was doubtful, those instructions related to a peace-time plan to spread fascism among the forces, which certainly existed but seems to have been discontinued during the war.

The most obvious trace of ideological action in the camp was furnished by two priggish little negativists named Denis John and Eric Reginald. In a dingy street in North London there is a baker's shop which cheers the eye by its clean and bright and not inexpensive window-fittings, and by its well-stocked shelves, which are neatly arranged with as attractive cakes and buns and breads and gingerbreads as anybody could hope to take out of an oven in these days. The owner, a stoutish middle-aged man, serves in his shop, and from early morning to late evening is either there or in the other shop in another part of the suburb which his thrift has purchased. He has his own quiet distinction, and has, as his only remarkable physical feature, watchet-blue eyes. He is the son of a German who came to England with his young bride in the last quarter of the last century, worked as a baker's assistant, bought his own bakery, became a naturalized British citizen, and died in London. When the First World War came, his son, who had been born a British citizen, fought against the Germans, and on his return married an Englishwoman. Their son, Denis John, inherited his father's eyes and slight but real difference from the run of the mill, and developed in much less favourable circumstances. His parents' marriage was not a success; it is to be remarked that most of the members of the British Free Corps came from broken homes. The baker and his wife separated when the boy was seven years old, and thereafter he was brought up by his German grandmother, who lived in London but took him to Germany every year and finally sent him to school there. At sixteen he went home to be instructed by his father in the mystery of their family craft; but difficulties arose, partly because of the unfortunate domestic situation and partly because Denis John had grown attractive in a way that was not of much use to him. He was a Lohengrin or Siegfried, with clear-cut features and waves of golden hair of the kind that shines as brilliantly and keeps as distinct as so much golden wire. Since Ophelia told us that the owl was a baker's daughter, it is not surprising that about Denis John, the baker's son, there was something of an owl: a lustrous, extravagantly blond owl.

He now drew to himself the attentions of some young men, born in circumstances superior to his own, who from the first, according to his family's friends, did him no good. When the time drew near when he should register for military service he felt a natural reluctance to fight against Germany, which, strangely enough, he, a German's grandson, knew and loved better than his father, who was a German's son. If he had gone to the proper authorities they would have explained to him the means by which people in his position could appeal for exemption from military service as conscientious objectors. But some of his new friends were connected with that ambiguous organization, the Peace Pledge Union, which in the name of peace was performing many actions certain to benefit Hitler. They persuaded him to go to the Union's offices and ask for assistance in evading military service, and it was arranged that he should take advantage of a scheme that the Union was running in co-operation with the Ministry of Labour which exported registered conscientious objectors to do farm work in various districts, including the Channel Islands. It is not clear how Denis John came under this scheme; he never claimed to have become a conscientious objector, and cannot have been registered as one, for he had never even been called up. But Denis John was sent off on a travel warrant issued by the Ministry of Labour to Jersey, which, neither in this war nor the last, would ever have seemed the safest of refuges, but was particularly unsafe on the day of his departure, which was on the 17th of May 1940, seven days after the Germans had invaded the Low Countries. It is not at all surprising that by August Denis John was working for the Todt organization, the Nazi sappers; and it cannot possibly have surprised the Peace Pledge Union. There was not even the sense of a treasonable agreement behind these proceedings. The Germans were not prepared to accept these unhappy children, and Denis John and a number of others were dragged about Europe, from camp to camp, for five years, exposed to every sort of degrading influence, till he and Eric Reginald landed in the British Free Corps. They joined it, apparently, only because the recruiting leaflets had caused an uproar in the English prisoner-of-war camp where they happened to be, and they wished to show how superior they were to the common herd.

When they all gathered together they developed an ideology, but it was strangely different from Nazism. Its perfect exponent was Alfred Vivian, a merchant seaman, a young man in his late twenties, very black of hair and very white of skin, who was plainly very clean and came from some clean home. He was not a Fascist and held, he said, no political views, but professed a vague pacifism. "I am a sailor," he said, "and as such have no hate for anybody, including the Germans." He was, in fact, strongly pro-German, and it illustrates the importance of truth in propaganda that he was first led to discredit the case for the Allies because he found when he got to Germany that the accounts of German privations which he had read in the newspapers at home were not true. Also he liked the Germans, and it is to be noted that some Germans showed these unhappy and inglorious men real kindness; the sullen and black-browed Ronald David was taken into one working-class household and given real sympathy and understanding. But the two factors which drew Alfred Vivian were remote from the particular facts of the international situation. The first was that he was a very clean man, proud of his personal appearance, and that in his prisoner-of-war camp he had acquired scabies and other skin diseases, and his transfer to a private house, where he could have baths and have leisure and facilities to apply medical treatment to his boils and blains, was relief from shame. The other was an obsession with rebellion. "In our barracks at Pankow and Hildesheim as well as Dresden we had a photograph displayed on the wall of the Duke of Windsor, whom we all admired as he was also a rebel", he said. "We all recognized him as the King of England. When we had parties, we always toasted the Duke of Windsor." In other words, those members of the British Free Corps who were not falling flat on their faces in the local brothels were engaged in re-creating Byronic romanticism, even to its self-distaste. Alfred Vivian once wrote, "I now feel thoroughly ashamed of myself. I realize now that I was a rebel and am sorry for everything that happened." So, sometimes, spoke Lord Byron.

But the rest of the British Free Corps went on falling on their faces; and were watched, at short range, with extreme distaste by Mr. Thomas Haller Cooper. This was a young man who had been born in consequence of an international situation. His father, a photographer in one of the less fashionable areas of south-western London, had been a soldier in the Army of Occupation after the 1914-18 war and had brought home a German bride, thus rushing forward and impaling himself on the next great international situation. When he was nineteen his mother took him back to Germany, as a woman taking her child to present him at the temple, herself returning to London. The year was 1939. A short time after war broke out he joined the Adolf Hitler Division of the Waffen S.S., and served in Poland, and then in Russia, where he was wounded. When he was convalescent he was recalled to do traitor's work, visiting the English prisoner-of-war camps and talking with the prisoners and giving them corrupting literature, and finally was made an N.C.O. in charge of the British Free Corps. At first he enjoyed the work, and many of the members of the British Free Corps liked him. There was probably a real geniality, an honest tenderness, between them. Cooper had come from the Eastern Front, the others had come from years of hunger and confinement; they found themselves clean and well-fed, and could exchange tales of woe in what was their native language and his father's tongue, in a good villa that was more than comfortable, that was cosy, among the woods, the sweet aromatic German woods.

Thomas Haller Cooper was beautifully built. He was very tall and slender, with a long supple waist and broad shoulders. He was very neat, with that neatness which means a religious state of mind, a cry to Heaven for approval. His forehead was very high, and his long face, narrowing from high cheekbones to a pointed chin, might fairly be described as coffin-shaped. His sleek seal-brown hair grew in a widow's peak deep down on his forehead, and receded sharply over his temples; he might have been wearing a close-fitting and peculiarly shaped fur cap. His dark eyebrows were very thick, and his mouth large and full, but hard. Many Germans look as he did; and such as do are usually Wendish in origin, descendants of a strayed Slav tribe that have lived in Germany for centuries, isolated from their own kind and interpenetrated with German blood, but remarkable for their special force. And he had the look of many young Germans who became Nazis, whether of his physical type or another: a look of the white-collar man who cannot climb up, because he has no special talent to make his own ladder and society will not let him use its existing ladders, which are reserved for other people. *Spiessbürger* is the German word for it.

It was one of the most remarkable fatuities of German propaganda that this young man was represented to the British prisoners of war as the son of Mr. Duff Cooper and Lady Diana Cooper. Enough prisoners of war must have listened to their wives reading aloud items from the gossip columns of the Sunday papers once a week over many years to know the only child of the most publicized character of our times was not of military age; and almost all of them would have known that that only child would not have looked or talked like Thomas Haller

Cooper. His English was poor and inaccurate; he made such errors as to talk of making an "observance" when he meant an "observation". But his German was rich, accurate, and happy. He had been born and brought up in London, had been to school in London, had been a clerk in London, but his mother had built a Germany around him, he was a German who had never been out of his fatherland. In the material world he had tried to be English. He had a great love of the East and, though he had not a remarkably good record of achievement at school, he had studied Japanese and Chinese; and as he grew into his later teens had tried to find employment in branches of the government service which might take him to the Far East, but was rejected because his mother was a German. His other passion was for order; and he tried to join various police forces, here in England and in the Colonies, but for the same reason he was rejected there also.

This meant frustration for him; but considering what his mother had done to him, the authorities were not unwise. It cannot be put down in black and white how she wove the spell about him, or what the other enchantresses who work the same magic brew in their cauldrons. The secret does not lie in the promise of conquest. Rather it lies in a lyricism that extends the kingdom of the nightingale, diffuses everywhere the perfume of the rose. The home where this man's mother lived was distinguished from all the other red-brick and stucco houses in a shabby suburban street by the wealth of flowering bulbs, jonquil packed beside narcissus, crocus beside grape hyacinth, which crammed the bow-windows of the ground-floor flat. They were not such compact growths as florists sell; the uneven flower-spikes and sprawling leaves showed that she herself, the loving amateur, busied herself planting them in fibre and shut them in cupboards while the winter fell. When the spring came they made a truly German window. Loving this lovely Germany, her son joined the S.S., which bled and died that there should be camps where starved prisoners fell on the bodies of their dead comrades and, if not too disgusted by the lice, ate their kidneys and livers and the soft parts of their thighs. This is a great mystery.

He travelled all over Germany with his charges. (It is one

of the curious features of the Nazi regime that it made the German passion for travelling into a guiding principle of its administration. Prisoners of war, whether loyal or traitors, were moved round and round and round the country long before the time when they had to be hustled out of the way of the invading Allies. It is as if in England we had moved the prisoners we held in the Isle of Man to the West Highlands, to Wales, to the Isle of Wight, and so on.) Always the billets were good, comfortable villas with gardens, set among woods and heaths. The custody of these louts was not the enterprise Thomas Haller Cooper had foreseen when he was detailed to it. He kept his sense of superiority by withdrawing into his favourite and unusual studies. In his room, instead of the usual portrait of Adolf Hitler, there hung a fine Japanese print. He had a solemn and sentimental love affair with a respectable young girl called Gisela, to whom he expounded Oriental philosophy in immensely long letters. He was really only a boy. In company he would murmur, as if in absence of mind, such phrases as *Om mani padme hum*, and, on being overheard and questioned as to what they meant, would start and explain that such phrases were always running through his mind, since he was, as a matter of fact, a Buddhist. But his boyhood had not been a nice one. Wishing to impress an Englishman he thought a traitor like himself, he boasted, quite untruthfully, that he had come to Germany because he had, during a street-fight in the East End of London, killed a Jew and had to get out of England in a hurry. This confession was unfortunate. His confidant was the British agent, John Henry Owen Brown.

But no amount of sitting about in the sun and mooning over Oriental grammars and writing to Gisela and swapping lies could reconcile him to the degradation of his charges. He tried to apply a mild form of S.S. discipline to them, and they mocked at him and staged a mutiny. That did not frighten Thomas Haller Cooper. But when D-day came and went, and the gales blew and did not blow away the invading Allies, and the Atlantic Wall was as if it never had been, then he was frightened. He said, "I have been a bloody fool", and announced his intention to work thenceforward for "the other side". Again it was the British agent, John Henry Owen Brown, to whom he spoke.

Thereafter this strong and proud young man had to cringe and smirk and flatter in the hope of survival, as it might have been thought that only old men would have to do, poor old men past their work whose children have died before them. He visited prisoners of war and thrust kindnesses on the prisoners under the sceptical eyes of non-commissioned officers, terrible beings, worst when they were little creatures burned up by Indian suns till they had not left in them a scrap of blandness. These looked straight at him and, without speaking, said things about rats that left the sinking ships. But these missions were better than his duties with the non-wits of the British Free Corps, who daily grew more drunken, more desperate, more maudlin amorous in the arms of their whores, themselves daily more desperate. Often they cursed him and flouted his orders; and sometimes he let it pass, because he did not care; it was as if he had never been a willing instrument of Nazi powers. But at other times he was prodded in the back by superior authority, which did not yet know whether it was definitely beaten, and which was not certain, if defeat was indeed certain, whether it was not going to die in its jack-boots; because, though it could pull them off and run away, pretending that it had never worn them, it had obeyed orders so long that it would not know where it should run. Everybody's brain was boiling.

Sometimes authority thought that, yes, it would pull its jack-boots off, and left Cooper to do what he would with the British Free Corps. Then he and his louts sat in a kind of vacuum, which slowly filled up with fear. But authority would change its mind and would buzz about Cooper's ears again, and he would disentangle the louts from their weeping whores and insist that they do a little drill, and see that they all kept up the pretence of an imminent dispatch to the Russian front. Sometimes events maddened authority into acts preposterous and tragic in their irony. On the night of February 13, 1945, the British bombed Dresden, in a legitimate attempt to end the war, for which no reasonable person can blame them, and slaughtered many thousands of refugees and turned to rubble one of the fairest cities bequeathed to our time by people possessed of virtues which we lack. The next day exasperated authority turned on the British Free Corps, which had just been brought there to improve

German morale by straggling through the streets, alleged that they were in some way responsible, and clapped them all in prison, including that Herbert George who had been in trouble concerning the chicken, the pennies in the gas-meter, the shirt and the scarf. At some point in this hubble-bubble, when authority was overcome by panic and felt that it must truckle to everybody, ear was given to the complaints of the British Free Corps against Cooper's attempts to discipline it, and he was sent away. He walked off with a straight back, determined to fight what was to come, down to the last ounce of his pride.

William Joyce now sat in his office, conducting his business with a quiet sacramental order. He had become wholly reconciled to his wife. D-day had been a crushing blow to him. All through his life he had been anxious, with the special anxiety of a very small man, not to make a fool of himself, and the first consequence of such wariness is to refrain from prophecies that may not come true. In his broadcasts he had mocked again and again at the idea of an Allied invasion of the Continent; and they had often been followed by songs, abominable and amusing lyrics coldly and lightly sung, which jeered at the Englishmen who were to lie dead under the Atlantic Wall. William Joyce was to afford, both in his broadcasts and in the programmes of which they formed part, proof that there are no half-measures in treachery; if a man does not love his country enough to concede its right to self-government he will end by not loving it at all, by hating it. Again and again Joyce had spoken with icy approval of murders wrought by the Germans on his fellow-countrymen. He did not feel he had to fear that this might make him unpopular if he returned to Britain, for he would return ringed with arms that would intimidate the British. Then the Atlantic Wall was broken; and it did not matter how much effort it had taken to break it; if it was unsubstantial, then it was unsubstantial as a dream. Henceforward, it was not to be Germans who were to kill Englishmen. There were perhaps to be more Germans killed by Englishmen than Englishmen killed by Germans, perhaps Germany itself was to be killed, perhaps William Joyce himself was to be killed, certainly William Joyce was to be killed. That possibility had always been clear in his mind. In his preface to his book, *Twilight over England*, published in Holland in 1942, he had written: "When, however, the writer is a daily perpetrator of High Treason, his introductory remarks may command from the English public that kind of awful veneration with which £5,000 confessions are perused in the Sunday newspapers, quite frequently after the narrator has taken his last leap in the dark." As a revolutionary he must have known a sort of dry-mouthed staring peace as catastrophe flowed towards him from the east and the west during the first months of 1945. There had been much doing and the fruit of it was to be nothingness; there had been a fullness of life, there was to be an emptiness of death. To this end he had worked since youth, and he would have been disappointed by victory. But that he himself should die must have brought to him the torment that the prospect of death brings to us all. It is no use talking of the death-wish at that stage. We wish for death, but we have developed the faculty of imagination, so that we can play out the drama of our death-wish in fantasy.

William Joyce sat in his office and distracted himself by exercises of the intellect. His last broadcasts were, in form, ably and carefully written political essays, much superior to anything he had put out over the air up to that time. In substance they were self-exculpatory. They warned England that she was being ruined by her participation in the war, and, destitute, would have to face a new and insatiable imperialist Russia; and rebuked her for having fought Germany instead of aiding her to fight against the Bolshevization of the world. This was nonsense. The week before Germany had brought England into the field against her by invading Poland she had signed a pact with Russia, and she remained in close friendship with her for the best part of two years; and no intelligent Englishman had wanted his country to go to war with Germany, because none was unaware that, if the price of defeat would be the reign of the Gestapo in England, the price of victory would be the disruption of Europe, the destruction of its political and economic and intellectual harmony, which is the highest level man has yet attained. It was the horrible and unique achievement of Hitler to force the West to fight the most terrible of wars without the sustenance of faith in victory. So the tired man, night after night, stood in the Hamburg studio of the Rundfunk and warned his fellow-countrymen of a danger which they had always anticipated and which now no longer could be avoided. There came a night when he spoke as if he were either very tired, or drunk, or perhaps both. Then, on April 30, 1945, he made a broadcast in which, speaking slowly and with dignity and obstinacy, he admitted defeat. It ended with the sentences: "Britain's victories are barren; they leave her poor, and they leave her people hungry; they leave her bereft of the markets and the wealth that she possessed six years ago. But, above all, they leave her with an immensely greater problem than she had then. We are nearing the end of one phase in Europe's history, but the next will be no happier. It will be grimmer, harder, and perhaps bloodier. And now I ask you earnestly, can Britain survive? I am profoundly convinced that without German help she cannot." Saying these words, he plainly thought himself a statesman, but he had said nothing that could not be answered with a phrase from an old comedy, " *Tu l'as voulu, George Dandin!*" This was the last time that the insatiable hunger of his voice was to travel over the air. English soldiers came into his office a day later and found it not disordered but empty. He had gone out on his particular path to the end.

VIII

EACH man took a different path to the end. Little Mr. Black got through the British lines and smugly reported at the British Embassy in Brussels, representing himself as having been engaged in anti-Nazi work in Berlin and having used his employment in the Concordia Bureau as a cover for doing kindnesses to victims of Nazi persecution. Not then, nor later at the Old Bailey, was he believed. He elected to go into the witness-box and give evidence in support of his plea. Since most of the traitors arrived in England destitute, they had to take advantage of the Poor Prisoners' Defence Act. A lawyer chosen under this act has not the control over his client that a lawyer has who is employed in the usual way, for he cannot tell such a client who disregards his advice to go to the devil and, elsewhere or there, find another lawyer. Hence many of the traitors made the mistake of giving evidence on their own behalf. Mr. Black did himself no good in the box. But he did a great deal of good to another traitor, out on bail, who attended his case. That traitor, at the preliminary police-court proceedings, had put up the same standard defence as Mr. Black, the same story of having broadcast for the Nazis in order to do undercover anti-Nazi work; but, having attended the Old Bailey and watched with a peculiar sick steadiness how Mr. Black was run up and down until he dropped under cross-examination, did not persist in that defence and put in a plea of guilty.

This trial, which was painful, was also comic. That was chiefly the fault of Miss Frances; of the American cabaret dancer whom he had met at the American Church in Berlin and negotiated out of Germany under a scheme for the exchange of civilian prisoners. The court looked on her with undisguised pleasure as she advanced towards the witness-box. In fantasy it raised its tongue to its palate and gave two sharp clicks. She was a lovely creature. Her lips and cheeks were brighter than paint because of the prodigiously healthy blood behind her thin and fine-grained skin; her chestnut-gold hair had the strong untroubled lustre of an animal's coat; the springing quality of her flesh recalled what claims it can make—and they are many—to superiority over marble. But she was also comic. For she was simple as puppies are. She was grieved, as all of us were, at the sight of Mr. Black in the dock, but it was as a puppy who sees its playmate locked in a kennel, and though such a puppy surely suffers, the simplicity of the world it lives in compared with the complexity of the world in which we live makes even its suffering matter for smiles. She was comic, too, by reason of a strangeness in her dress, for she was one of those women who, perhaps because of some childish infatuation with an old photograph, hark back in their appearance to the ideals of a past generation. She had a lot of clothes on. So far as the saleswomen had let her she had gone back to the days when Ruby de Reymer wore so wide a hat and so many yards of tucked and frilled chiffon that fifteen ospreys could alight upon her person. Miss Frances had not the ospreys, but their home was ready for them. The spirit of our age, however, cut off all this plenitude at the knee.

There the skirt stopped, and it was seen that her lovely legs could have been snapped at the ankle by a cruel finger and thumb.

She would have been well advised, if she wanted to convince the court, to stand on her head in the witness-box. The ordinary way up she was not a good witness. Her voice flowed past the judge and jury, giving them no more information than if it had been a rivulet of melting ice-cream. From the melodic lure of her voice it could be inferred that she was telling a romantic story of misfortune borne with courage, but the only time she could be heard an old music-hall jest found itself functioning on the other side of the footlights. She was asked what she was doing in Germany that she needed Mr. Black's help, and she replied plaintively, "Why, I was in trouble". This phrase in an English female mouth limits the range of her possible predicaments to one. The court was suddenly sympathetic. But when she cooed on, softly as a distant dove, "Yes, for two years I was in trouble", it showed its relief too cheerfully. But all this did Mr. Black no good. Her counsel, a handsome and at that moment intensely embarrassed young man, tried in vain to control his witness; but it was as if he were taking a puppy for a walk and had got the leash wound round his legs, and on the bench Mr. Justice Oliver put down his pen and held his reeling head between his hands. In his summing up he referred to Miss Frances, with an almost abnormal detachment, suggesting that the law is a tomb and he was speaking out of it, as "a young lady to whom, I am sure, we would all be glad to be of service, if the occasion arose". Speaking less like a broken man, he went on to point out that Mr. Black's obedience to what must be a universal inclination to be kind to Miss Frances was no evidence that he had indulged in his traitorous activities as a cover for anti-Nazi activities.

While the jury was considering its verdict she stood in the corridor with the two sad-faced friends of Mr. Black who had put up bail for him to the amount of a thousand pounds and had loyally accompanied him to the court that morning; gentle elderly men who were probably friends of his family and had admired him since he was a boy for his great gifts. Her mouth, which was soft as a child's, was trembling; her voice, which was at once the voice of Desdemona and Minnie Mouse, ran up the scale as she complained, "Every time I tried to say something that terrible old man wouldn't let me". So she tried again when Mr. Black's appeal came up. The Court of Appeal, held in a dusty library, is conducted on the most abstract terms possible considering that the subject-matter of the law is humanity. No witnesses are heard, only counsel, who spin the legal thread finer and finer till, in the opinion of the three judges, it breaks. But Miss Frances was there. She saw herself running along the railway tracks, waving a lamp to warn the oncoming express of the broken bridge ahead, or leaping from ice-floe to ice-floe with her little brother in her arms, like the heroine of an early Griffith film; and indeed in her excess of scarfs she recalled Mary Pickford and Lillian Gish, though it was with skirtage they were so encumbered, and her skirtage was—and why not?—brief. Glowing she rose and, throwing her head back and her classic bosom forward, cried out that she wished to speak for Mr. Black. The Lord Chief Justice inquired whether she was a member of the English bar. A less necessary question never was put. That thick varnish of beauty could have been preserved intact only by strict abstinence from study. But doubtless dedication to certain sorts of wisdom implies a duty to ignore others. She replied that she was not. Lord Goddard announced that, that being so, the court could not hear her. This was not an early Griffith film. So Mr. Black went off to prison to serve his ten years' hard labour, which was an extremely severe sentence, indeed the most severe sentence passed on any of the persons charged under the Defence Regulations; and Miss Frances returned across the Atlantic, to make or break the American stage.

Probably Mr. Black had been at his best in his companionship with this artless child, so sweetly soaked in the lucent sirops of her own beauty. Doubtless in some of those days of concentrated spring that Berlin knows, when the south wind at last brings warmth to a land long blown clean by the other winds, he had stood beside her while she cried how cute a snowdrop was, and softly settled beside it like a mothering dove; doubtless he had sat by a fire in a big soft chair, forgetting the maniacal Dr. Hetzler and the way the war news had gone, and explaining something about Plato, while she, although mending something, listened to every word, as she proved every now and then by telling him that he was making it all so wonderfully clear. It was for such friendships that the little man was made. But he had too liberal an allowance of the sin by which most of the traitors fell: which was pride. When one of the prosecuting counsel mentioned the title of his book, *Woe for My Comrades,* he said tartly, "It's a quotation from Sophocles", and tossed his head, as if to say, "You wouldn't know about that. It's poetry. And Greek. People like you don't care for that sort of thing, they only care for material success. Poetry and Greek, those were the things I and my wonderful German friends cared about. And today my sort of person is in the hands of your sort of person." But the prosecuting counsel was in fact a man of culture who knew much poetry and much Greek, and was treating him with civilized charity. Mr. Black had rightly supposed that he himself knew more than many people about poetry and Greek, and he had based on this fact the fiction that his intellectual gifts were so prodigious and commanding that they entitled him to a position of power. The case of William Joyce was slightly different; for he possessed the structure though not the substance of such a prodigious and commanding intellect, and it was not possible for such an oddity to know what it lacked, having none of it. But most of the traitors not simply procured by their appetites had fallen into this error of regarding their slight superiority to the average as an overwhelming superiority over all people of all places and all ages, which gave them the right to reject all traditional values and assume that every action and opinion of the community was wrong. Thomas Haller Cooper was correct in his observation that most of the youths he met as a suburban schoolboy or a City clerk were not, as he was, studying Oriental languages, and that they were abstaining from these studies because they were inferior to him in brains and imagination. But he forgot that in the world there are countless people who have had so much intelligence and so much imagination that they had become not merely students but masters of Oriental languages, and that he had not yet proved that he belonged to this class. Forgetting this, he had, in the event of the war, gone counter to the rules as laid down by the wisdom of states and had behaved as if he were already a German national when he was too young to go through the legal formalities of becoming one. But, indeed, he is no perfect example of pride, for his love of his German mother and of Germany would have forced him into that illegality in any case. The issue was confused.

Indeed, no trial was as confused as his. He was charged under the Treason Act and therefore had to be found innocent and let go free or found guilty and hanged; and the reason for this rigorous form of prosecution lay beyond doubt in the part he played as procurer of the British Free Corps. He was a member of the S.S.; they had found under his arm-pit the blue tattoo-mark of his blood group which was its secret and indelible sign. That he might not have been able to help. But to seduce prisoners of war, to tempt men weakened by captivity into giving up their birthright, that he could have helped, that he should have helped. What cruelty this was can be guessed from the hatred, too awkward and unexpansive to be feigned, with which the men in charge of the prisoner-of-war camps gave evidence against the traitors who tampered with their men. One such, a wizened little non-commissioned officer, brown and dry as a good potato crisp, snarled as he told of how Cooper came to his camp, and tried to see the boys separately, and how he had reminded him that that was forbidden under the terms of the Geneva Convention. As he described the big Foreign Office car in which Cooper used to travel, he spoke with a winking contempt, as if he had been speaking of a kept woman or a man who lived on the earnings of a prostitute. Indeed Thomas Haller Cooper was a pimp; but he was also naïve. It is said that at the preliminary police-court proceedings his jaw dropped when there came into the box, as one of the chief witnesses against him, an Englishman who had been working beside him on a seeming parity of treason, and he heard that the man had been a British agent. This was John Henry Owen Brown, to whom he had expressed consternation when D-day came and went and the Allied invasion stood its ground, and said that he meant to change sides; to whom he had made his boast of having had to leave London because he had killed a Jew. The boy was astonished. He and his S.S. friends had meant to be the ones that were hard, that were sly, that gave evidence for the prosecution.

He was naïve when he went into the witness-box, as of course he insisted on doing. There he too told the same story as Mr. Black of having worked for the Nazis only as a cover for underground work for the Allies; but he lied with a brassy fluency which announced to everybody who might otherwise have missed it the spuriousness of his story.

He was naïve, yet he was self-possessed. He was at ease in the court, and that was tragic. A court of law is the antithesis of a home, a place where people live, speaking easily and with only reasonable truthfulness, since they have not been sworn, and pleading guilty and not guilty at one and the same time, and passing sentences on each other and never carrying them out. But the difference did not appal the young man, for he had not lived in a home for years, for something like a quarter of his young life. He had been either in barracks or at the Russian front, or acting as jailer to the poor brats of the British Free Corps. He was so naïve he could not keep hidden the source of his self-possession in all its dreadfulness. When he left the witness-box and returned to the dock he tried to carry on the good impression which he quite falsely believed he had made by his evidence. So he threw out his chest and brought his feet down on the boards in a smacking strut. Not so has any Englishman, even the most highly drilled English soldier, ever walked. He could be seen for what he was. It had to be recognized that had there been a ring at the bell in the early hours of the morning, and one had opened the door and found this young man standing in the passage with a comrade or two just like himself, all in their jack-boots, one's heart would have missed some beats; and one would have had reason, for there would certainly have followed some hours in a cellar, or as like as not some years in Buchenwald or Belsen, or, not improbably, no years at all anywhere. Of course he was found guilty and sentenced to death. But the character that made his story of having worked for the Allies a plain imposture saved his life. "Do not class me with the other bastards that have been standing in this dock", he said to a police officer. "I am half a German." This view was shared by authority, and for that reason he was reprieved.

The world can bear to shed blood. It has done that often. What it cannot bear is to see all its hopes drowned in that blood.

In this war that has happened, and the war was the work of Germany. It is a mystery that a young man, seeking to be acquitted by a court full of people who had suffered in this war, should seek to win their favour by making himself a perfect example of the kind of German that shed the blood of the world and drowned its hopes. Of course it cannot have seemed to him that he was doing that. He was saying to himself, like a child, "I must please them, I must try to look a nice young man". To him all niceness was in Germany, a nice young man was a nice young German, which by German consensus of opinion was a Nazi. But it is still a mystery why to him, with a choice between England and Germany, all niceness seemed to lie in Germany. Perhaps the answer lies in that suburban street where the German woman's home could still be told at a glance because the windows were packed with the small heavy bulbs of that small massive flower the hyacinth, with the daffodils that encourage the weak spring sunshine with the strong summer sunshine of their rich yellow, with flowers that bloomed long before they were flowers, when they were still brown bulbs without a single sprout, in the mind of the woman who planted them in winter, who planted far more of them than her English neighbours, and planted them more cleverly, because she cared more for them. That window is a great mystery; if one could understand it one could understand Germany, which has its flowers, its songs, its Buchenwald.

This confusion of loveliness and all that imperils it is no new vice, it has its roots deep in the soil of Germany, its prehensile growths take to themselves all those who have drawn their being from the soil. It took back Denis John, the golden owl, the son of the North London baker whose parents had been born German and had become naturalized Britons. It determined the course of his path to the end, which was not what would have been predicted for the young prig who circulated in the safe and evasive London of the Peace Pledge Union with his pretentious friends. He and his companions had moved across Western Europe after their capture by the Germans in the Channel Islands, where they were evading military service, and had passed from camp to camp, everywhere defying authority but not without cost to themselves. They were silly, complicated, quarrelsome, courageous; not unlike the characters in the *Nibelungenlied*. They joined the British Free Corps chiefly in order to flout the old-fashioned prejudice of their fellow prisoners of war, and once in it, organized a revolt against the conditions, beating up some support from the confirmed rebels such as Ronald David and the misfits such as poor Herbert George. For that they were sent to a *Straflager*, a punishment camp, and there they learned what it could be like to be entirely unprotected, either by the police or by the recognized authorities of a prisoner-of-war camp. After seven weeks they petitioned the German authorities to let them go back to the British Free Corps on any terms, and were told that they might do so, but that if they ever gave any trouble it would be the end of all of them. This was in the autumn of 1944, when the authorities felt the chill of doom falling on them, and nagged and bullied the wretched little British Free Corps as a slum mother, fearing a visit from the rent collector, will scream at her children and drag them about.

In the early months of 1945 the British Free Corps, which had been on exhibition in Dresden, was sent to Berlin. "We had nothing to do here," said Denis John afterwards, "and we all used to get around the town all day visiting hotels, cafés, etc." Very soon he fell in love with a girl called Lena; and this is perhaps the one real love affair amongst all those matings which were at once a prime motive and a consolation for the treachery of the men in the British Free Corps. For this girl had been a pupil at the school in Germany to which his German grandmother had brought him, and as schoolchildren they had been great friends. She had been in some trouble during the war; she had been brought back to Germany from Bulgaria, where she had been working as an army clerk, for having expressed anti-Nazi sentiments. Now she was working in an office of the S.S. in Berlin and had a flat in the suburb of Duhlendorf. The discipline in the British Free Corps was so slack that very soon Denis John was living in her flat and going to the barracks only to draw his pay and his rations. As their passion grew they applied for permission to marry, but this was refused. It was a curious quirk of the Germans that though they often ordered German women to have intercourse with the traitors they never gave these people permission to marry, though why that particular egg seemed better to them raw than cooked is hard to see. But terror was driving duty out of German offices by then, and one could at least get a forged travel permit. With this the boy and girl went to Bremen, and there they went to a church and tried to persuade the pastor to marry them; and perhaps persuaded him to perform some ceremony. There was at any rate throbbing emotion; there was kneeling before an altar, while mystic authority recited spells relating to the eternal, and the heart swelled and burst and melted into the circumambient cloud of solemn bliss.

Later it was learned that the authorities intended to send the British Free Corps to the Russian front as that swept from Polish to German soil, and at this news the British Free Corps took to its bed as one man. It is not surprising that the authorities took not much trouble to get it up again. The degree to which German life through despair had become frivolous can be judged from the curious hospital routine followed by Denis John. He had been taken in as a patient suffering from tonsillitis, but he spent only his nights in the hospital. Every morning, with nobody raising any objection, he used to rise and dress and go out to console Lena, who was with child. Their position was as preposterously dramatic as opera. He, a traitor, had to be got out of Germany before the British came; it is to be emphasized once again that most traitors of normal mind from prisoner-of-war camps perfectly understood their position, for it had always been explained to them by the British officers before they left the camp, except in the rare cases where our security organization had broken down. She, who had been adjudged too anti-Nazi to be safe company for the peoples of occupied Europe, could not get a permit to leave the country. The pregnant girl rushed about Berlin appealing to her friends with the various Ministries, who with the calm of delirium gave her what she wanted: an order transferring Denis John from the British Free Corps to the English propaganda department of the Milan radio, a forged travelling permit for herself.

This was in early April. The journey from Berlin to Milan took eleven days. Dirty and tired and young, they stumbled out into the Italian spring which shone eternal among the confusion. At the German radio station a German officer shouted that he had been warned by Berlin that Lena's papers were forged, and that he meant to arrest her, but, turning aside to make provision for his own safety, let them both walk out of his room. Fortunately for them, the German system had not entirely broken down. One cell of this unit was still functioning. There was a cashier who in a reeling world retained the knowledge that everyone holding a travelling permit had the right to draw eight thousand lire, and so paid Denis John and Lena sixteen thousand lire. With this money they went out into streets perilous with the sniping and counter-sniping and grenade-throwing of partisans and Germans and Fascists, and found a hotel, and slept off their fatigue for two or three days. Then they crept out of the city along the road to Pavia, and stayed at a village called Bressane which looks from the flat lands, among the Judas-trees and the poplars, to the chestnut-covered slopes of the Ligurian Alps. There they stayed until the end of May, until the American troops came. Then they were put in a camp; and soon the boy was sent back to England and prison, the girl to Germany and the bearing of a child in hunger and among rubble. The type of such experience is the "*Liebestod*": a great work, were it not for the feeling that the composer and his creations alike sucked suffering like a toffee in the mouth. It was doubtful from Denis John's statement if he would ever have fallen in love with Lena had there not been curving over the city where they met the breaking wave of a historic catastrophe. The North London baker who is Denis John's father, who stands in his neat lounge suit ready to serve his customers with the gingerbread made in the Continental fashion and the buns made in the English fashion, both as good as they can be in these times, his watchet-blue eyes heavy with sorrow, his skin shining like glazed china, as fair men's skins do when they are ill and tired, is perhaps more romantic than his son, because he tried to save his son from romanticism. The emigration of Germans to England and America was not wholly economic in its origin. It was in part a desire of the uncorrupted part of the people to save its seed from the "*Liebestod*" which sang itself in *Tristan und Isolde*, and was to be privately practised by Lena and Denis John and many another, and publicly consummated in the wide ruin from the Rhine to the Oder.

Denis John was sentenced to three years' penal servitude. It was not a harsh sentence. For it must be remembered that while he was acting out his version of the *"Liebestod"* many young men of his age had experienced the *Tod* without the *Liebe*. He had been dealt with by the civil courts because he was not a member of the British armed forces; and in that he was lucky. It is regrettable that any serious offences should be dealt with by court-martial, other than those which have to be dealt with as quickly as possible by military or naval units operating in areas remote from civilization. The constitution of a court-martial is in itself highly objectionable. Six officers who know nothing about the law and may not have the capacity to learn about it act as both judge and jury; and though they have a professional lawyer sitting with them, in the person of a Judge-Advocate, who directs them on questions of law, this does not correct the disadvantages of employing a panel of amateurs instead of a judge, and it drags out every case of any complexity to intolerable length and tedium, as every time a point of law is raised the court has to be cleared while the six judges ask and receive instruction. Just how unsatisfactory such a court is can be grasped by imagining that one day the judge should step down from the bench at the Old Bailey and order the jury to take over his functions, appointing a stray K.C. to explain the law to them as they went along, and clear the court while he made his explanations. The poor prisoner has not only to endure this unnecessary prolongation of his trial, he is faced with a dilemma concerning his defence. Either he has to employ an officer as his amateur counsel, or employ a professional lawyer, who will be regarded by the judges with suspicion as a tricky outsider who is trying to pull fast ones on them. When the trial comes to an end he is subjected to an ordeal far greater than usually experienced in civil courts. The six judges deliberate, just as a jury does, on his guilt. If they bring in the verdict of guilty, they then take evidence as to his character and previous convictions and retire again to consider the sentence, which is usually, but not always, announced only when it has been confirmed by the Army Council, which may not happen for some weeks. The anguish caused by this delay is increased by the lack of any standard of sentences. Groups of amateurs dotted about the country, functioning once or only a few times in their lives, cannot found or transmit a tradition of appropriate punishment; and they sling out sentences which are likely to be, if they are unimaginative, savage, and if they are imaginative, frivolous.

It is possible to appeal to the Army Council against these sentences, but such an appeal is held in secret, and the authority does not disclose its reasons. The prisoner is also hardly dealt with by the impossibility of ensuring a public trial by court-martial. Any member of the public can attend a court-martial which is not being held *in camera* for reasons of security; but how any member of the public is to hear of a court-martial is not so plain. It can very easily happen that a man whose home is in a remote part of England and whose trial takes place in London will be tried without a single person being present except the officers of the court. It also often happens that courts-martial take place in premises entirely unsuitable for the purpose, where the correct legal procedure cannot be followed without deviation and there is no proper accommodation for witnesses.

The prisoners of war who joined the British Free Corps and the S.S. or who broadcast, who were tried by court-martial, were to illustrate the arbitrary character of this obsolete institution. Almost identical cases of a mild type were sent to prison for six months, two years, seven years, ten years, and fifteen years; almost identical cases of a depraved type were sent to prison for five years, ten years, fifteen years, and for life. Such a diversity of sentences must mean injustice and must bring the law into disrepute. One case was uniquely unfortunate. A boy named Henry Alfred Symonds joined the army in 1941 when he was fifteen years of age. It is not clear how, in those days of identity cards, he can have been accepted by the army authorities. Two years later he was captured in Italy, and was induced to join the British Free Corps. He was sentenced in 1946, at which time he was just twenty-one, to fifteen years' imprisonment. He did not serve any great part of his sentence; but it is not easy to compute the agony such sentences inflict before the reversion. There was, moreover, an interesting antithesis between the policies of the civil and service courts. The civil courts obviously pursued a firm policy in their prosecution of treachery which was designed to make it perfectly plain to the public mind what that offence was and what traitors must expect. They brought to book the chief exemplars of the crime: William Joyce the broadcaster, John Amery the inventor of the British Free Corps, Walter Purdy the informer, and Cooper the volunteer in an enemy armed force, and got them sentenced to death. Then they prosecuted with an obvious anxiety not to gratify any desire for revenge, not to deprave the community by blood-baths and excessive use of the *oubliette*; and the cases gradually faded out, except for one or two who might have been forgotten and had plainly forced trial on themselves by their eccentricity. The armed forces, on the other hand, brought their prosecutions forward with extreme dilatoriness and an increasing animus, so that some of the earlier sentences were fatuously light and the later ones remarkably severe.

Alfred Vivian, the black-browed romantic who had been genuinely pro-German and had drunk the health of the Duke of Windsor in the mess of the British Free Corps, was one of the lucky ones, for he was a merchant seaman and was tried at the Old Bailey, and got seven years. Throughout the trial a handsome matron had been sitting in the court; but there were four other merchant seamen in the dock and it was not clear whose kin she was until, when this sentence was delivered, she raised her clenched fist and struck her knee with it, and rose, and left. Fuseli, painting Mrs. Siddons as Lady Macbeth, painted such a woman, such a gesture. Fate constructs round people of this type dramas in which they play the leading part, and doubtless she had made her life in a riverside suburb into a very moving and uplifting drama, using her personal relationships as a fiery but solemn argument for pride and decency, and worth. It was a great misfortune that her son, forced by his inherited blood to build such a drama round himself, had not known where to look for a theme, so had fallen into this nonsense. When in the spring of 1945 he realized how disastrous this nonsense was likely to be for him, he acted in the same way as most of the British Free Corps. He rose from his hospital bed, stole or was given some civilian clothes, and, turning west to fly from the Russians, walked into the Allied lines, and was there well received as an escaped prisoner of war. The men who followed this course enjoyed a false sense of security that lasted for some time. Their stories were naturally accepted; those of them who had acquired a good working knowledge of the German language during their captivity were useful as interpreters to the advancing British and American troops. These men continued in this magical state of immunity for a matter of weeks or months. Till VE-day and for a long time after, the army had many other things to do than to chase unimportant traitors; and during this period of disorganization the men were sheltered by the rule of the British Free Corps and the British section of the Rundfunk that all traitors except the most important should work under assumed names. This did no more, and the Germans must have known it would do no more, than give them a short respite before arrest.

Sooner or later nearly all of them received the message they expected: that some officers of the Intelligence Corps wanted to see them. The one man who forced his arrest before its time was Ronald David, the Byronic wastrel who had been adopted by a spinster in New South Wales. He was in a sense one of the most debased members of the British Free Corps; he had liked the soft life, the whores, and the drink. On him were found the photographs of thirteen German prostitutes, as well as mementoes of a steadier attachment. But he confessed his connection in the British Free Corps of his own accord, in order to gain permission to give evidence for the defence at the court-martial of one of the "Big Six" of the Corps. The rest were led away; and statements were taken from them, usually by the Scotland Yard inspectors who had been lent to the War Office for such work, and who were to show in these exceptional circumstances what qualities of heart and brain we take for granted in the police.

The statements varied from the suicidal and pretentious apologia of John Amery to the artless inventions of Herbert George, the Disney dwarf who had fought with the International Brigade in Spain and deserted from it. He described how he had met a German girl called Hilda Henschel, and after speaking to her "found she was pro-English. I told her I wanted to escape and she said she would help me. I told her I had studied the theory of piloting a plane and eventually she told me she could find out where I could get hold of a plane, which she did. The plane was in an aerodrome about thirty kilometres away from Hildesheim. On the night we had a nasty raid and the airfield was damaged so I could not carry out my plans." He returned to England and at his Thames-side home rejoined his wife in perfect domestic bliss, although he had taken steps to divorce her when he was in the prisoner-of-war camp; and, determined to pick up all the threads, he became the life and soul of the local Communist Party. The poor little man had to leave this happy and busy life for two years' hard labour.

It would have seemed a pity to have bothered about this odd little soul, but such segregation was in his own interests. It was certainly a great relief to the licensed trade of his Thames-side town. On Saturday nights Herbert George would come into a bar and, after a drink or two, would be filled with a desire to entertain the company and would therefore relate his adventures, first in the International Brigade and then in the British Free Corps. This never worked out well. His imprisonment must also have been a relief to the officers of the local Communist Party, who are doubtless serious-minded men. This odd creature, and all the other odd creatures, then went into a world abhorrent to contemplate: a world of cold cells, of dirt, of mind-slaying monotony. "I never worry", said a legal official, "about men who are merely hanged. What worries me is that a man who has been in prison for ten years is no longer a man but an automaton, and that there are a certain number of men who must be sent to prison for ten years if certain crimes are to be suppressed." But penal reform is impossible without new prisons and more warders of a high type. Not for a generation will our bankrupt people be able to build new prisons; and the labour shortage means that it becomes more and more difficult to induce men to enter the exacting life of prison service if they are fit to do anything else. There is pain here, and it cannot be avoided. The thought of Herbert George is here reassuring, so certain is it that he will pass unscathed through his two years in a convict prison and will add this to his list of experiences and regard it as yet another source of distinction. All of the rest of them will come out as they went in, unchanged in their essential and dangerous quality. Because of their fundamental neuroses and the stimulus applied to these by their environment, they will be timber for the next international revolutionary movement.

IX

WILLIAM JOYCE, of whom that cannot be said, left his Hamburg office and went out, in the company of his wife, to seek a safety which he did not by then believe could be found. First he slipped into his pocket a passport made out in the false name of Wilhelm Hansen: who was described as a teacher. He liked teaching, he was proud of his gifts as a teacher. It was dated November 3, 1944, but the date may have been as false as the name. Till the end he had refused to admit to himself that his Germany might be defeated, and it is unlikely that he would have taken such a precaution up to the last moment. Then it would be easy, for all over Germany people were sitting in government offices forging papers to deny their curious Christs at the third cock-crow. Joyce's wife had a separate passport. It had occurred to them that anything might happen: the worst might happen; they might have to part. So they started on their journey, and, like all the traitors who then closed the door behind them on the misery and futility which had grown thicker and thicker round them for the previous five years, they stepped out into the spring. But not for the Joyces any season of respite, for they could not, like their underlings, go into the British or American lines and tell a lying story and be given work, and be at ease for a little and hope for the best. Joyce, who at that time had only a vague suspicion that there was any doubt about his British nationality, knew that there was no hope for him at all if he fell into Allied hands.

So they took to the forest, the German forest: where the trees make a sweet shade and the family can picnic, where the trees make so deep a shade that at their roots the dark traditions germinate and grow. The Joyces lived out there. By then the first birch leaves were small green flames against their silver bark, and the pines and the larches manifested their soberer sort of spring, and on the open heaths the tufts of young grass surprised against the dark ling. The genius of the country took them to itself. They were obliged to enact their "*Liebestod*". Sometimes they spent a night in the towns or a village, more often they found their bed in barns and sheds at the wood's edge and heard the hoots of the owls, that mourn so softly, as ghosts might mourn for their own destinies; and by day they lay on the soft pine needles, while the sun shone on them between the tree-trunks as between the bars of a prison window, or, wanting to wash themselves or their clothes, knelt at the edges of lakes, and shuddered because the water was still too cold for the flesh, which has an inveterate preference for remaining warm. The love between them, which Joyce had so often mauled and man-handled, at this time established its value for ever. Now that everything else had failed them, it survived, not only intact, but intensified. Their joy in each other must have been transfused with agonizing self-reproach; for they might so easily have stayed in England. Both must have said, "No, it was not your fault, it was mine". Sometimes death must have seemed to be already standing beside them; sometimes they must have felt that everything would be all right, because it always had been. At all times they were horribly uncomfortable. The British troops were everywhere, and they were under a real necessity to hide. William Joyce had always been very exacting about his food. His mother had been a very good cook; and a fellow-student of his at the Battersea Polytechnic, questioned about him many years afterwards, could remember almost nothing except that he had once taken him home to tea at Allison Grove and the cakes and soda-bread had been wonderful. His wife had made it her pride never to ask him to sit down to a cold meal. Now they ate at irregular intervals where they could. They grew very thin and could not keep themselves clean or neat. William Joyce developed a skin disease affecting the scalp.

On May 28, 1945, they had been on the run for some weeks. We had been told of what that day brought to Joyce at his trial. Now we can know what was behind the odd incidents told in his captors' story. In the evening he was walking in the forest when he came on two British officers. Had he gone on his way they would probably not have noticed him, for he was by then a very miserable figure, and they were busy looking for loose wood to build a fire. But he halted and watched them, and in the end he had to speak to them. Into the void which is a revolutionary's mind when a revolution has been effected there rush old passions, faiths held and forgotten. He had been reared by his father to regard the British Army as the symbol of the power and the glory on earth; he had hoped to be a British officer himself; he had boasted as a boy that he had served under the orders of a British officer. Also they were men of his own people, from whom he had been exiled for five years and more. He told them where they would find more wood; and he spoke in French. Nothing could have been better calculated to draw their questioning attention to him. But William Joyce had always been proud of his French, which was correct and fluent. Perhaps an ingenuous part of his mind was saying, "You are British officers. I had hoped to become a British officer but I abandoned my hope. I was not a gentleman, I was not the sort that is given a commission. But I can claim other values. I have a good mind. Listen to my French, which I speak better than most gentlemen." When the two British officers stared at him in interest, he committed the act which any man except him could have committed with impunity, but which was for him suicide. He said in English, "There are a few more pieces here". To every man in the world there is one person of whom he knows little: whom he would never recognize if he met him walking down the street, whose motives are a mystery to him. That is himself. It is possible that William Joyce did not know that he alone among men spoke with the blended voices of Tamerlane and Punchinello, and that whatever he said he also said, "I am William Joyce". The two officers, startled, conferred together. Then the junior of the two, Lieutenant Perry, asked Joyce in the idiom of his time, "You wouldn't happen to be William Joyce, would you?" Joyce put his hand in his pocket, meaning to take out his forged passport, and was struck down by the reality he had provoked, for the Lieutenant, nervous as every member of an invading force must be, thought that he was feeling for a revolver, and drew his own and shot him in the leg. Joyce fell to the ground, groaning, "My name is Fritz Hansen". So little store had he set on the sole means left to him for escaping detection that he had not troubled to memorize the details of his forged passport, which was made out in the name of not Friedrich but Wilhelm Hansen, nor to throw away his real military passport, made out in the name of William Joyce. The idea of any precaution being of any use any more had deserted him.

One of the officers went away and made contact with authority; and eventually Joyce was taken to the military hospital at Lüneburg. Mrs. Joyce had been arrested and taken to a prison camp, spent and dishevelled, saying in her habitual manner, which was jaunty and mechanically cynical, that she and her husband had expected this for a long time and that there was no use making a fuss about it. They were not to see each other again until after he had been sentenced to death. The news that Joyce was coming to the hospital arrived before him, and his stretcher was carried from the ambulance through a crowd of soldiers who were chiyiking and crying out "This is Jairmany calling". This must have been the first intimation to him that he was considered by the British public as a comic character, and there could be no more perplexing anticlimax. On May 31 an Intelligence officer came and sat by his bed and interrogated him. To that officer he dictated this statement:

I take this opportunity of making a preliminary statement concerning the motives which led me to come to Germany and to broadcast to Britain over the German radio service. I was actuated not by the desire for personal gain, material or otherwise, but solely by political conviction. I was brought up as an extreme Conservative with strong Imperialistic ideas, but very early in my career, namely, in 1923, became attracted to fascism and subsequently to National Socialism. Between the years 1923 and 1939 I pursued vigorous political activities in England, at times as a Conservative but mainly as a Fascist or National Socialist. In the period immediately before this war began I was profoundly discontented with the policies pursued by British governments, first, because I felt they would lead to the eventual disruption of the British Empire, and secondly, because I thought the existing economic system entirely inadequate to the needs of the times. I was very greatly impressed by constructive work which Hitler had done for Germany and was of the opinion that throughout Europe as also in Britain there must come a reform on the lines of National Socialist doctrine, although I did not suppose that every aspect of National Socialism as advocated in Germany would be accepted by the British people.

One of my dominant beliefs was that a war between Britain and

Germany would be a tragedy, the effects of which Britain and the British Empire would not survive, and I considered that a grossly disproportionate influence was exerted on British policy by the Jews, who had their reasons for hating National Socialist Germany. When, in August 1939, the final crisis emerged I felt that the question of Danzig offered no just cause for a world war. As by reason of my opinions I was not conscientiously disposed to fight for Britain against Germany, I decided to leave the country since I did not wish to play the part of a conscientious objector, and since I supposed that in Germany I should have the opportunity to express and propagate views the expression of which would be forbidden in Britain during time of war. Realizing, however, that at this critical juncture I had declined to serve Britain, I drew the logical conclusion that I should have no moral right to return to that country of my own free will and that it would be best to apply for German citizenship and make my permanent home in Germany. Nevertheless, it remained my undeviating purpose to attempt as best I could to bring about a reconciliation or at least an understanding between the two countries. After Russia and the United States had entered the war such an agreement appeared to me no less desirable than before for, although it seemed probable that with these powerful allies Britain would succeed in defeating Germany, I considered that the price which would ultimately have to be paid for this help would be far higher than the price involved in a settlement with Germany.

This belief was strengthened from month to month as the power of Russia grew, and during the later stages of the war I became certain that Britain, even though capable of gaining a military triumph over the Germans, would in that event be confronted with a situation far more dangerous and complicated than that which existed in August 1939; and thus until the very last moment I clung to my hope of an Anglo–German understanding, although I could see that the prospects thereof were small. I know that I have been denounced as a traitor and I resent the accusation as I conceive myself to have been guilty of no underhand or deceitful act against Britain, although I am also able to understand the resentment that my broadcasts have in many quarters aroused. Whatever opinion may be formed at the present time with regard to my conduct, I submit that the final judgment cannot be properly passed until it is seen whether Britain can win the peace. Finally I should like to stress the fact that in coming to Germany and in working for the German radio system my wife was powerfully influenced by me. She protests to the contrary but I am sure that, if I had not taken this step, she would not have taken it either. This statement has been read over to me, and it is true.

(Signed) WILLIAM JOYCE

This was a remarkable statement to be dictated by a man who had been brought into hospital three days before, not only wounded but suffering from malnutrition and exposure. But the mind that framed it was remarkable only in its structure. The substance was poor; and greatness depends on the substance of the mind, which is the mirror of all substances, and chooses between them, between good and evil, love and hate, the agreeable and the disagreeable. The situation of England was as he saw it. It was to her interest to form an alliance with Germany; for without a strong Germany the balance of Europe must be disturbed and world trade disorganized. But the substance of the mind, reflecting the substance of Germany, should have, if it were a true and bright mirror, reflected cruelty and murder and fatuity, a character with which the sane could conclude no alliance, however terrible the alternative, because it was itself the limit of terror. The substance of William Joyce's mind was not a true and bright mirror; he might know that A and B and C were linked by certain causal connections, but he would never apprehend with any exactitude the nature of A or B or C. But at the time he dictated his statement he must have learned the nature of Nazi Germany from his own painful experiences, working with the frenetic Hetzler, learning what happened to those that fell out with his masters. He must have known why Great Britain had had to fight Germany, and been lying when he pretended that he did not. That pretence, however, was too late. Our troops had been in Buchenwald and Belsen. It was certain that whether Britain could "win the peace" or not, it had certainly been imperative that she should win the war. Nevertheless it remains true that that statement was remarkable both as an intellectual and a moral effort.

Sixteen days later he was flown to England. One of the soldiers in the plane asked him for his autograph as they were crossing the Channel, and he wrote him a scrawl—"This is the most historic moment in my life, God bless dear old England" —which reeked of that illiterate quality never dispelled by his University education. He was taken to Brixton Prison, and there he did well. When he first appeared at Bow Street after his arrival he struck spectators as a scrubby little creature of the sort that has never known anything but scrubbiness. One of the reporters likened him to a dusty London sparrow. But he soon improved and put on weight and dignity, and an air which was not unlikeable and which was new. In the past he had always startled the people he met, unless they were in the Fascist nexus, by the real or affected brutality of his egotism. Now he startled people as much by his quiet pleasantness; by his humour, which was no longer boisterous and teasing, but gentle and remote and self-satirizing; by his contentment.

Of all plants contentment is the last which would be expected to grow within prison walls. But William Joyce had much reason to feel that Wormwood Scrubs was not such a bad place to be. He was out of the alien forest, he was no longer enacting a tragedy which was part of other men's tradition but not his. He had food to eat, a roof over his head, and was among his own people again: among the unexcitable, matter-of-fact, controlled English whom he had despised. If a warder now and then was mean or surly, there was no Dr. Hetzler here and this was no concentration camp. But for the most part he found the prison officials very kind and responsive to his efforts to give them as little trouble as possible. It is to be remembered that William Joyce had always liked the police, and his passion for discipline was so great that he may have found a sort of pleasure in conforming to prison routine. Into this cold grey snugness came his family; most often his beloved and loving young brother Quentin. From them, it is true, he must have learned that the revolt against his parents which he had carried on throughout his life had come to an end, because they had both been vanquished in the world of fact, and, if they had not actually been killed by the forces whose cause he had espoused, had been tormented by them in their last hours. Though it is possible that he may have heard of his father's death not long after it happened, for Michael Joyce had died before America had come into the war, and the Joyces had relatives in the United States, it must have been now that he heard for the first time of the death of his mother. That tiny and spirited being, though she had been persuaded to go into the country after her widowhood, had returned to London to be with her sons and daughter, and when she was stricken with a painful disease she was taken to St. Mary's Hospital, Paddington, where she lay dying during the summer of 1944, while the V-1's broke over the town. This news must have brought William Joyce a grief which, though intense, was warm and purging. Fantasy applies to our personal relationships a chill and commonplace formula which forces the members of our families to cast aside their individualities and play certain obvious and inferior parts, in order to throw what we hope is our obvious superiority into relief. Now that fantasy had to relinquish this material in William Joyce's mind, all its ends having been dreadfully attained, reality could reassert itself. Now in his cell there was room, as there had not been in the wide liberty of London, for his mysterious and loving father, his gay and loving mother.

In his cell there was also room for an intellectual exercise more complex, more absorbing, and more novel than any he had engaged in when he was free to study as he liked. When he entered Wormwood Scrubs he believed he had no defence to the charge of high treason which had been brought against him. But his solicitors drew his attention to the passage in his statement in which he had alluded to his belief that his father had been a naturalized American citizen, and had forfeited his naturalization by failing "to re-register". If his father had been a naturalized American citizen when he was born, they told him, then he himself was an American citizen by birth, and nothing which had happened afterwards could affect that. Did he ever believe that safety lay in that resolution of his doubts regarding his status? It may be so. But it is said that, in conversation with a prison official, he described the defence which was to be put up for him and added, with a faint smile, "It will be amusing to see if they get away with it." Perhaps the gentle cynicism was honest enough. He had lived by his ambition.

That part of his ambition which lived on his lips and in the forefront of his mind had been utterly frustrated. He was not going to be king. In all the world there was not one man, not the most pitiful blind beggar nor the most eroded leper of whom it could be more certainly said that he would never, till the end of time, exercise the smallest grain of power. The other ambition, which lived in his heart and in the secret governing chamber of his mind, was as utterly fulfilled. The revolution had succeeded. He had seen Hamburg, and knew that more than a city had been destroyed; he had a nice historic sense and perhaps he recognized that a continent was dead; he had grown wise enough latterly to realize that a civilization had been murdered. Into his cell, each morning brought the white light that comes at dawn into a house where a corpse lies awaiting burial. If the dead were loved, then those who wake and see such light feel grief; if they were hated, their enemies wake to emptiness and bereavement, because the hunt is over. If the corpse were both loved and hated, then those that still live feel agonizing conflict; and if the corpse died not a natural death but had been helped on its way, then the immortal justice in their hearts tells them that they should pay for their guilt with their own lives. All these several pains torment the successful revolutionary. For him death is truly a release. Joyce's shrewdness knew enough to make him serene.

So he went to his trial, which was not like most earthly trials but was the pattern of such trials as must happen in the hereafter. For we shall be judged at the end unjustly, according to the relation of our activities to a context whereof we, being human and confined to a small part of time and space, knew almost nothing. Such judgment depends not on the blowing of a trump but on the existence of a mind that, being aware of the sum of experience and therefore able to estimate our worth in relation to it, shall judge us by taking cognizance of all the facts we did not know, as it must since we are an integer in that sum. It is said that in few murder cases has it been wise for the accused person to give evidence on his own behalf; but here was a trial where a person under a capital charge could not conceivably give any evidence bearing on his guilt or innocence. He might, indeed, have embarrassed the prosecution to the point of impotence if he had given false evidence that he had not used his passport for the purpose of leaving England for Germany; and he must surely have known enough of the means employed for getting German spies in and out of England to have been able to spin a plausible tale. But he was not a perjurer. He had at least chosen to play out his drama in the real world. If sentence was to be passed on him, let it be based on the truth. But that condition was all he could contribute to his own trial. He could not speak of his own knowledge concerning his father's naturalization, or his status at birth, or the kind of allegiance he owed to the Crown, or the consequences flowing from possession of a passport. He might have been the poor soul in a theologian's dream waiting to hear if the divine caprice poured wine of grace into his cup and made it saved and unbreakable or left it empty and damned. But that is the dream of a finite mind. In the infinite mind there is reconciled justice and injustice. The moral sense of a man is clairvoyant: he knows if he chooses to love rather than to hate he shall be right both in time and in eternity. William Joyce, knowing that he had struck against his own flesh, had written it down over his own signature that every time he had broadcast he had committed treason. Thus he took a short-cut to the same conclusion reached by the lawyers who knew so much about him that he did not.

He was found guilty and he was taken to Wormwood Scrubs: a prison standing on the western edge of London among flat and greasy fields where the sea-gulls gather in time of storm. It has a peculiar character, for it was built about seventy years ago in the full flush of the late Victorian enthusiasm for social reform, with the intention of reclaiming prisoners serving their first sentence by providing them with beautiful surroundings. Though, like so many Victorian buildings, it seems stuffy as stale seed-cake by reason of a marked prosaic error in the proportions and the drab colour of the materials employed, it is a work of great vigour, not irrelevant to its function. It is built round three places of worship, an Anglican chapel, a Roman Catholic chapel, and a synagogue, which wear about their Italianate façades certain clouds of solemnity; and the surrounding mass of administrative and cell blocks is broken by a number of *campanili*. Though the place suggests not only Ravenna and Pisa but a giant model of a lodging-house cruet, it nevertheless has the virtue of presenting extraordinary shapes which the inmates may well find appropriate to their own extraordinary destinies. A prison built with the simplicity of a hospital or a school might well seem heartless to convicts who know that they have lost their liberty by no event so natural as falling sick or growing up; but this alien and emotional ornament and these superfluous towers might be taken as implying knowledge on the part of authority itself that life could become completely strange, as it had been at the moment of their disaster, when a demon entered into them and they said "Yes" when they should have said "No". It was there Joyce waited for the hearing of his appeals, in which he did not believe. There he changed to the man we saw at his later trials, who seemed no longer to trouble himself about his demon's unfortunate reply, but to ponder on an answer he must make to another question.

His destiny was to be honest; to be wrong; to have his habitation "south the river". Wormwood Scrubs lay on the scabbed edge of London, but nevertheless on the same side of the Thames as the imperial city, so his place was not there. The prison was seized by a spasm of madness and ejected him. The news that Joyce was within its walls spread amongst the other prisoners and they raged against his presence. Perhaps they were trying to upset the social verdict of worthlessness passed on them at the same time as their legal conviction; perhaps they were idiotically responding to the call of tradition, for throughout history treason has always been the crime most abhorred by the English, as parricide has been the crime most abhorred by the French; perhaps it was true of the criminal population, as it was of the rest of us at the end of the war, that the sanest were a little mad and the half-mad quite demented. Whatever their reasons, they howled against him with the simplicity of wolves. In his cell he heard the riot, lifted his eyes from the book he was reading and forced them back again, but finally laid the book aside and said hesitantly to the prison official who was sitting with him: "Those people are not calling out against me, are they?" He received an evasive answer, but was later to learn the truth, for one day as he was taking exercise some prisoners in cells overlooking the yard realized his identity, and, though they knew they would be punished for it, shouted curses at him and threw down on him what missiles they could find through the windows. It is said that some of the craziest convicts formed a plan to make a dash past the warders at a favourable moment, to seize William Joyce, and to murder him.

There was not the slightest danger that this plan could have been carried out, but this was not the atmosphere in which a man under sentence of death could be left to await the hearing of his appeal. So Joyce was taken away from Wormwood Scrubs and sent to Wandsworth Jail, a shabby old prison, black as a coal-tip, set among the trodden commons and the discoloured villas, the railway viaducts and the long streets of little houses, which lie "south the river". His last days of his life in London were to be spent only a mile or two from the house in Long-beach Road where it had begun. Now his second wife, with whom he had lived only in his aspirant exile north of the Thames, was received into the district which was his real home. A man condemned to death has the right to see whom he chooses, and the authorities brought his wife over from Germany and lodged her in Holloway Prison, sending her over the river to visit him almost every day. They took great delight in each other's company; and on the morning of his hanging she retreated into a frenzy of grief which for long did not abate. It was necessary afterwards to send her back to Germany, for she had automatically become a German subject when her husband became a naturalized German. There it was necessary to put her in a camp from which she was not released for two years, for she was passionately pro-Nazi and could no more be let loose than any other Nazi propagandist; and, indeed, had she been allowed to return to England and her own family, she could not have been left at liberty, for her own sake. These two people had contrived their own ruin with a finality that not their worst enemy could have achieved by unremitting malice. Iago was a gentle child compared to their suicidal selves.

Thus the white light which came into Joyce's cell all these last mornings shone upon utter desolation. But he maintained his pinched serenity. That was the fruit of courage; and to say this is to say nothing, for courage of a sort which is not dimmed during months of waiting must have its source in something other than itself. It cannot be said that he was upheld by his faith in fascism, although he never recanted and his impudent hand scratched a swastika on the wall of the cell in the Old Bailey where he waited to be taken up to the dock. Of course he could not recant. It would have looked as if he were a coward trying to beg for his life, and he would have falsified the situation as much by giving the impression of repentance as he did by not admitting his disenchantment with Hitler's Germany. It is possible that the long book which he wrote while he was in prison, and which should certainly be published as soon as possible, as a matter of vital historical interest, attempts to explain why National Socialism would have worked if it had been handled by other personalities than the Nazis. That would be the way of retreat which would suggest itself to most minds. But in truth he had lost his faith. The old William Joyce, when he was asked by the judge if he had anything to say before sentence was passed on him, would have thrown back his head and hawked out, "God save England and to hell with Russia", or some such slogan. This new William Joyce kept silent. If he was illuminated by a certain satisfaction it was not because he felt himself supported by fascism; but it was perhaps because he felt himself a Fascist. Men who are perfect specimens of a type feel pleasure in their representative perfection, even though the type itself is not happy. Byron was sleek at finding himself the archetype of the Romantic, although the essence of romanticism is suffering; and Tolstoy enjoyed being the archetype of the Anarchist, although anarchy is the most hopeless of faiths, being an aching discontent with time, which inexorably engenders order. A work of art gives satisfaction to the artist and the spectator because it analyses an experience and synthesizes its findings into a new form that makes people eager for fresh experience. It is natural enough that something of the same sort of satisfaction should be enjoyed by a human being who finds himself so thoroughly and comprehensibly what he is that he can fairly be ranked as a work of art.

X

THERE are several growths from the Fascist stem. Of these William Joyce could represent but one. He had nothing in common with the rank and file of fascism, which was drawn from the mindless, traditionless, possessionless urban populations that are the children of the machine. Those have wholly lost their sense of process. They have forgotten that whatever is not natural is artificial, and that artifice is the fruit of thought and effort. To them a loaf of bread is something they can buy at a bakery; they do not think of the earth and the weather and the plough and the wheat and the harvest and the threshers and the mill. To them light and heat are what they summon by putting a match to a gas-jet or a finger to a switch; they do not think of coal and the pithead and the shaft and the dynamo. They therefore believe that all benefits can be obtained by quite small efforts, and they cannot understand why governments have not already given them full employment, preferably of a light character, high wages, cheap food, free recreations; and they therefore will work to put into power any men who say that they will be able to conjure up those goods by command. Such simplicity is infantile, and must be tainted by the first ugly brutishness of the emergent mind; so cruelty is inevitably an associate of the demand for dictatorship. Only in his love of street-fighting had William Joyce any tie with this kind of Fascist, whom he regarded cynically as the medium in which he had to work. His Irish peasant background had given him a sound enough understanding of process, and he thoroughly grasped the practice and the theory of the modern political machine. It is certain from his broadcasts that he did not hold the essential doctrine of the Fascist rank and file, which is that government is easy. The kind of Fascist he represented was the leader drawn from the small, uninfluential home as distinct from the leader drawn from the armed forces or from the aristocracy.

He was therefore representative of the newer type of Fascist leader. Of the older types, the professional soldier who turns his arms against his own kind and seizes political power is old as man. The king, whom the foolish sneer at as a reactionary figurehead, is this man tamed by law, forced by the Church, which was the noble cunning of early Europe, to enter into a contractual relationship with the people, to give them protection in return for their allegiance. Sir Oswald Mosley, too, is a type that reappears in age after age, not to be abolished. The aristocrat who has a flaw in him which is recognized by his own kind but who will not take their verdict on him and tries to rush over their dead bodies to the place in the council chamber which they denied him, he also is a familiar figure. From the time of the Plantagenets he, on our island, has had again and again to be told to stop pushing; and on the Continent he has revisited again and again, choosing the name of Wallenstein for one of his most positive reincarnations. But the Fascist leader drawn from the small uninfluential home is new as our own century.

He is the man who, whatever his origins had been, if he had been born in favourable and not in unfavourable circumstances, could not in any age, nor in any place, have been given a position of power by the community, because of some innate flaw in his character, such as made Mosley or Wallenstein unacceptable to their equals. Till now he could pretend that the cause of this failure lay not in himself but in his stars. He could maintain, with a fair measure of truth, that it was impossible for him or any other man without fortune, or useful connections, to become a national leader; and nobody could disprove his claim. He could go to his grave, therefore, in the rounded contentment of a genius who could have saved his country had he but been permitted. But now this simple and profound order of satisfaction, which benefited millions, has been destroyed by the development of the democratic system. It is no longer true that any person of political talent can be debarred from exercising it by poor or mediocre origins. Joyce was born and bred in much easier circumstances than Ernest Bevin or Herbert Morrison or Ellen Wilkinson, and if he could not rise to the same heights the reason must lie in his inferiority to them. He knew, too, that intellectually he was probably not inferior to them, for his academic attainments proved that he had at least the foundations of a good mind. Therefore he was forced to search in other fields for the cause of his unacceptability, which he must have recognized immediately it declared itself, possibly in the days when he tried to become an army officer.

He was bound to suspect that it was a moral deficiency which rendered him unattractive. It might have been that he was in his secret heart not truly trustworthy, and that the world had spied it out; and that would be a horrible fear, since in his youth he certainly meant to be good, and if his intelligence recognized his latent capacity for cynicism and brutality it would be with stoicism rather than with exaltation. But he could rebut that suspicion simply by remembering the guarantee of high principle which he and his family, isolated in an enclave of history, believed themselves to possess as Irish supporters of the British ascendancy. Only the strongest moral fibre would have empowered them to thread their way among assassinations in service to the splendid symbol of the crown. Beyond all doubt William Joyce was not prevented from winning political eminence by external circumstances, nor by intellectual inferiority, nor by moral baseness. There was but one other possible impediment. It must be that he was rejected because he did not please. But that is what none of us can bear: to realize that we do not please, that we are not liked, that we are not loved.

Rather than make that admission William Joyce would tear out by the roots the process by which, throughout the ages, the leaders of the state have been accorded their leadership. For the making of a king is twofold. He is consecrated by the Church, and he is chosen by the people. That is, he promises to follow the law that is the reflection of heavenly order in the mirror of man's mind; and he is liked by the people, he is loved by the people, they lift up their spears and shout when they see him crowned, their hearts are warm within them when they see him given the compliment of power, they have no fear that he will misuse it. This relationship is not essentially altered between the electors and the elected in a modern democracy. There is the same promise to discover and execute the law, the same reliance for dynamic force on the heat of liking. But since William Joyce was not liked, he would drive out the element of liking from the governmental situation. He asserted that power should not be won by love but should be seized by force. If the masses would not like him and choose him as their leader, then he would find a few men who liked him and they would help him to seize power. In fact, that prescription would not have answered, for if the mass did not like him it was probable that the few also would find something in him unpalatable: and indeed the private history of Fascist parties depicts a confusion of unpalatable men whose gorges rise at one another and who look angrily about to see if they themselves are not having a like effect on the gorges of the others. It is for this reason that fascism develops its international character. The leaders must look outside their country for supporters to aid them against their enemies and their friends, who are perhaps also their enemies, inside their own country; so these will have an invasion up their sleeves, to trump all aces. Mussolini, the first Fascist ruler of our times, cultivated the friendship of Fascist-minded men in the Balkans. Hitler cultivated the friendship of Mussolini; Franco cultivated the friendship of Hitler and Mussolini. Treason is inherent in fascism, and in that William Joyce was a traitor he was more respectable than those half-Fascists who would not take the last fence and spent the war in Brixton Jail. What he had chosen to be, he was.

But there remains a mystery in William Joyce and all those others who are Fascist leaders because they are debarred from high positions in the state by reason of intellectual inferiority or moral baseness or failure to please. Why is it so important to them that they should stand on the political platform, hold office, give commands with their own voices and be personally feared? A man who is not acceptable as a national leader is given by our system the opportunity to exercise as much political power as is necessary for his self-respect and the protection of his rights. He can vote in Parliamentary and local elections; and he can serve his country as a private Member of Parliament or a member of a local authority or as a member of a special committee. Why should William Joyce and his kind howl after impossible eminence when in the common run they had no occasion for humiliation? There are other means of establishing exceptional value. If Joyce was not loved by the mass he was loved well by some near to him, and to some was a good lover; to his brother Quentin and to his second wife he was light and warmth. He was also a good teacher. Happily he transmitted the tradition of knowledge, happily he saw it happily received. That surely should have been enough for him: to be a good brother, to be a good husband, to be a good teacher. Many are given less. Yet he hungered for the mere audience, for the wordless cheering, the executive power which, if it be not refined to nothing by restraint, is less than nothing.

Perhaps right was on his side. Perhaps it is not enough to be a good brother or to be a good husband, or to be a good teacher. For human relationships are always qualified by questioning. A brother, and a wife, and pupils have their own selves to maintain, so they must sometimes defend themselves and keep back their secrets; they will sometimes pass over to the attack and seek out the secrets of the brother, the husband, and the teacher; and often time changes them, so that there is no acceptance, only this questioning. It would be better for a man to have a relationship with a person who knew all about him and therefore had no need to question him, who recognized that he was unique and precious and therefore withheld no confidence from him, who could not be changed by time though by his steadfastness he might change time and make it kind and stable. Those who believe in God enjoy such a relationship. It would be impertinent to speculate about Joyce's relationship with God, about which we know nothing relevant save that he left the Church in which he was born and that he inscribed himself on the Nazi records as "a believer". But it can be taken that his mind had been trained over the trellis erected round him by society, and that that trellis was cut in a non-Christian or even anti-Christian pattern. Whether he enjoyed his relationship with God or not, he must often have believed that it did not exist.

Those who have discarded the idea of a super-personal God and still desire an enduring friendship must look for it in those fields of life furthest removed from ordinary personal relationship, because human personality lacks endurance in any form of love. The most obvious of these is politics. There a leader can excite love in followers who know nothing of him save his public appearances, and who, even if they achieve the closest oratorical union with him, would be deterred by a sense of impertinence from questioning him about his private existence. That love is unqualified; for no party can cause its enemies to rejoice by admitting that its leader has any faults, and what parties profess they soon sincerely feel, especially in crowded halls. That

181

love swears itself undying, too; for no party can afford to let itself be overheard contemplating the exchange of its leader for another.

Therefore many men who would have been happy in the practice of religion during the ages of faith have in these modern times a need for participation in politics which is strong as the need for food, for shelter, for sex. It feeds their soul, it keeps them from the wind, it drives out that terrible companion loneliness. Such persons never speak of the real motives which impel them to their pursuit of politics, but continually refer, in accents of assumed passion, to motives which do indeed preoccupy some politicians, but not them. The chief of these is the desire to end poverty. But William Joyce had never in his life known what it was to be hungry or cold or workless, and he did not belong to the altruistic type which torments itself over the plight of others; and indeed there was probably no callousness in this, for surely had he himself been destitute he would have been too completely absorbed by his rages and his books ever to notice it. His was another hunger, another chill, another kind of unemployment. But the only people in the generation before him who attacked the governing class had been poor or altruist, and since their attack had been successful, their vocabulary held a tang of victory.

So William Joyce and his kind borrowed their phrases, and spoke of economics when they thought of religion, thus becoming the third wing of a certain triptych. In the third and fourth centuries of this era Europe and North Africa and Nearer Asia were racked by the economic problems caused by the impending dissolution of the Western Roman Empire. The study of economics was then barely begun; there was as yet no language in which the people could analyse their insecurity and design their security. But during the preceding centuries the earth had been visited by Christ, and several men of genius had been impressed by his personality and excited by its bearings on the discoveries made by the ancient philosophers. Hence the science of theology was developed to a stage where quite simple minds could grasp outlines with which it firmly delineated universal experiences, and the inarticulate learned from it to use confidently phrases more expressive than they could have invented. Therefore those suffering economic distress complained of it in theological terms. They cried out to society that its structure was wrong, in terms that, taken literally, meant that the orthodox Christian faith was mistaken; they rushed from the derelict estates where they must starve to towns where they lived as leanly, into the desert where they could eat well on brigandage, and said that they did it because they had had a peculiar revelation concerning the Trinity. Now, in our day, those suffering from religious distress complain of it in economic terms. Between the two wings of the triptych shone the rich panel of European civilization.

It is undignified to be the victim of a historical predicament. It is a confession that one has been worsted, not by a conspiracy of enemies nor by the hostility of nature, but by one's environment: by the medium in which one's genius, had one possessed such a thing, should have expressed itself. As harsh is it for an actor to admit that he cannot speak on a stage, for an artist to admit that he cannot put paint on canvas. So the victims of historical predicaments are tempted to pretend that they sacrificed themselves for an eternal principle which their contemporaries had forgotten, instead of owning that one of time's gables was in the way of their window and barred their view of eternity, so that possibly they had been wrong in relation to the sum of things, and were at any rate obviously not really right. But William Joyce pretended nothing at his trials. His faint smile said simply, "I am what I am". He did not defend the faith which he had held, for he had doubted it; he did not attack it, for he had believed in it. It is possible that in these last days fascism had passed out of the field of his close attention; that what absorbed him was the satisfaction which he felt at being, for the first time in his life, taken seriously. It was at last conceded that what he was and what he did were matters of supreme importance. The police car brought him up from the black Wandsworth Jail through the streets, never grand, thronged by the people, never great, of South London; it slid across Waterloo Bridge to the fretted neo-Gothic outline, alluding to Christianity, associated with power, symbolizing tradition, of the Houses of Parliament, where the tower raised up against the winter skies Big Ben, the portrait of time, wrought large, to be seen by those on both sides of the river, who are alike subject to its discipline.

He had thought that because he was not yet accepted on the imperial side of the Thames nothing that he did was of great moment, but now it had appeared that he had been involved by his birth in a war between the forces in the community which desired to live and those which desired to die, in a war between the forces in himself which desired to live and those which desired to die. Time was the battlefield set apart for the waging of such wars, and in time he had no other value than attached to his bearing in that battle. If he had borne himself well he would be saved, but if he had been an evil soldier he would be damned.

Surely he felt pride and relief at understanding how he stood, for it had been his fear that, bearing no great name and never having been allowed to earn one, he and his doings were not priced in any catalogue. It was an end to mediocrity. It was the beginning of such distinction as would ideally be conferred on him in a society which believed that a man's soul was immortal and precious to the high powers. Thus made serene (for all who saw him would concede his serenity), he waited his time. It cannot have been easy waiting, for events made mouths at him, as they always do at people who have been spatchcocked by history. In all trials of importance there are strange coincidences, oddities in name, overlappings of time. William Joyce would not have been human if he had not hoped for his life when it was appointed that the result of his appeal to the House of Lords should be given out on December 18; and it was on December 18 that he had been tried at Lewes Assizes on a charge of riotous assembly, and had been acquitted. Confined in his cell he knew moments of hope, succeeded by moments of despair when that hope failed; and certainly these must have been succeeded by moments of another hope when it appeared that all previous estimates of the imbroglio were false, and that even if justice executed its harshest imperatives it would have another outcome, cutting across its length and breadth and depth in a direction not till then predicted, which would be glorious; though what was inglorious would not be forgotten.

Such alternatives of hope and despair, such visions of hope and despair relating to eventualities not of this earth, are known to all of us, confined in the flesh as in a cell. On the floor of the courts where William Joyce was tried there was tested an issue

184

of how far the letter is divorced from the spirit; it was debated whether a man can live all his life among a tribe and eat their salt and in the hour of their danger sharpen the sword that their enemies intend for their breasts, and then go free because of something written in an old book which said that this man was not truly of that tribe. But in the upper air above these courts it was argued whether the God with whom man can have a perfect relationship is the dream of disappointed sons imaging a Father who shall be better than all fathers, or is more real than reality. This other trial was not concluded, not being confined to time or space. For it was expansive as the life of clouds, which overpass the horizons binding any human habitation; it began with some remote birth and will not now end till the last death. It is this uncertainty which gives life its sickening and exquisite tension. Under that tension the fragile body of William Joyce quivered as he sat in his several docks; for though his speech was a blunt instrument his substance was not dense, it offered no gross resistance to the wave of this pulse. Now his silence had the terrible petitioning quality we had heard in his voice in the past. Though he was calm, his wonder at time as it streamed away from him could be felt. There was visible through his flesh the thin shaking flame on which, by the direction of other thin shaking flames, a white hood was presently to fall as an extinguisher.

So William Joyce was condemned to death for the crime of treason, yet fared not so badly. For his trial gave him the chance to wrestle with reality, to argue with the universe, to defend the revelations which he believed had been made to his spirit; and that is man's glory. But treason took to itself others who were not so fortunate, for they were madmen and children, and for them there is no glory.

II

THE INSANE ROOT

JOHN AMERY AND NORMAN BAILLIE-STEWART

I

THE first people to come into Room No. 1 of the Central Criminal Court, where John Amery was to be tried for high treason, were two American officers, who sat and stared about them for some moments before any came to join them, drab figures in a court sallow with November. They were the soberer sort of soldier, their faces lined and greyish with the prolonged overwork that led up to and away from D-day. There arrived next the Director of Public Prosecutions, Sir Theobald Mathew, a long-headed, slender Irishman with jutting eyebrows. He watched his clerk set down an enormous file at the counsel's table and turned away, moving as if he had reason to feel something like pleasure: better put it down as unusually acute interest. Then the regular personnel of the court filtered in. First came the chief prosecuting counsel, the Attorney-General, Sir Hartley Shawcross, just home from the trial of the war criminals at Nuremberg. The fall of those desperate men to their last place in the pit can also be looked at from another point of view: a creditably conducted incident in a sunnily successful career. There is nothing callous or even smug about him, he has indeed the gentlest and most charitable of tempers; but he is fortunate, visibly fortunate. Had Pippa passed him she would have added him to her list of proofs that all's well with the world. He was followed by the counsel for the defence: Mr. Gerald Slade (now Mr. Justice Slade), who was counsel for Joyce, who pecked at his cases like a sparrow, as tireless and as careful of the smallest grain; and his assistant, John Foster, he who spent the first years of the war at the British Embassy in Washington, dark and high-coloured and genially menacing, like a Renaissance bravo.

The three long tables in front of the judge's bench were soon filled up with lawyers and those two strongly contrasted types who had to be present at all the trials—the men with iron faces who belong to the special police, and the Military Intelligence officers, who are usually of notably mild appearance, having been detached from the ordinary army service because of their clerkly gifts. Indeed the court looked very much as it was during the trial of William Joyce except for the spectators. When Joyce was being tried, the court became a background for him and his followers, who, though they were scattered in twos or threes, achieved by their emotions an effect of unity, so that the remembered scene has the quality of a chapter in a legend of martyrdom. The people who had come to see John Amery tried were drawn by an interest in the treason laws, or by a recollection of his broadcasts, or by curiosity about the black sheep of a deeply respected family; but there were no apostles, for there was no leader. The eyes turned towards the dock that day were certain to be dry. The trial of John Amery was the end of a long story desiccating to the heart.

John Amery, who at the time of his trial had lived thirty-three years and had been in trouble for most of them, was the son of an Englishman of many gifts who had rendered liberal service to his country, and his wife, who was loved by many for her kindness.

John Amery was not insane, he was not evil, but his character was like the kind of automobile that will not hold the road. As a child, he would be taken by his parents to a hotel at some holiday resort and would be discovered in a corner of the gardens or in the lounge, after dinner, amusing the guests with some mimicry or musical fooling. But the entertaining monologue would become a dribble of nonsense, the dance would go on too long, and there would break in a hint of frenzy. The child would turn from a pet to a pest, and sooner or later there would be trouble, trouble of an odd unpredictable kind which could not be guarded against, which was not cruel or cowardly but slapped the normal human process in the face. What is one to do with a boy of fifteen who from school issues prospectuses for a film-producing company and collects money from investors, not with the intention of embezzling it but inevitably with that effect? What is one to do with him when he is so pitifully delicate that it is not possible to subject him to the discipline of work? One can but say hopefully that he will not always be fifteen. This is, however, not necessarily true. There are some who are always fifteen. John Amery continued, into his twenties and thirties, to like glossy, costly automobiles as an adolescent likes them, and as an adolescent he liked glossy, costly companions, disregarding the plainest whorishness. And in such automobiles and with such companions he delighted to visit those grandiose hotels which delight the immature and revolt the mature as the very antithesis of home.

But on these adolescent appetites was superimposed a wholly individual gift for complication. He was convicted seventy-four times for automobile offences which for the most part were not just breaches of regulations but quite unforeseen embroideries on the commonplace process of travelling from point to point aided by an internal-combustion engine. Marriage he complicated as effectively as transport; he made it into a game like snakes-and-ladders, with his family and himself playing against each other. He fell in love with a lady older than himself, and when his family had employed the most recondite legal means to prevent their union, circumvented them by marrying her in an Orthodox church in Athens, a place not covered by their strategy. As for those hotels, credit was to him what orchestral tone is to a conductor. In business, an obsession with films led him to persistent though always brief connections with the industry. He once stranded an entire motion picture outfit in Africa in extraordinary circumstances. Nobody could imagine how he had got the credit to take them out there; but there they were, in quite the wrong continent. It is only just to say that his closest intimates knew a John Amery who was loving and capable of profound emotions about people and causes; and it is not possible to prove this John Amery less real than the John Amery known to the world.

When John Amery was only twenty-four his loyal but exhausted family had let him become bankrupt. He failed for five thousand pounds, with assets nil. That was in the autumn of 1936. The following summer he evoked a yelp of protest, oddly passionate for official proceedings, from the receiver in charge of his estate, though such men are usually inured to the financial optimism which soars like a lark from the heart of the imbecile. Amery had asked for a discharge from bankruptcy, so that he could add another and crazier story to the crazy edifice of credit which he had built on the site where, given his nurture, a more noble structure might have been raised. Could nothing in his life be simple, nothing be of good repute? The answer, through the years, in various sorts of court, was that there seemed indeed to be some such necessity. After his bankruptcy he left England, his family giving him an allowance. Let this not be counted as unkindness on their part. It is an offence for a bankrupt to obtain goods on credit without disclosing his situation, and he could not possibly have fulfilled this obligation. The new, immensely long, and shark-nosed automobile would have been too tempting; another hotel might have been opened in London. He would have had to go to jail.

Once abroad, John Amery was absorbed into a bath of purity which was washing clean many a poor tarnished body. At that time the Spanish Civil War obviously offered a theatre for Left-wing gallants, and so generously did they play their roles that the labour movement in every country in Europe is the poorer for the young men who died there. But the war also offered its opportunities to the Right Wing, and John Amery became not an unsuccessful volunteer on Franco's side. He apparently had a fairly continuous career as a gun-runner and as a liaison officer with the French Cagoulards; and in these capacities received a *laissez-passer* which gave him as much right to come and go as a Franco Spaniard. When the Second World War broke out, he was living on the borders of Spain, at San Sebastian. He crossed over to France, possibly under orders, and lived with a Cagoulard group, knowing or at least meeting the French Fascist leaders Jacques Doriot and Marcel Déat. Among the Cagoulards were a certain number of enthusiastic and shapely young women. With one of them, Jeannine Barde, John Amery contracted a permanent relationship which some said was an actual legal marriage. Mark now the peculiarly flimsy silliness which does not know enough to come in out of the rain, which, indeed, stays outside while it is raining and, when it stops, goes inside just as the ceiling is falling. John Amery remained inactive throughout 1940 and 1941, when there was a very good chance that Germany might win the war. He was called into activity by the Germans when they wanted some person who would catch European attention to conduct an anti-Russian campaign at a time when they were making peace overtures to the Russians; but it is unlikely that the idea of using him would have come into the Germans' heads had not Amery himself, instead of lying doggo in a Savoy village, repeatedly volunteered for service with the Germans. So in 1942, when it was becoming obvious that the Allies had at least a chance of winning, he began to broadcast from Berlin. In 1943, when the Allies' position was improving daily, he went into a camp of British internees at St.-Denis, near Paris, and attempted to raise an anti-Bolshevik Free Corps to fight with the Germans against the Russians. This is the classic type of treachery which every educated person knows at once for the base and fatal act it is, for Sir Roger Casement committed it during the 1914-18 war and was hanged for it. In 1944, when it was practically certain that the Axis was defeated, the poor young idiot travelled all over Europe, visiting Norway, France, Yugoslavia, and Belgium, and talking to large audiences that inevitably contained many members of the resistance movements. It is not true that he was caught up in the machine and could not break loose. If he had been a little more eccentric the Germans would have let him go back into obscurity. They found him almost impossible to handle as it was, and conceived a lasting hatred for him which was to find expression after the end of the war. But, like a child who tries to obey an angry nanny, Amery tried to behave well, and behaved well enough to carry on this job long enough to leave no possible loophole for his safety.

Again and again throughout John Amery's life his family must have said to themselves, "He can't be doing that, but, my God, he is!" They must have said it to themselves with unimaginable agony when they heard him speak on the radio; for in this supreme folly was disclosed his private sweetness that forbade them ever to free themselves of their love for him. His voice was young and eager and honest and good-natured, and he spoke as a crusader when he declared that London was in a state of shame because the Lord Mayor was a Jew (and so he was, and a very decent body too). There could be seen the city of his desire, rising in the radiance of unspotted honour, its purity a fitting casket for his own, for he was one of those who are reborn every day no matter what the night has brought. It is a curious example of the fatuity of German propaganda that these broadcasts should have been widely announced as by the elder son of the Secretary of State for India; the public felt a wave of sympathy for the Amery family, and an increased disgust at the Nazis.

At the end of the war John Amery was captured by the partisans in Italy; and when he was questioned by a British Military Intelligence officer he asked for a typewriter and proceeded to type a statement some thousands of words long, which was brilliantly composed, put the noose around his neck, and gave the history of two different people. One of these was a wise young man of lofty principles who sought to reconcile England and Germany in order that together they might fight the rising tide of communism, and to that end travelled about Europe, a weary Titan urging common sense on statesmen who for some reason would not heed the voice of sanity; the other was a crazy harlequin enmeshed in unfortunate adventure. "After a few days in Paris and travelling under the names of Mr. and Mrs. Browne, I arrived in Berlin early in October 1942", he wrote. For a time this inveterately companionate "I", who was always travelling under the names of Mr. and Mrs. Somebody, was to be alone. "On April 7-8", he wrote, "my beloved friend and political revolutionary, Jeannine Barde, died." The poor creature's death was said not to be natural. By some accounts she killed herself, life being rendered unendurable by the sour flavour of treachery, the air raids, the humiliations of life dragged out in dependence on the Nazis, who knew that these two had no alternative employers. By other accounts she died because of a blow received at a wild party. The circumstances of her death, whatever they were, increased the Germans' distaste for Amery; and their feeling for etiquette was further outraged by his failure to attend her funeral, though as like as not it was through unbridled grief that he absented himself. But to the wandering wit sorrow is no prison. "In the end of September", he wrote, "I returned to Paris. Once more much political talk, and on October 4 I remarried at the German Consulate. Politically, the situation remained almost unchanged." And at the end of the statement comes Harlequin's supreme antic.

This man awaiting a capital charge writes: "Moreover, the colonel commanding the Piazza di Milano, who brought me from Saronno to Milan, undertook at the time to have returned my property that was seized by the partisans when they arrested me. Of this nothing has so far been seen. It consists of one suitcase (important documents and personal effects), one overcoat, one fur coat, and two silver foxes, a 20-litre petrol tin, full, one Lancia Aprilia motor car No. 78410 MICDI."

When John Amery was brought to England, it was widely believed that he was not going to die. His case was postponed several times in order that evidence might be collected for his defence, which rested on a claim that he had become a naturalized Spanish citizen, and it was known that a relative had gone to Spain to collect evidence in proof of that claim. It seemed quite certain, when the court assembled, that the search had been successful, for nearly a whole side of one of the three tables in front of the bench was taken up by a number of trim and plump and florid young men who were said to be Spanish lawyers. Before them there appeared presently that famous figure of the courts, Mr. Salzedo the interpreter, a Spanish Jew, lean and brown and white-haired and antique in courtesy, who passed around the table shaking hands with his compatriots, not perfunctorily but as if they would presently be engaged in a considerable enterprise together. A young relative of Amery was talking to the defence counsel, and it was said that he was to be the principal witness for the defence. This could hardly be, unless his search for evidence of John Amery's naturalization had been successful. There had been distress among the kindly officials of the court because Mrs. Amery had applied for a seat. It might be that they had no reason for perturbation; she might joyfully witness her son's acquittal.

But if there was a wealth of Spanish lawyers, there were lacking some of the court's most usual features. There was no judge, there was no jury, there was no prisoner. The Lord Mayor and two aldermen, in their fine black gowns and jewelled chains, took their places on the bench, but the chair under the sword of justice was empty. In the jury box, leaflets of instruction lay yellow on the dark wood at each juror's place, but there was none to pick them up. The kitchen chairs in the dock were naked in their discomfort. (Surely that is the last ungraciousness of society, that it should make its failures learn their doom sitting on a hard wooden chair.) Half-past ten had passed, though that was the hour at which the trial should have begun, and one could set one's watch by the law courts. Half an hour passed, and still there was no judge, no jury, no prisoner.

Just after eleven a messenger came to the lawyers' table and spoke to John Amery's counsel. The dock is a shallow square box without a lid, with glass walls rising on all sides except the side which faces the judge. A staircase runs down from the dock to the cells where the prisoners are kept from the time of their arrival in the prison van at the court till they are brought up for trial. From the gallery of the court one can look down into the staircase, which is lined with those obscene creations, white sanitary tiles. There was seen a sight rare in an important case: the counsel going through a door in the glass walls of the dock and down the stairway to the cells. They looked like ravens in their black gowns, stooping as they gathered up their skirts. While they were gone, people in the court, particularly the lawyers, began to laugh a great deal as they talked among themselves. This had nothing to do with anything they were thinking or feeling about the trial of Amery. It was a collective nervous reaction, like the storm of coughing that sometimes sweeps through a theatre when a play is going badly. After twenty-five minutes, Amery's counsel returned. There was talk with Sir Hartley Shawcross, from whose look of gentle, reflective well-being nothing could be learned, and with the Director of Public Prosecutions, who nodded as if something had happened which he had foreseen. There was a flurry of messengers. The trial began.

The judge entered in shrivelled and eccentric majesty. It was Mr. Justice Humphreys, a very old man whose age was crisp as a fine winter night, with a fierce wit on his tongue and a fiercer wit on his face, where there is often written what he will not let himself say lest necessary institutions fall. He had a son whom he named Christmas, who grew up to be president of the Buddhist Society and chairman of the Ballet Guild. To such a fantastical world, resembling Peacock's novels, does Mr. Justice Humphreys belong. He made a little, stiff, old man's bow to the court and sat down, small in the depth of his red-and-purple robes, to try the poor shadow who had been brought into the dock. It had been said that John Amery was deeply diseased with tuberculosis. There was no truth in it. The prison doctors, who are nowadays able men, pronounced him free of this or any other disease. But it was with his body as with his mind. He was, judged by any accepted standard, not mad, but he was not sane. He was free from disease but it would have been absurd to call him healthy. His skin was yellow and grooved round the small bones of his face by long exhaustion and fear and the immediate strain of the moment, which was evidently frightful to him. His face was the muzzle of a little monkey; and it could be seen that in youth there must have been here much animal vitality and charm, as well as an animal secretiveness that would make him incomprehensible. He wore an overcoat that was the colour of the bloom on grapes, and a black-and-lime scarf of the heavy and subtly coloured sort that used to be sold at the expensive shops on the Croisette at Cannes. The weight of these good clothes was too much for the worn trifle of his body. He leaned on the ledge of the dock, his small, bare hands very white and limp. By his appearance he made, as prisoners so often do, the ultimate appeal against human justice. It is not fair that some vessels should be made for honour and some for dishonour. The lawyers in front of him seemed guilty of a kind of theft in having so much prospering vitality while this poor child had none. The two American officers who had been the first in the court seemed grasping in having secured those lines on their faces which spoke of fatiguing, honoured service.

Again the kitchen chair in the dock seemed monstrous, and it could hardly be imagined that John Amery would be able to sit through the trial upright on this bleak piece of carpentry. But such anxiety was immediately proved unnecessary. They read out the indictments against him, charging him with having made treasonable broadcasts and speeches and having attempted to seduce British subjects from their allegiance, and asked him whether he pleaded guilty or not guilty. It had been supposed that he would answer "Not guilty". Then the jurors would have been called in and sworn, and the counsel would have addressed the court, and the routine would have rolled on for perhaps as long as four days. But when the question was put to him he answered, "I plead guilty to all counts", and the trial lasted eight minutes. A murmur ran through the court which was horrified, which was expostulatory, which was tinged with self-pity, for this was suicide. If he pleaded guilty he must be sentenced to death. There is no alternative sentence for treason. It is not in the power of any judge to substitute imprisonment, and there is no appeal. There is only the possibility that the Home Secretary may advise the Crown to reprieve the condemned man; and this happens only in certain circumstances, not to be found by any eye in the case of John Amery. In effect, the young man was saying, "I insist on being hanged by the neck in three weeks' time", and the strength of his desire to die was forcing his weak voice through his shuddering lips and ignoring his pain, which was great, for he was blasted by what he did. He was like an insect that falls on a hot stove and is withered, and what he did felt like an act of cruelty to the whole court. It rejected the life that was in all of us. It could be perceived that the legal tradition whereby a man under a capital charge must be urged by every possible means to plead not guilty is no meddling excess of humanitarianism but is an expression of the fundamental belief of living things in life. It relates to that saying of Charles Dickens which so profoundly impressed Tolstoy, that whatever power gave us life, and for whatever purpose, he was sure it was given to us on the understanding that we defend it to the last breath. It is true, of course, that there are conditions in which a man can die without betraying his life, because his death will give it the spiritual value without which material existence is worthless, but these conditions do not usually arise in the criminal courts, which practise on the plane of simplification.

The old judge leaned forward and said to the clerk of the court, "Before that is recorded . . ." and broke off. Then he said to Mr. Slade, "I never accept a plea of guilty on a capital charge without assuring myself that the accused thoroughly understands what he is doing and what the immediate result must be, and that he is in accord with his legal advisers in the course he has taken". Mr. Slade stood up and answered, no longer like a bird, but speaking with obvious careful fidelity to a prepared model, "I can assure you of that, my lord. I have explained the position to my client and I am satisfied that he understands it." This passage had the quietness of the worst sort of nightmare. It was as if he had said, "Yes, this man chooses to be walled up, and all proper arrangements have been made to get suitable bricks". The old judge's eyebrows and the corners of his mouth made a queer pattern. Yes, life has to be defended to the last ditch, but what a damned thing it is! He said, "Right. Let it be recorded." Then the clerk of the court asked John Amery if he had anything to say. The young man answered, weakly and politely, "No, thank you". The attendant placed the square of black cloth on the judge's head, but the judge did not deliver the death sentence. Instead he leaned forward and asked, "You do not want to say anything?" Still in the same well-bred and dying voice, the young man said, "No, thank you, sir". It was quite clear that he was morally satisfied and that he was congratulating himself on having at last, at the end of his muddled and frustrated existence, achieved an act crystalline in its clarity, an act which fulfils the conditions in which a man can choose to die without betraying life. Yet none of the hundreds of people who were watching him with the intensest interest had the faintest idea what that act was, with perhaps the exception of the lawyers, who were bound by professional etiquette to keep silent.

It was immediately spread about that John Amery had suddenly insisted on pleading guilty for the sake of his family, to spare them the prolonged humiliation of his trial. That would have provided a simple explanation had it not been for the Spanish lawyers. They must have attended to give testimony in support of John Amery's story that he had been naturalized as a Spanish citizen; and their testimony must have been previously examined by Amery's counsel and judged to be conclusive. Had it been so, then he would have been acquitted, and by that his family would have been spared much of the pain and humiliation inherent in his case. And if John Amery's motive for pleading guilty was really concern for his family, it was odd that his counsel did not mention it when the judge questioned him about the plea, thus softening what was an oddly stark statement. There was also the suggestion that he pleaded guilty simply because he wanted to die as quickly as possible, without enduring the slow torture of the trial, but the impression given by his flinching flesh was that he wanted very much to live, and there was that in his air which suggested that by his conduct he was serving more than himself. It is, of course, possible that his counsel did not know his motive. That animal secretiveness may have made him put forward nothing to them but some babbling nonsense such as used to break his teachers' hearts, or he may have been cut off from their comprehension and their kindness by his old gift for complication. His inhabiting devil may have long ago set forces working which had produced an event so monstrous that it was almost as hard to grasp as it would have been to foresee, so monstrous that even he would have recognized it as intractable and surrendered to despair. In any case, his end was as his beginning. What should have been light was dark. There never was a more turbid martyrdom.

Perhaps there was a clue to the nature of that monstrous event that day in court. It could be seen by those who looked about them during that period of waiting that the Spanish lawyers did not all belong to one party. They seemed to be split into two groups. Perhaps one group had come to give evidence in support of John Amery's claim to be a naturalized Spaniard, and the other to controvert that evidence. How that situation might have arisen was indicated some months later to a traveller in Spain who found himself at a dinner with a member of the Franco government. This traveller remembered that a relative of John Amery had gone out to Spain with letters from the British authorities asking the Spanish authorities to give all facilities for searching the records for proofs of this claim to naturalization, and that shortly afterwards a British law officer, bearing credentials from the same fount of authority as Amery's relative, had also gone out to Spain, apparently on some errand of investigation. It occurred to the traveller that perhaps the Spanish politician might have met one of these visitors, and he mentioned their names. "Now, tell me", said the Spaniard, "just what happened in that case. What made the British government change their minds about John Amery?" "Change their minds?" echoed the traveller. "Yes", said the Spaniard petulantly. "First they wanted not to hang him, and then the next thing we knew they wanted to hang him."

It must be remembered that John Amery probably believed that he was a Spanish subject. Once he heard of the defence that William Joyce was raising, his feather wits would easily convert the *laissez-passer* he had received from Franco when he was a gun-runner into a certificate of naturalization. His relative must have gone to Spain to look for the evidence of that naturalization in the belief that it existed, and unprepared for complaisance. It would not have crossed his mind that any Spanish official would misinterpret the request of the British authorities that he should be given facilities for such a search, since such credentials would have been given to any reputable person in a like position. In good faith he must have brought back the evidence of John Amery's Spanish citizenship, in good faith his parents and their legal advisers must have accepted it, and John Amery, in his mental twilight, would not have been surprised that his myth had become a fact. But by then Amery's private papers had fallen into the hands of British Intelligence officers. It was unlikely that a Spanish official, however willing to oblige, would find a date on which an imaginary ceremony of naturalization was performed which would fit into the account of his life contained in these papers, and indeed it is said, in a story coming from the German Embassy in Madrid, that the official who was thus willing to oblige had the maladroitness to choose a date on which, according to Amery's passport, retrieved from the Germans, he was not in Spain. It was inevitable that the deception should bemuse all persons concerned with the defence, inevitable that it should be uncovered by the prosecution. It is not possible to imagine a more torturing complication of destiny. A persecuting destiny had for long inhabited this young man's body, inextricably confused with what was lovable in him. Those round him had conquered it, for it had never made them fail him. Now it must have seemed to them to have broken loose and ranged the earth, acting at a great distance, acting through men so stupid that they were dangerous even when they meant to please—that they could not recognize what pleases the civilized; acting through the supposed neutrality of inanimate objects, through volumes in the shelves of a register office, which could have been judged eternally innocuous through dedication to uninteresting fact. But this astonishing doom could not imprison

John. He escaped into another fantasy. Now he saw himself as a martyr in the Fascist cause, and swaggered as he had done when he drove the high-powered automobile he had not paid for at ninety miles an hour on the wrong side of the road to the hotel where he would not be able to meet the bill. That was the source of his faintly consequential air in the dock, his air of knowing something.

The judge spoke some words to him before passing sentence, expressing hatred of his crime. Many people thought the judge heartless, forgetting that a very old man might well feel himself on an equality with a prisoner under sentence of death, and might even think that the prisoner would find a precise evaluation of his position more interesting than tenderness from a stranger. Also the judge seemed baffled, like the rest of us, and there was a certain ineptness in his enlargement on a passage in the depositions which described how John Amery had visited the camp at St.-Denis to enlist internees for his renegade British Free Corps and had been warned by some of the men that he was committing high treason but had taken no notice. It was not a point worth making, so far as Amery was concerned, for by that time his magic circle was sealed, and he must have thought that he was giving the internees an opportunity to join the winning side. Yet, if what the judge said had little application to Amery, he seemed to say it because his mind had been shocked into flight underground to some place near the sources of our general destiny. The judge said slowly, with accusation and querulous wonder in his voice, "They called you traitor and you heard them". It was as if he spoke to all men, marvelling at their knowledge of good and evil and their preference for evil, and looking at his own heart from far away that he might see the cause.

II

THE ghost of William Joyce certainly haunts the Old Bailey, for there he knew what must have been—to that gallant exhibitionist and obstinate confessor of his faith—in a profound sense the happiest days of his life; and during the treachery trials which followed his, he was surely the most contented of ghosts.

Not then were the courts crowded; not then was it difficult to find a table in the neighbouring restaurants; not then did people wait in the streets outside. Such things happened only when he and Amery were up for trial, and he could fairly claim that Amery had family behind him and that he himself was the only traitor to cause such a stir by his own personality. Greatness went from the treason dock with Joyce; and no other case was a work of art, a posed picture, like the trial of John Amery. But the other traitors were nevertheless strange and disturbing figures, and their trials were full of dream-like incongruities, evoking laughter even while they dismayed by recalling something which it would be preferable to forget and which cannot be completely remembered. For people do not become traitors unless they are unable to fit into the society into which they were born, and the cause of that incapacity in their case is a disturbing personality which catches those around them off their guard and therefore provokes them in their turn to strange behaviour. Hence their lives become a chain of fantastic events. And the trials were certainly a debauch for the connoisseur of the law. Machinery set up in the past was acting on the material provided by a present so novel that it was almost as mysterious as the future; and the results were never more astonishing than in the case of Norman Baillie-Stewart.

He might be considered the most tragic of the traitors, for he started with great natural advantages. He, the officer whom British officers would most wish to blot off their rolls and out of human memory, looked like the ideal Guardee of Ouida's dreams. When he came into the dock the noble sculpture of his head and the dignity of his tall body were astonishing. But his handsome face was so sullen that it was impossible to imagine that he would ever laugh or weep again. He looked the more inhuman because he was wearing one of those thick and shiny German raincoats which are dead black with white highlights. The addiction of the Nazis to these garments is an extravagant present to the psychoanalysts. These people who wanted to drench the earth in blood could not stir from home without protection from the rain; so, as like as not, Freud is right and aggression is the other side of fear. Baillie-Stewart's gloomy aspect could not simply be put down as natural in one standing in the dock, for he had a very good reason for feeling relief. He was not going to be hanged, and in any other age that would have been his fate. But of course the life that had been given back to him was not going to be worth living. It is the essence of treachery that those who commit it would still be severely punished if the law did not lay a finger on them.

Baillie-Stewart's initial advantages were not only physical. In 1927, when he was eighteen, he passed tenth out of the Royal Military College at Sandhurst. During his subsequent career in the Seaforth Highlanders he attracted the attention of his superior officers by his general competence and a marked mechanical gift. But there was something very strange going on in his head, of a sort that can be grasped by consideration of his name. For he was born Norman Baillie Stewart Wright, but in his early twenties took the name of Baillie-Stewart by deed poll, thus, so to speak, rebuilding himself in the Scottish baronial style. He explained this step later by saying that it was his mother's maiden name and that as her brother had died it had been thought advisable that he should carry on the name. In fact, his mother had been a Miss Stewart, and Baillie was one of the Christian names borne by his father. No family called Baillie-Stewart exists. His justification was that he considered himself the "heir-at-line" of his mother's family, but it was an archaic act. Formerly it used to be the custom for the husband of an heiress to add her name to his, and for the inheritor of property from a testator of a different name to adopt that name, especially if the inheritance took the form of an estate. The creation of a double-barrelled name in these times is rare in this country, though still not infrequent on the Continent, and it usually comes of fidelity to one of these customs. It would be interesting to know how the Wright family reacted to this curious event. Probably suspicions were aroused which might have been confirmed, if families were reasonable, in 1932, when he was charged with having communicated information about certain military matters to the German government. The arrest caused a sensation, because it was the first of its kind in living memory, and because he awaited trial in the Tower of London and was therefore known to the newspapers under the good romantic title of "The Officer in the

Tower". But the trial took not a romantic but a comic course. It turned Baillie-Stewart into a comic character of a peculiarly indecorous kind. He was to England in the early thirties as widely known as the Jubilee Juggins to his Victorian day, but the mirth he evoked had a Restoration quality.

His offence was the minimum which could have brought him into the sphere covered by the Official Secrets Act. The information he gave to the Germans was minuscule and no more than they could have derived from a careful study of the photographs in English periodicals. It is said that he had shortly before met a young German woman resident in England, in whose company he had learned to appreciate the art of love and to disapprove of the Treaty of Versailles; and here is the first sign of the difference between Baillie-Stewart and the other major traitors. He is the only one of them who might have been diverted from the road to jail by a competent psychiatrist. In Joyce there was a false deployment of the forces which fight for human victory. In the case of Amery there was a large and unhappy coincidence: a man who was too mad for psychiatric treatment but not mad enough to be certified happened to be born at a time when two important European powers were experimenting with rule by the insane. But if Baillie-Stewart had been sent to a sound analyst it is probable that he would never have found himself in the dock. He was never interested in fascism. It was first and last Germany, whether under the Weimar Republic or under the Nazis, which obsessed him, though it is doubtful if this obsession turned easily to espionage. He was also interested in women; and a German woman would obviously have a double interest for him. Hence, if this young woman threatened to withdraw her favour from him if he did not give her some information to send home to Germany, he was willing to yield. When it became known that he had handed over this information, and he was questioned by his superior officers, they would probably have accepted his plea that this information was too worthless for it to matter whether he handed it over or not, and allowed him to resign quietly from the service, had it not been for one damaging fact. He had received some money from Germany: ninety pounds. It was his attempt to account for the receipt of this money, and the effect it had had on the officers who interrogated him, which appealed to the ribald side of the British public.

Norman Baillie-Stewart, *né* Wright, alleged that this payment related to an incident which had occurred when he visited Germany in 1931, as he in fact had done on a holiday when he was waiting transfer from one regiment, where he had found himself unpopular, to another. During his travels he had gone to see a gentleman called Herr Obst, who had introduced him to a young lady called Marie Louise. He was at that time, as it appeared in the trial, engaged in the pursuit of a German film star, but Marie Louise became enamoured of him and asked him to correspond with her under the pseudonym of Alphonse Poiret. It was never clear why a pseudonym should have been necessary. There were suggestions that Marie Louise's friends and relatives might have objected to such a correspondent, but it was never explained why they would have objected less to a correspondent named Alphonse Poiret than to one named Norman Baillie-Stewart. In the course of the correspondence which followed, the story continued, she had sent him ninety pounds out of gratitude. Pressed by the colonel who was examining him as to the reason for this gratitude, he stammered out that it related to a tender scene which had reached the extremity of tenderness. The colonel suggested that it would be useful if he could recall at what hotel in Germany he and the young lady had stayed. Baillie-Stewart confided that this was not possible, for the tender scene had taken place in a park. This is in line with an ancient tradition; but all the same it seemed an odd venue for a young lady so strictly brought up that her correspondence was supervised. But what park? He did not know. But there was a lake in it. The tender scene had happened beside a lake.

This story is an index to the peculiar quality of Baillie-Stewart's mind. He is a stranger to humanity; he does not share the common reactions of humanity. This means he cannot lie; he cannot imagine the normal patterns of behaviour. It had come to his knowledge, since he himself was a handsome young man, that sometimes handsome young men are paid for their embraces by infatuated ladies. It had come to his knowledge that people who feel the desire to embrace often yield to that desire in very odd places. But he could not make a credible story based on these quite sound observations. Tears ran down people's cheeks as they read the reports of the case, so madly ludicrous was Baillie-Stewart's story. They laughed even more loudly at the naïve evidence of the colonel to whom this singular evidence had first been told. Asked at the court-martial what effect it had had on him, he replied, "When he told me the remarkable story of getting ninety pounds for one act of intimacy in a public park, I was so astonished that I asked for an explanation". It was unfortunate that other remarks made during the trial also suggested that Baillie-Stewart's real offence was that he had disregarded a recognized ceiling-price. The Judge-Advocate in charge of the trial once asked him, "Do you consider that the ninety pounds which you received was in respect of services rendered to her over a fortnight and eighteen hours?"

The trial was brought nearer reality and propriety by the improbable appearance, as a witness, of the English Benny Goodman, Mr. Victor Silvester, a musician famous as leader of the Strict Tempo Band. The prosecution had laid some emphasis on the inability of Baillie-Stewart to provide any but the vaguest particulars about Marie Louise. She was fair and about twenty-two, and that was all he was able to say. He did not even know where she lived. The prosecution took this blankness as proof that Marie Louise did not exist and that Baillie-Stewart had had dealings with German officials and had received the money from them. But Mr. Victor Silvester gave evidence which brought the image of a real woman into the courtroom. He said that when he and his wife were fulfilling an engagement in Berlin shortly after Baillie-Stewart's visit to Germany, they had been approached at a hotel tea-dance by a young woman, fair and about twenty-two, who gave her name as Marie Louise. During their conversation, which touched only trivial things, they asked her if, as she had a French name, she was French, and she laughed and replied that, on the contrary, she was very German. From Mr. Silvester's report there emerged a picture of a real person, and what is more, of a real person who was in high good humour and had found a particular amusement in searching out English company at that particular moment.

After the trial was over Mr. Silvester sent to the War Office a letter which had been posted to him from Berlin, written in Tarzan English and signed Elsa Schutz. Schutz means shield, protection. "Dear Mr. Silvester," it said, "I write for my friend Fräulein Marie Louise to ask you not to make the inquiries for her any more. She has done all she can, but the conditions are so, she cannot do what she would like. If she come to England, it must be that she is taken for a bad woman. . . ." It is impossible not to hear the faint sound of a distant giggle. Here it must be remarked that Mr. Silvester is the most respectable of men, whose integrity cannot be doubted. It is psychologically significant that he chose the title "Strict Tempo" for his band.

Baillie-Stewart was found guilty and was sentenced to five years' penal servitude. During his imprisonment his father, who had spent much of his capital on his son's defence, sickened and died. He was released in January 1937, and he must have emerged in a state of joyous hope, for he had become more and more pro-German while he was in prison, and during his sentence the Weimar Republic had given place to the Nazi Reich. It should have been a case of "I run, I run, I am gathered to thy heart"; but there came a curious impediment to the embrace.

An English convict does not usually serve the full term of imprisonment to which he was sentenced. He earns a remission of so many days according to his good-conduct marks, which may amount to as much as a third of his sentence. This remission amounted to very little in Baillie-Stewart's case: only two months. Till that period was up he was, according to routine, released only on a licence which required him to report to the police at regular intervals and forbade him to leave Great Britain until the date on which his sentence expired. Baillie-Stewart could have gone abroad in March 1937. But he did not leave England until August, and then he went not to Germany but to Austria. This was not the result of any preference; for he made the most vigorous efforts to become a naturalized subject, not of Austria, but of Germany. These efforts, strangely enough, met with a curious lack of encouragement. In Vienna he was taken under the wing of a Nazi agent, an English or

English-speaking woman who had assumed the name of Edith Shackleton, a celebrated London journalist, and falsely claimed to be the sister of Sir Ernest Shackleton, the explorer. She introduced him into Nazi circles and he was notable for his enthusiasm for Hitler. n 1938 the Austrian police accused him of pro-Nazi activities. All the same, his naturalization papers did not come through. Long after the normal period of completion had elapsed he was still petitioning the German authorities to admit him to citizenship. This might seem evidence that there is one real International: that, diverse as the human mass may be, and severed by natural and artificial barriers, there is one body which, scattered over the whole earth and serving beneath the myriad banners of the sovereignties, acts in real unity. It might be that Baillie-Stewart's papers were held up because a civil servant had lost them: that while innumerable officials in Washington, London, and Paris were losing the papers of people who wanted to get away from Germany, their counterparts in Berlin were doing the like for this refugee who wanted to get into Germany. But that was not the explanation.

That there was another reason for the delay was proved on the outbreak of the war. The Nazis allowed him to enter Germany and took him into their employment, but with the most noticeable coldness. He was given none of the opportunities to work against his country which one would have thought the Germans would have offered to a trained English soldier who might, dropped by parachute, have been a most dangerous *saboteur*. He was put into broadcasting, and the Propaganda Office and the Foreign Office played their usual game of battledore and shuttlecock with him. He finally got his naturalization papers; but he was kept in one small room or another, usually under orders from William Joyce, whom he detested, writing broadcasts which were often revised and sometimes scrapped. He was not even allowed to recruit for the British Free Corps, though the value of an authentic officer of attractive appearance would obviously have been very great. Unless he had been actually interned, his reception could not have been chillier. And on Christmas Eve in 1941 an intoxicated employee of Goebbels gave away the reason. He was talking to an American resident in Berlin, saying that some time during the evening he had to look in for a moment on a party given by the traitor broadcasters, and he went over their individual characters and cursed them one by one. "As for Baillie-Stewart," he said, "he is a spy the English have planted on us, and we know it."

That remark rings true when the incidents of the trial are recalled. The story told by Baillie-Stewart must have been valid to some extent. It cannot be doubted that on his German holiday he did meet a man and a woman who called themselves Herr Obst and Fräulein Marie Louise, though later he was to claim that Marie Louise was a myth. For the interrogating colonel gave evidence that Baillie-Stewart seemed genuinely surprised when he learned that *Obst* is German for "fruit", that Marie Louise is the name of a variety of pear, and that *poiret* means "little pear". It is almost beyond belief that he invented the story and hit by chance on names that fell into the orchard category; or that he should have invented the story and chosen such an implausible batch of names. But the colonel does not seem to have pointed out to him, and may not have known, that the slang meaning of *poire* is "a credulous fool, a dupe". The merriment of the Fräulein Marie Louise encountered by Mr. Victor Silvester comes back to mind, and the hardly disguised facetiousness of the letter from Elsa Schutz. It appears certain, in the light of the official's remark, that a gang of German counter-espionage agents had met Norman Baillie-Stewart and had been just too clever in their estimate of him. His story of wanting to be a spy had struck them as odd; and they did not realize that its oddity was due to the fact that he was a very odd man. They sent him the ninety pounds to encourage him to come closer to them. Perhaps they were startled when Baillie-Stewart was arrested. But then the peculiar evidence given by Baillie-Stewart must have aroused their suspicions that his was a bogus trial. Why should a sane man make such a poor job of defending himself? Then, too, that suspicion was bound to be nourished by some of the evidence which was brought against him. In the train that took Baillie-Stewart into Germany when he was going to see Herr Obst, there had been a very attractive young woman to whom he had introduced himself. In the course of conversation with this stranger he explained that he was going abroad "to do the most difficult thing he had ever done in his life", and had rambled on with such hints at an exciting mystery, stopping so nearly on the hither side of explicitness, that as soon as she read of the case in the papers she wrote to relate her experience to the prosecution. The Germans might well have said to themselves that the man was not born who would behave like that when he was going abroad to act as a spy, whether he was moved by a genuine desire to commit treachery or whether he was only going to pretend to be a traitor. It must have seemed to them false evidence, brought as part of sham proceedings. This suspicion would be strengthened by the circumstance that the young woman had been allowed to appear before the court under the title of Miss D. It would become ineradicable when the Germans found out that he had changed his name. Why would a man who was born Wright call himself Baillie-Stewart on the ground that that was his mother's name when it was not? There was, of course, no reason at all, except perhaps some remote misadventure, such as the failure of the two halves of his brain to synchronize or an excess of protein in his blood. But the Germans had, put into their hands, the tempting hypothesis that Baillie-Stewart, having committed himself to an enterprise bound to bring shame on him, had changed his name to spare his family.

Therefore the German War Office smiled sardonically when Baillie-Stewart sought entrance to Germany after his release in 1937. There began then for this young man an existence which reproduced in reality the fancies of the most unhappy type of lunatic. The man at the corner table was really watching him. His letters were being opened. His friends were his enemies. The bogus Miss Shackleton, after the charming evening, went home and wrote it all down in a little book. If it had not been for Baillie-Stewart's neurosis he would have recognized these things and returned to England. It is true that there went with him everywhere a fair woman who was said to be the same who had induced him to be a spy, though whether it was Marie Louise or the earlier mistress was not known. But it is very difficult indeed to believe that he did not notice for what it was, the German refusal to use his services, since he had not been a fool when he was in the army; though it may not have struck him, so conscious was he of his integrity as a traitor, that by putting him in the British radio office they were keeping him in a box and could lift the lid at any moment they pleased to see what he was doing. But it must have galled him, with his social ambition, to work under the control of William Joyce, who was indubitably not a gentleman; and he must have shared the resentment that all the traitor broadcasters felt against the insane bully that supervised them. But in the statement he made after he was arrested by the Allies there is no indication whatsoever that his obsessional love for Germany had diminished.

When Germany collapsed, Baillie-Stewart escaped from Berlin and was found some months afterwards wandering about the Austrian mountains in a Tyrolean costume very ill-suited to his height, in a very sad condition. Like most of the traitors, he was hungry when he was taken, and, though he was fed, had to be roughly lodged until he was sent to England, as conquered Central Europe was in no tidy state. He was charged, on his first appearances at the police court, with high treason. A convicted spy who after serving his sentence had gone abroad and re-entered the service of the foreign power for which he had betrayed his country could not hope for anything else. In the course of these preliminary proceedings he made a remark oddly incongruous with his virile appearance. When he was requesting the magistrate for time to prepare his defence he said, "I learn that my mother has died during my absence, and I have no one to turn to". The atmosphere of these treachery trials was extremely matter-of-fact, and an appeal to sentiment was rarely heard; the accused knew that that was not a profitable line to take. Moreover, "I have no one to turn to" is a phrase with a definite character of its own to the English ear. It would be natural only on the lips of a fragile and elderly woman or a deserted wife. His statement also exhibited a peculiar defection from masculinity. He gave his affection for a German woman as the cause of his treachery. It is interesting to contrast that admission with the allusions made by Joyce and Amery in their statements. Joyce mentioned his wife with classic protectiveness. Amery praised his companions as fellow-Fascists. They would certainly have felt that they were making themselves ridiculous if they had ascribed their political opinions to the influence of a sexual infatuation. What is more, if their political opinions had been due to any such cause, they would have had the sense not to mention it in a court of law, which would find it far from endearing.

The sum of the confusions within this dour creature was a habit of feeling passionate emotions which were not reciprocated. He loved Germany and Germany did not love him. He hated England; and when he had betrayed England it had laughed at him for a week, sent him to prison for a moderate term of years, and then forgotten him, and on being reminded of his existence and told that he had betrayed it again, still could not bring itself to be bothered about him. When he came up for trial at the Central Criminal Court the charge against him had been reduced to an offence against Defence Regulation 2A; and the prosecuting counsel and the defending counsel and the judge wearily agreed that it really seemed absurd for the English courts to concern themselves with an Englishman who had acted with perfect legality in his desire to abandon his British nationality, and who had started taking out his German naturalization papers so long ago that, had it not been for the sluggishness of Berlin officials, he would have become a German citizen at a time when the countries were at peace and such an action was no offence against the English laws. In fact, England yawned in Baillie-Stewart's face and said, "Have it your own way". The humiliation of his position was emphasized at the trial by the personality of the judge, Mr. Justice Oliver, a large, handsome man who had probably never done anything not very sensible in his whole life, and whose sense was so sound that he had missed very few of the good things of life. In the dock Baillie-Stewart was piteous and inconvenient, but more inconvenient than piteous, like a dray-horse that has fallen in the street. When a dray-horse falls there always appears an efficient person who inquires where ropes can be got. Mr. Justice Oliver was that person. Contemplating the closed door of Baillie-Stewart's face, he reflected that if this man wanted to be a German the best thing was to let him have his wish. So he asked Baillie-Stewart's lawyer to find out whether his client would give his promise to go back to Germany and never to return to Great Britain; and he asked

213

the prosecuting counsel to make inquiries as to whether the Allied Control Commission would find it convenient to receive Baillie-Stewart in Germany. So the court adjourned.

The next morning Baillie-Stewart was very gloomy when he entered the dock. The ropes found by Mr. Justice Oliver had not put the dray-horse on its legs again. Baillie-Stewart had been offered, as a great concession, the prospect of returning to the rubble and ashes which was all that was left of the country to which he had given all he had and which had grinned at him with the misplaced acuteness of an idiot. He had accepted this offer, making in exchange the promise that he would never return to the place where he was born, where he might find the irrational affection, springing from ties of the blood, which was all he could be sure of attracting. But that grim contract was too favourable to be permitted as part of his destiny. The Allied Control Commission had been forced to object. Since it was bound to penalize people who had actively collaborated with the Nazis, it would only have to take in charge this extreme collaborator the minute he arrived back in Germany. It was not said in court where in Germany he had been domiciled. But had it been necessary to return him to the Russian zone, his story might have been short. It is possible that this decision of the Allied Control Commission gave him back his unhappy life a second time.

The judge could do nothing else than send him to prison. This queer creature could not be allowed to go free. It would have made the punishment of others for like offences seem unfair; and assuredly he would have found some new way of getting into trouble. Quite a few of the traitors were arrested only because they drew attention to themselves, not from any loyalty to Nazi principles but from a desire to push their personalities into the limelight. So Mr. Justice Oliver had to pass sentence on Baillie-Stewart, who faced him like a dead man standing upright, a dead man who had died alone, with nobody to shut his eyes. He told him that he was perhaps the worst citizen that England had ever produced, which was not a very apt or precise description. He had obviously done far less harm in his life than John Amery, and was less politically dangerous than William Joyce. It would have been more accurate to say that he was the most alarming citizen that we had ever produced. For it is man's terror that the magic which created the universe out of nothingness may one day start working backwards: the rabbit will recede into the empty top-hat, the lent watch will never return, when the screen is taken away there will be no magician, and as the audience rushes forward to seek him they too will abruptly be nothing. That this might indeed befall us was threatened by the singularly perfect negativism of this man, who had cancelled everything in his life by its opposite, who had felt the extreme of patriotism for a country which was not his own, who had gone about the business of spying as noisily as a postman, who was now to be a prisoner on terms antithetical to any previous condition of captivity. For the judge sentenced him to five years' imprisonment, with a recommendation to the Prison Commission that he should be released and sent back to Germany as soon as the state of the country permitted it. That time was not to come during his imprisonment. When he was released he was still barred from Germany. He spent some time with a benefactress of high character not previously known to him, who had been drawn to him by reports of the case; and afterwards he went to Eire where he took employment under a German manufacturer of paper bags. That might seem not perfection but somewhere in the direction of his heart's desire. But the German manufacturer, on hearing of his employee's past, immediately discharged him, and he had to become an itinerant seller of "Westerns" in rural Eire, a fate which surely has no relevance to his needs. It is as if there has at last been translated into terms of existence one of those negative mathematical quantities which till now have seemed to mean nothing, merely to indicate that the symbolic system on which they are based has outrun its business of representation.

III

NEITHER John Amery nor Norman Baillie-Stewart was certifiably insane. They never saw things that were not there. They never committed actions which gave the community an instantaneous shock. Their suicidal policies were long-term, and they could successfully apply logic to their experience on a small scale. The actions by which they offended normal standards could well have been committed by men who were not mad but bad; and Amery has been matched in incoherence and Baillie-Stewart in sullenness by countless people who conduct their lives in the most reasonable way. Nevertheless, the minds of both these men were not so adjusted as to bring them happiness or favour their survival. They leaned towards the state of psychosis: they fell into the darker of the two categories into which the maladjusted are divided. Neurotics, who cause less distress to themselves and their neighbours than those in the other category, are at war with their own natures. Their right hands are in conflict with their left. Psychotics, and it is those who commit purposeless crimes and prefer death to life, are at war with their environment. Right and left hands strike against the womb that carries them.

This has its bearing on power politics. The psychotic will very readily take sides against his own country. He is as if decreed by Heaven to be a prop for any neighbouring power which desires to swallow his fatherland. He hates the people round him, he hates his fellow-countrymen, because he hates the real world, which he knows through the testimony of his senses. His power of fantasy enables him to build any country which is the declared enemy of his fatherland into an ideal and beloved world; and it will perform that miracle whether the enemy be Great Britain, America, Germany, or Russia. Throughout any international movement which seeks to destroy the independence of nations there must run a vein of madness.

III

THE CHILDREN

KENNETH EDWARD AND STOKER ROSE

I

THERE were also the children among the traitors, the ones who thought like children, and felt like children, and were treacherous as children are, without malice, only because someone was giving away sweetmeats or because the whole gang was chasing the dog. Most of these were children with men's bodies; but some were children in body as well as mind.

When the Second World War started, Kenneth Edward was a moderately naughty little boy of thirteen living in a Cornish town with his father, who was a policeman employed in a naval dockyard. When he left school he worked for three or four months as a kitchen boy in a Cornish hotel, which must have found that he exaggerated rather than relieved their labour difficulties. He did not get on with his father, and he went to sea at the beginning of 1940, as deck-boy in an ammunition ship. In May he transferred to a steamer called the *Cymbeline*, and in September, when he was not yet fifteen, he was aboard the ship when she was sunk by a German raider. For six weeks he was kept a prisoner on the raider, and then he and two of his shipmates were landed in France and put in an internment camp. In November they were taken out and he was separated from them, and was sent to another camp, and to another, and then to another. He was not sure where these camps were, or how long he stayed in them. Eventually he was put in a camp near Besançon, where there were some Englishwomen among the internees. One of these women was released and allowed to go to her home in Paris, and she got permission to take the boy with her. Even during his trial, when years of anxiety had made his face puffy and glum, it could be seen that he must have been a charming boy, pretty and jolly and impudent. For some time he was mothered by this woman, but as he grew nearer military age this situation was naturally not tolerated by the Germans. He describes what happened in these words:

Then I was sent to a camp near Drancy near Paris, in which I found myself alone with a lot of Jews I stayed in this camp with them for three months and then I was transferred to St. Denis with all the Jews on August 29th, 1942. On June 9th I escaped from St. Denis and I could not get away from Paris So I gave myself up on the 10th of July 1943 when I returned to Camp I had a dogs life from the Jews because they believed I gave one of there number away seeing he had escaped and was hiding unbeknown to myself quiet near to where I was an he was caught three days after. I stayed in camp then in a hut to myself because even my best Friend would not speak to me until it was found out that I never gave him away. Soon after a man Came to our Camp and he Called himself John Amery he called some men to a hut in the Camp and spoke to them about a Legion of St. George that had been formed in Germany. Then he put some big Poster in the Camp, which said that a said Legion had been formed and the strength of this Legion was a little 1800 men P.O.W. and those R.A.F. planes that had come from England to fight Bolshevics which I can truly say I did not understand what it meant untill a few months ago, he said it was our duty to come and fight for England and Europe. So I spoke to the Camp Captain Gillis a German who said it was good and that most of my friends had vol. but he could not tell me their names, so I thought if he said it was good it must be so. I told him I would join too.

This letter explains why offenders like John Amery had to be prosecuted: why such seducers of prisoners of war must be ranked as criminals. The boy Kenneth Edward was by now not quite eighteen and had undergone two and a half years of imprisonment, varied by life in Paris under the occupation. A fortnight after his interview with Gillis he was taken to a private house where he met a German called Plack, of the Foreign Office, and John Amery, who was introduced to him as the Foreign Secretary of England. They took a great deal of trouble to persuade this illiterate child with no military training to enlist in the Legion, and this was not folly. A gay and good-looking boy, in high spirits because he had regained his liberty, and bubbling over with talk of the fine time the Germans were giving him, might have been a very successful recruiting agent in

English prisoner-of-war camps. To John Amery, who knew nothing of the puritanism of the hero, he must have seemed a much more potent instrument than he was; and Plack was helping to put on a performance for the outside world. England had to be persuaded that Germany was more hostile to Russia than ever before, so long as the peace proposals were being discussed. In order to get hold of the boy the German told many lies which he must have known to be lies. He said that several of the boy's friends in the camp had joined, but he would not give their names, on the pretext that he had been asked not to disclose them. In fact, none had joined. He also declared that three British submarines had been brought in to St. Nazaire, and three British planes had been grounded, one in Holland, one in Belgium, and one in Germany, all by crews anxious to enlist in the Legion. It is not possible that he could have believed this.

Kenneth Edward did not immediately yield to this persuasion. So he was taken back to the camp and told that he had a week or ten days to make up his mind. It was at this point that his naughtiness passed to a degree of culpability which deserved and later received punishment. For the camp was seething with denunciations of Amery. Nearly all the internees had recognized his speech as the raving of a crazy traitor, and a number of them had remembered his criminal record. There were other boys there, as young and as unfortunate as Kenneth Edward, who kept their heads and their courage. But it must be remembered that Kenneth Edward had had his differences with the camp when he was under suspicion of betraying the escaped Jewish prisoner to the Germans. It was probably resentment against this injustice which made him succumb after a few interviews with the Camp Commandant. So about three weeks after he saw Amery he was handed over to an English member of the Legion named Tunmer, who took him to Paris. There they lived in a house managed by French collaborationists in the bleak and surrealist district on the outer edge of Auteuil, where gaunt buildings tower over a landscape made unnatural by the attack of the fortifications on its contours, in the Boulevard Exelmans, not far from the solid yet fantastic viaduct of the Pont-du-Jour. Tunmer took Kenneth Edward to see the sights of Paris and gave him some money to spend on amusements, and promised him he would soon be having as nice a time in Berlin and that the war would soon be over, for Britain and Germany were drawing together. There was doubtless a real tenderness and pity in the older man's dealing with the boy, for after eight days of this holiday-making two men in civilian clothes came to the house and took Tunmer away. He was a British agent.

Kenneth Edward did not know what to do; and later that same day John Amery paid him a visit to see how he was getting on. When the bewildered boy told him what had happened he showed signs of surprise, and on the plea that it did not seem safe for him to stay in the house when such things were going on, he rang up the Gestapo. Whether he took this step in good faith or not, the consequences were alarming. Three Gestapo men came and interrogated Kenneth Edward about Tunmer, and threw him into jail for about a week. Amery, with his long experience of Franco Spain and collaborationist France and the radio traitors' circle in Berlin, must have known perfectly well into what an unending night of terror he was leading the boy when he recruited him. At the end of the week's imprisonment Kenneth Edward was taken under guard to Berlin, where he was met at the station by Amery, his Cagoulard wife who had succeeded Jeannine Barde, and Herr Plack. They greeted him affectionately and took him back to Amery's rooms in the Kaiserhof, a luxurious hotel looking out on a great square. It was not in the same class as the Adlon on the Esplanade, for the Germans would not have given Amery their first-class accommodation, but it was in the same line of vulgar splendour as the Eden. Kenneth Edward was dazzled by it, and greatly impressed by John Amery's good looks; and he enjoyed playing with Amery's dog. Amery gave him three hundred marks and kept him with him for some hours, lying about the growing strength of the Legion and preaching a crusade against Russia. Finally he took him over to the German Foreign Office, which was not far away, and introduced him to a Dr. Hesse, who inquired with what must have been inhuman irony as to his readiness to fight the Bolsheviks, and gave him the three propaganda books *England Faces Europe*, *Root of the War*, and *Fire over England*, which were supposed to have been written by Amery and probably were in part. It is unlikely that with his lack of stability he should have written all of them. Kenneth Edward was then taken by Plack to a boarding-house and settled in a comfortable room.

But he did not see Amery for a month. Plack kept him supplied with money and cigarettes, and he drifted about Berlin with nothing to do. Then Amery summoned him to the suite at the Kaiserhof, and introduced him to Thomas Haller Cooper and a group of German officers who had been engaged for some time past in spotting likely traitors in the prison camps, and had brought along their chief catch, an English public schoolboy of Lithuanian origin who had volunteered for the British Army in New Zealand. "Drinks", Kenneth Edward reported in one of his statements, "were supplied by Amery." The British Free Corps was launched onto the sea of alcohol on which it was to sail until its shipwreck. At the end of the evening Amery said to the boy, "You will soon be with your unit now, and will start training soon with the Corporal". But no call came for him, and it was the last time he was ever to see the man who, pitiful himself, had been so pitiless towards him. By now it was September. For the next three months Kenneth Edward was to live in a peculiar limbo. Berlin was constantly raided. Plack ceased to take any interest in him, and he was so poorly fed that he missed the Red Cross parcels he had had in camp. He was unable to write to his family or receive letters from them. As he spoke very little German he was repeatedly put under arrest; he thought it happened on as many as twenty-three occasions. Again and again he wrote to Amery asking him what he was to do, but received no answer. The last time he was arrested his captors put him in a cell and beat him with a blackjack in revenge for the damage the R.A.F. were doing. In desperation he went to the Foreign Office and reminded the authorities of the interview he had had when he first came to Berlin; and on the 1st of January 1944 he was sent to a house on the outskirts of Berlin where there were a handful of men who had volunteered to join the British Free Corps and were now under the command of Thomas Haller Cooper.

Kenneth Edward was not very kindly received. The German authorities issued an enlistment form which required the recruits, with touching trust in their good faith, to state whether they were of Jewish blood and had any criminal record. He was not asked to sign this, because, he thought, "I wasn't very trusted and had been brought in by Amery". That there was some feeling against him was indicated by his position as the one and only private in the British Free Corps. All other volunteers, without a single exception, were made officers. The explanation he gave was probably correct. The Germans had by this time found that John Amery was more than they could stomach. Nevertheless, they used Kenneth Edward by sending him on recruiting tours through the camps. But they had fallen into the pit which is dug for all corrupters of youth. Despoiled innocence loses its innocent charm. The happy and pretty boy they had enlisted to speak fair things to melancholy prisoners was no longer happy or pretty, and his words had had little power to lift the heart since he had seen Tunmer spirited out into the interminable curve of the Boulevard Exelmans and exorcised into nothingness by two quiet conjurers in civilian clothes; and since he had first known Amery so well that he could sit in his grand room and drink his liquor and play with his dog, and then found that he did not know him at all, so that in hunger and during raids and under blows from a blackjack it was useless to hope for his help.

He made no recruits; and, on finding himself, in the month of May 1944, in the course of a tour, at the merchant seamen's camp near Bremen, he heard something of the Security Officer who was in charge: Captain Notman. This man was as all men would wish to be: comely, strong, courageous, never perjured, much beloved. Learning his repute, Kenneth Edward wrote him a letter in which he threw himself on his mercy:

But it's not been for the last month that I have realized I am a traitor to England and by what I am doing I am causing my Mother the greatest agony she has ever felt so I implore you not for my sake but for my Parents' sake to help me get out of the mess I am in. I'll face anything if I can get out, but if it is possible to see Brigadier-Major Interne I think he will see that I don't get down the mines Because I am scared for my health and I would (I have realized) like to come to Milag with Real Englishmen, I thank you Sir.

224

When Captain Notman got this letter he came out of his office and talked to the boy, whose presence in his camp on these tours he had till then ignored. He formed a good opinion of him, and wanted to take him to the Kommandantur to make his statement before the Kommandant of the camp and trust to this man's humane feelings. But another Englishman in a position of authority advised Kenneth Edward not to go; and it is possible that this was the wiser counsel, for Captain Notman was not aware how John Amery's prestige had fallen in Berlin and how the Germans were savaging the traitors. As an alternative Captain Notman advised Kenneth Edward to stay in the British Free Corps, and, since Switzerland was the neutral power named by Great Britain to protect the interests of its prisoners of war, to go to the Swiss Embassy in Berlin and put his case before the officials there.

This Kenneth Edward did, a month or so later, and a Swiss official promised that he would find out what could be done for him and then write to him. But of course the boy never heard from him. Prisoners of war who lose their status through treachery are not a class which it is possible to protect by international action, since it would be impossible to make the threat of reprisals against a similar group which is the only weapon which guarantees the protection of prisoners of war. In his misery he made another attempt to get in touch with Amery:

DRESDEN, 4.11.44

DEAR SIR.

I write you a few lines and hope that you may receive them. Well Mr Amery it is a long time since I saw or heard from you last and I sometimes wonder how you are getting on. I hope you are in good health the same as this leaves me. I saw in the French papers that you were wounded on your way to Lyons, but I am glad to know that you have recovered. I am still in the British Free Corps we expect to go to the front in two week's time, but I don't think there is anything in it. We are doing Pioneer Training for the past six weeks and I like it very much I speak a great lot of German so I can tell a few were to get off. How is your wife and dog? I hope they are still in good health. Have you heard from Mr and Mrs Plack. How are they? would tell them I should like to be remembered to them and I would like to have a line from them some time, I cannot write to them because I have not there present address, also would you be so kind as to give Mr Adami my best regards. I must close now because it is time for me to go on Garde duty. All the Boys sends there Best Regards so goodbye for the time.

Yours truly,

KENNETH EDWARD

The forced cheerfulness of this letter contrasts strongly with the honest misery of the letter he had written six months before to Captain Notman. His motive in writing it was probably the hope of getting in touch with Plack, who had once helped Kenneth Edward when he was in desperate straits, as he was again. But nobody helped him. He was inevitably one of the unhappy residue of the Corps which was hustled to the Eastern front and forced toward the fighting line under the leadership of Thomas Haller Cooper, who, himself just released from arrest by the Germans for the sole reason that their power to hold anything was vanishing, was going on fulfilling the orders they had given him; partly because his German blood found content-ment and swelling music in death among flames, partly because he was at a loss to know what else to do. He dragged Kenneth Edward into the battle somewhere near Schöneberg. "The minstrel boy to the war has gone", never less gloriously, never with less comradeship to sustain, never with much more than mere fear to distress him. When the collapse of the German army was complete he passed without difficulty to the Russian lines and there surrendered, and he was presently handed over to the Americans, who sent him back to England by air, and in the following February he was tried, with Denis John and Alfred Vivian and Ronald David, and the eccentric Herbert George, all of them being merchant seamen. The reason for his prosecution must have been the part he had played in the recruiting campaign, for certainly the policy of the Crown in bringing these charges of treachery was to assert the sacredness of the prisoner of war and guard him from molestation in any future war. If it be objected that he was young, it should be remembered that among the prisoners of war whom he had through weakness attempted to seduce were boys younger than himself but of sturdier soul. He was given nine months' imprisonment, which was the lightest sentence passed on any traitor. As he left the dock he gave the V sign to some members of his family who were sitting in court and went down to the cells looking plumply stoical. Without doubt he would be able to support another nine months added to his four years of continuous hardship; he was physically robust. Without doubt he would forget the terror and the loneliness and the beatings and the bullyings. He was not sensitive. There had been done to him, however, an injury which struck not at the body nor at the nerves but at a deeper part. Captain Notman was the kind of person whom he respected, and he had committed himself to a way of living which the captain held in contempt, which he was unable to abandon even after the captain was aware of him.

II

THE hotel at Portsmouth had once been famous for its claret and its port; many an admiral had enriched the purple patina of his complexion in its panelled dining-room. Now the taxi driver could hardly find it. "Nobody comes here now," he grumbled, "they all go up to the new hotel in the town." That, indeed, had been the intention of the female journalist whom he had brought from the station; but every room in that had been booked weeks ago. Very few hotels were still standing in the town. "People don't like coming down here to the docks now", he went on grumbling as he crawled along, poking his head out each time he passed one of the few houses that stood up like towers among the rubble on the harbour's lip. "I don't like coming down here now myself." Within, though the war had been over for nine months, the windows were still boarded up. At this spot as rigorous a blackout had been imposed as anywhere in the world, and there was no labour available to take apart its firmness. The female journalist, arrived in her bedroom, found that there were no towels. She had forgotten that this was possible, and indeed it might not have been so; though nearly every hotel in England was short of linen and asked the clients who booked ahead for lengthy visits to bring their own, they usually did something for transients, if it were only to give them a quarter of a worn-out bath-towel. But it was too late to bother anyone about that, so she dried herself on cotton-wool.

In the morning she rang for the maid and asked for some sort of a rag but was refused. The maid was slow and pleasant, with the pleasantness of Western folk. Mournfully she said, "The mistress won't give out any linen, not an old dish-cloth, and I can't ask her for it. Her nerves are so terrible bad. She was here all through the blitz, and her son was in Japanese hands as a prisoner of war, and has come home very ill. He is yellow, quite yellow. It is as if the Japanese had wanted to make him like themselves. But about the towels, I'll tell you how most people that don't bring their own make do: they take the part of the sheet that's folded under the mattress and dry themselves with that. It's quite safe, you can leave it hanging when you go to bed, then the damp won't mount through the mattress and you won't get rheumatics."

The female journalist was anxious not to make difficulties, but she pointed out that this prescription would hardly help her when she wanted to have a bath. "But how long are you going to stay?" asked the maid. She was plainly going to argue that in two or three days the issue need not arise. "I don't know", said the female journalist. "Just as long as the court-martial of Stoker Rose goes on." "Oh," she said, her calm face clouding, "are you here for that? It is a most terrible thing. The only naval man to be charged with treason, and him a Portsmouth man. But I don't believe a word of it. They are trying him for telling the Germans all about radar equipment, but what would a stoker know about radar equipment?" She was behind the times, not only our own times but our fathers' times, about the elementary matter of bathing, but she could speak sensibly about radar, for she could speak of naval matters just as such a woman brought up at Newmarket might speak of racing. She had moved all her life among people who were masters and slaves of a certain technique, and they had made her wiser than herself.

The morning brought no light because of the boarded windows; and as the powdered-egg omelette was eaten in the panelled room where the admirals had drunk their port a rat ran across the floor, a horrified waiter running after it and striking at it with a napkin. It was not that the place was dirty. It was remarkable for its dogged cleanliness. But a house near by was being torn down, and its rat tenants were looking for new homes. Outside was a Portsmouth made oddly idyllic by destruction. In this district round the harbour the houses had been so close-pressed that neither streets nor houses made any individual impressions. Now quite a quarter of the houses had gone, and most of those which remained disclosed the comely character of homes built for simple but prosperous people two hundred to a hundred years ago. Where fire or blast had torn down an outer wall, rooms shone with the clear pastel colours to which weather turns even the vilest wall-paper, and were marked with vertical lines of fireplaces where the dead had warmed themselves when they were quick. Where the houses had gone entirely there now grew wholesome country grass, not merely the purple willow-herb which alone will grow on the poor soil of London bombed sites. It was as if a mad village green were wandering through the town.

The court-martial was held at the Royal Naval Barracks, which are built round a vast asphalt square with sides of three or four hundred yards. The wind which sweeps over it is salt. One remembers what is easy to forget in this town where the harbours and quays are as private to the state as the Kremlin: that one is by the sea. In one corner of the square some hundreds of blue-jackets were marching and counter-marching in a mass that looked as threatening as a thundercloud, though today men with arms no greater than they can carry are, relatively speaking, innocent as lambs. Beyond the square, red barracks, a clock tower and a chapel—dreary buildings set up by convict labour in the nineteenth century, with gaps filled up with black huts where bombs had struck to the very earth—drew the landscape and established the confines of a huge, enclosed, and unfanciful community. On the nearer side of the square were tall red blocks of barracks, a labyrinth of them, some scalped or hollowed by bombs, with lines of two-storied huts set in the alleys between them, to house the departments left homeless by the damage. In and out of this chipped solidity there tripped the sailors, dark as priests in their long full coats and long full trousers and close round caps, gay as children, nimble as ballerinas, and as grim as they were gay and nimble, by reason of the courage and discipline that stiffened their faces. Their gaiety was odd, considering that the bomb damage inflicted acute discomfort on nearly all of them. At night many of them were sleeping in hammocks under tarpaulin roofs that leaked under downfalls of any persistence, and others who could not support that discomfort were spending their own money to lodge in overcrowded rooms in the town; and all day they were working and playing in quarters so scant that everyone had someone's elbow in his ribs.

The air chattered. Loud-speakers were perpetually roaring that one bearing this name and that number should report somewhere immediately. At every corner the men who were obeying these calls were running full tilt towards each other, swinging clear with a grin at the very last moment, and skipping on their way. At the end of the labyrinth of alleys between the tall barracks, near a boundary wall, was a squat little house ordinarily used as a school for certain courses. Here they were to try Stoker Rose. "But", said the rating who was guiding the journalists from the gate, "we don't reckon he's guilty. A stoker wouldn't know nothing about the radar on his ship. Nor about the defences of Portsmouth Harbour, and they say he told the Germans about them too." Stoker Rose, he added with pride, was to be defended as well as he could be, not just by an officer, as usually happens in courts-martial, but by two professional lawyers, a King's Counsel and a junior. Their fees had been subscribed by naval stokers who wanted to clear the good name of their comrade and their kind.

To make a courtroom, folding doors had been opened between two school-rooms. In the larger one, on rising tiers, sat the spectators, who were all naval personnel, male and female. The women all looked charming, for the black tricorne felt hats worn by Wren officers make all but inoperable cases charming in a high-bred eighteenth-century way, and the non-commissioned ranks were like a chorus of soubrettes in their sailor caps. The men, officers and ratings alike, had the beauty given by health, the dignity given either by the possession of character or the long-continued imitation of character, and that not monotonous uniformity given by submission to a common discipline. Sickliness and weakness, which one would have taken as part of the pattern in any ordinary crowd, here seemed remarkable; so, too, would any sign of the uncertainties of thought. In what had been the smaller room seven captains, glorious in gold braid and wearing their swords, sat at a long table covered with red baize, their backs to the only wall in which there were windows. These were the court. The one in the centre was the President of the Court. Facing them across the table sat the Deputy Judge-Advocate, a naval officer trained in the law whose duty it is to instruct the court in the legal problems presented by the case, though he cannot advise them on matters of fact, nor on the verdict, nor on the sentence. At a small table covered with green baize, right in front of the court, almost touching the press table, sat the Prosecuting Officer, who was in full naval uniform and wore a sword, but who was in private life a lawyer. He was a heavily built man who moved with a slowness that was aggressive, a criticism of all who were more speedy. At another table covered with green baize, set against the opposite wall to the court, sat the two officers who were the Accused's Friends—which is the technical term used for the officers acting as amateur lawyers for the accused person in a court-martial—and the two professional lawyers who had been employed by the stokers to defend their comrade. These two lawyers were the only people on the floor of the court who were not wearing the uniform of the King's navy. They had, of course, in their white wigs and their black robes, some sort of repartee to the blue serge and gold braid, but they had no equivalent of the sword. They were always slightly at a disadvantage. Actually the King's Counsel had fought in the last war, and his junior had seen active service with the navy in this war and had been gravely wounded. Nevertheless the naval men and the lawyers looked at each other across the gulf which always opens when a professional fighter faces a civilian. The service man, pinned down to specialist studies and a limited discipline, feels inferior to the civilian with his greater range and flexibility, and libels the civilian by pretending that he uses all his advantages to develop craftiness. The civilian feels inferior to the service man because the other is usually physically fitter and is dedicated to the primitive virtue of courage, which often atrophies in the civil life of peace, so libels him as a thick-skulled martinet. It might have been thought that the war, with its immense conversions of civilians into service men, would have ended that conflict. But it reasserts itself today as if we had all just come back from Waterloo.

There was only the flimsiest of docks: practically a symbolic dock, a hip-high screen of varnished wood, such as children might make to use in a charade. Behind it stood Stoker Rose; and behind him was standing the petty officer who was the Master-at-Arms of the court, holding a sword pointed upwards. The Deputy Judge-Advocate, who was an elderly captain, frank in kindliness as proved men of action can dare to be, gave them the signal to sit down at the first possible moment. Stoker Rose sank down in his seat in an attitude of collapse which was surprising. He and Dr. Alan Nunn May were the only traitors who did not pull themselves together in the dock and try at an appearance of courage; and of both of them it may have been true that they were perhaps compelled to make a poor show by their physiques. Rose's head lolled on the long stalk of his neck, and when he was standing his body had that vertical sag which is one of the least admirable attitudes of the lily. In face he resembled an idealized version of the Duke of Windsor. His hair was pale gold in the light and mouse-coloured in the shadow; under his blue eyes there were pouches; and his lips were full. At the moment his colour was earthen. It was obvious from his demeanour that he had little physical courage. One at least of the spectators was in a like case. But the two were the whole minority. Physical courage was an element in the climate of the barracks.

It appeared from the statements of the prosecution that this young man, who was now twenty-three, had been a stoker on a motor torpedo boat, known as an M.T.B., on a night in March 1943, exactly three years and ten days before the court-martial, when it was sunk off the Dutch coast. He was picked out of the water after some hours by the Germans, who took him to Wilhelmshaven, where he remained while a tremendous R.A.F. air raid flattened the town about him, and then to the celebrated prisoner-of-war camp near Bremen known as Marlag-Milag Nord. There in the pleasant month of May he was approached by an American sailor named Williams, who had formed a plan to escape in company with another American sailor named Schaper. Williams asked Rose if he would switch identities with him. This was a common device to confuse the authorities during an escape.

It meant that the police searched the countryside for someone looking like the man who had failed to answer the roll-call, not like the man who had actually escaped. After this request had been endorsed by Williams's commanding officer, Rose consented. As soon as Williams and Schaper had gone he was arrested by the camp officers and grilled for some hours. In the end this lad, who till he joined the Royal Navy had driven a coal-cart in Portsmouth, was forced to admit that he was not a native of Boston, Massachusetts. All this grilling was a sham, a device not to extract information but to excite fear. Rose's tormentors had known from the first who he was. For as soon as Williams and Schaper had got clear of the camp they had been arrested, for the simple reason that Schaper was not an American sailor but a German Intelligence officer who had learned his English in America. Schaper then saw that Williams was put in a concentration camp, and transferred his attentions to Rose, for some reason not immediately comprehensible, as he was of no special value to Intelligence. His attentions were formidable and repellent. From evidence given in other cases it is known that he was a fair man, six feet two inches in height and broad for that. His teeth were very badly stained; and he suffered so much from varicose veins that his vast limbs were always swathed in elastic bandages. He had curious pleasures: he seems to have enjoyed having sexual intercourse with women in the presence of other men.

It was on the ensuing events that the three charges against Rose were based. He was charged first with traitorously holding correspondence with the enemy between, roughly speaking, the time of his first intimidation and the end of the war; secondly, with traitorously giving intelligence to the enemy, during the first two months of his intimidation, concerning the fitting of radar equipment on British ships and aircraft; and, thirdly, with traitorously giving intelligence to the enemy concerning naval and harbour facilities at Portsmouth.

The first two witnesses for the prosecution turned out to be, to all intents and purposes, witnesses for the defence. The first was the captain of the M.T.B. on which Rose had been captured, who was eager to admit that Rose had had no opportunity to observe the nature of the radar equipment on his vessel, and that

233

by some oversight Rose had never been instructed, as all soldiers and sailors should have been during the war, that if he should be captured he must tell the Germans nothing but his name, number, and rank. The second was a radar expert who defined the kind of radar equipment that was installed on an M.T.B., and added that a stoker would know nothing about it.

There then passed into the witness-box in slow succession two Canadians named Edwin Barnard Martin and John Gordon Galaher and an Englishman named John White, who had led lives during the war that were singular not in themselves but in the peculiar renown they attained without knowing it. They were among the half-dozen men who were living in a hut outside the prisoner-of-war camps at Lamsdorff in Silesia to which Rose was brought to meet Schaper after he had connived at Williams's escape. Martin and Galaher had been captured in 1942 at the raid on Dieppe. White had been captured in 1940 outside Dunkirk. It had been already proven against Martin and Galaher, who had already been tried and convicted when they gave evidence against Rose, and it was alleged against White, who was at that time awaiting trial, that they had been engaged in the least attractive of the activities open to traitors: when a new batch of prisoners came into a camp they mixed with them and pumped them for information which they then reported to the German Intelligence officers. In return they got the same rations as the German soldiers, which were twenty-five per cent more than those given to the prisoners of war, and slightly more comfortable quarters; they were given enough money to buy liquor, and a number of German women were detailed to supply their sexual needs; they were allowed to wear civilian clothes and go to the pictures and walk in the woods and, sometimes, visit the nearest big town; and for some of them, such as Martin and Galaher, there was reward in the work itself.

Edwin Barnard Martin, of Riverside, Ontario, must have been a pretty baby, and later the small boy for whom old ladies spread scones thick with jelly. His like can be seen at the picnic and on the steamboat, a girl swooning love-silly in his arms, himself trim and upright and ready to make a getaway. His eyes were clear blue under eyebrows that arched like circumflex accents, and his tiny mouth parted under the shadow of a moustache. His nails were badly bitten. He had been sentenced to twenty-five years' imprisonment by a Canadian court-martial. An allusion to this by one of the lawyers appalled the spectators, for though in Great Britain we sentence people to imprisonment for life, this actually means twenty years, and that is often remitted by years; but Martin himself was cool and brisk. Doubtless his hobby can be pursued in jail. Some fellow-prisoner or warden will one day, probably as a result of doing him a kindly act, come down suddenly when he thought he was going up. And at this moment he was happy because he was having a day out of prison which he was spending in an attempt to condemn to prison, and perhaps to death, a young man with whom he had lived in comradeship for two years.

He described how Rose had arrived at the informers' hut in a state of misery which could be imagined from the boy's present aspect in the dock. His head was drooping towards one shoulder, and he was staring out of the window at certain treetops which showed above the barrack-walls. His lids were bluish-silver, the colour of the eye-shadow which women used in the 'twenties. Occasionally the blood rushed backwards and forwards through his body so that his face was white, then scarlet, then white. This was in Shakespeare. "Death is a fearful thing", he had said, like Claudio. "And shamed life a hateful" had answered the traditions of the service. And, like Claudio, he had persisted, "Ay, but to die, and go we know not where. . . ." To settle this argument in Claudio's favour, Schaper had one night made him drunk with spirits and had in the morning produced a paper covered with compromising statements bearing his signature. He had pointed out to the boy that his switch of identities with Williams had one dangerous consequence for him: now if he disappeared there would be no necessity for the German authorities to account for him.

It was then, according to Martin, that Rose began to give information, which he himself claimed was always false. But Martin said that he had given information first about the radar equipment on the M.T.B., of which his captain had proved that he knew nothing. He also insisted that Rose had given information about Portsmouth, where Rose's parents were still living. To prove this, Martin alleged that he had one day gone into

Schaper's office and had passed the leisure hour examining the files in which he had found a folder of eight pages concerning the harbour and naval facilities of Portsmouth, signed by Rose. There was charm in the conception of a German Intelligence officer who left his files open for inspection by his alien and highly unreliable employees, and was of such an amiable disposition that his employees would risk being found ransacking his office. Martin could not say how Rose had signed himself, nor undertake to recognize his signature.

He told another story which was as poor as evidence, yet was probably true. One day during August 1943 the traitors had turned on the radio in their hut and had heard the B.B.C. announcing a raid on Portsmouth, and one of them had said to Rose, "I suppose this is some of your work. I hope you are proud of yourself." He had not denied this accusation, and had blushed. This news was, in fact, never given out by the B.B.C., yet the incident may have occurred. It was probably given out on the broadcast in English by the German radio. In the picture of the traitors' life which was built up by the testimony in this and other cases it was apparent that they spent much of their long idle days in almost meaningless chatter about treachery, just as prostitutes fill their leisure with babble about sex; and, like prostitutes, they were always being shocked by each other's impudicity, which, they alleged, passed the bounds of legitimate trade. Probably Schaper, as the Madam of the establishment, asked Rose questions about Portsmouth, though he must have known nothing a stoker knew would be likely to supplement the excellent maps drawn up on the basis of our English maps, their espionage, and aerial reconnaissance. Doubtless Rose signed nonsensical answers. Doubtless the other traitors taunted him with the supposed effects of his alleged treachery, though they must have known that Portsmouth had been bombed again and again before his capture.

John Gordon Galaher, of Windsor, Ontario, followed Martin into the box, and because prison was a horror to his goatish disposition and he had been there for six months, stood like a dead man not so efficiently raised as Lazarus. When he was asked a question his mouth worked under the stubble of his moustache and then hung open. Usually his hands were clasped behind him; sometimes he brought them forward and rubbed them together.

They were curiously marked, as if by untidy stigmata. Staring upwards at nothing, he repeated names of men with whom he had lived for years as if they were words in an unknown language whispered to him from a great distance. The next morning he was not so purely and simply a corpse, his earthly attributes could be perceived. From his dark ginger hair his receding forehead sloped to a long nose, a stalactite of a nose under which his hungry mouth continually twitched. His eyes, which were dull grey flecked with hazel, winked about him in libellous apprehension, imputing to his surroundings a malignity of which they could hardly ever be capable. In the middle of his forehead were three short deep lines, expressive of the same denigrating fear. His career had been inevitable. A man who saw the world as he did, vile in cunning, would have no resource but to outmatch it by vile cunning.

The story he told was the same in substance as Martin's, and differed only because he was a simpler man. Martin might have been an automobile mechanic or a clerk. Galaher had been a barber, and the establishment which employed him was probably not elegant. Martin had given a miniature performance; all his life he had been careful to do as little as he could and keep his brittleness intact. But the goat in Galaher's loins made him skip high, whatever pipe was played, and he gave a bravura performance in a role of repellent baseness and heart-rending naïveté. He saw the court as comprised of persons who, like all persons gathered together in public, proposed to believe in virtue. Or did they really believe in virtue? Perhaps so. He could believe in virtue too if he bade himself. Then let them all be virtuous together. At his own court-martial he had been described as "the ears and the eyes of the Germans". He had been the informer to end all informers. With his wide grin and his wide hands that could fall so brotherly about a fellow-comrade's shoulders, he plucked out secrets from the most honest hearts, through the most disciplined lips. Even before the war he had been able to persuade; often and often he had induced the gang in the bowling alley to believe what was not true concerning his prowess with women and his defiance of the boss. Well, now he was back in peace-time again, and he was ready to set about persuading this gang at the Portsmouth court-martial that his activities among the prisoners of war were so benevolent that a just comparison could be found not among the heroes but the heroines of war, in such figures as Florence Nightingale or Edith Cavell. He described how, when he and the other traitors searched the prisoners for private possessions and took them away, they were careful to set aside maps and compasses and cigarettes and smuggle them back to their owners, and how he and his friends took pains to get them their rations. "There were a hundred and one little things we could do for the prisoners", he declared priggishly. He declared that the German houses he and the traitors visited in the towns near the camp, which were in fact mostly brothels and beer-houses, were the homes of anti-Nazi civilians. But in this orgy of self-justification he spared time to say a good word for Rose when he could. He repeated Martin's improbable stories of Rose's giving information to the Germans about radar and Portsmouth, but he described how the boy had gone more than once to see certain German officers and, weeping, had begged them to release him from this servitude and send him back to an ordinary prisoner-of-war camp, but had been told that this could never be allowed because "he knew too much". Though Galaher certainly lied in saying he aided these attempts, his account of them was probably exact in all other respects, for it tallied with other stories told in similar cases. Only active resistance to orders which would have led Rose to Buchenwald or death would have freed him from his association with the traitors. We were back to Claudio and Isabella. "Death is a fearful thing." "And shamed life a hateful."

Galaher's simplicity gave him sometimes a sort of childishness. "What did you do with your time?" he was asked, when he was speaking of the life he and his friends had led in huts outside various barracks. He answered, "We played cards. We read books. We went walks in the woods. And sometimes", he said, with sudden gusto, "we went swimmin'." One saw his hairy and sweating body raising a diamond spray of water in the sunlight, one heard the harsh and meaningless cries with which he would have banished tranquillity in order to proclaim his pleasure. The traitors were often disconcerting in their appreciative references to the simpler delights. It is as if, called upon to enact the austerer chapters of *Pilgrim's Progress,* they had insisted on living the lives of Huckleberry Finn and Tom Sawyer. But Galaher's sensuousness, which was apparently immense, had its graver consequences. He was himself not content with his servitude, as he found Schaper a brutal master, and once agreed to make an attempt to escape in company with Rose. They collected maps, compasses, and food, and made a plan to dodge the guards; but at the appointed hour Galaher was missing. He had been given one of those leaves in civilian clothes to which the traitors were entitled, and twenty-two guards were sent out in search of him while he lay lost to time in the unfortunate bosom of a prostitute.

Now that things had gone ill with him, his simplicity had not matured into wisdom, it had acquired no dignity; it had merely become grotesque like a gargoyle. He was asked why he had come to give evidence against Rose, and it was suggested that he had hoped thereby to re-establish his reputation and increase his chance of winning his appeal against his sentence, which was, incredibly enough to our ears, even longer than Martin's. "You are serving a life sentence, are you not?" asked Mr. Curtis-Bennett. "And by Canadian law that really does mean imprisonment for life, does it not?" "Yes", said Galaher, staring at a nothingness which was within a few feet of him, which he could have touched. "But I know I'll never serve it." He spoke like a seer. All of us thought he must mean either that he knew himself to be so far advanced in some deadly disease, or so resolute in the intention of suicide, that he would serve no term of imprisonment at all. But he had meant simply that he believed he had established this preposterous story of his innocence by his appeal. He did not know what was known to several persons in court: that his appeal had already been rejected. This situation made him pitiful, but left him still repulsive.

The third of these tainted witnesses, John White, came from Durham, that county of rocky sea-coast and upland moors and coal mines, and therefore spoke in an accent which English hearers associate with austerity and the more rugged type of trade unionism. But he was a tiny little creature, built like a jockey, with bright and shifting blue eyes and a slight harelip, which gave him a surprised and petitioning expression, and a mass of brown hair rising from his forehead in the cast-iron undulations of an old-fashioned marcel wave. He surveyed the world with the bogus loving-kindness of a Riviera bar-tender. He would strike naïve people, when they first met him, as ready to do anything for anyone. Stoker Rose, who had hardly looked at Martin and Galaher, turned on White an eye heavy with hatred. The young man, however, was not abashed. He had given evidence against Galaher; he had given evidence against Martin; now he was giving evidence against Rose, and it was not his fault if the results were any less serious.

He seemed as repulsive as Galaher. Yet in another court another aspect of him was to appear. It is the besetting sin of the recorder to see those who make victims as fixed in that role, and to overlook the instances, so frequent as to be the rule, when they, in some other relationship, are also victims. On the psycho-analysts' couches women, mothers themselves, learn to reproach their mothers, and in the next world their mothers must resent the injustice which forgets that they too had mothers whom they might have reproached, but forget their resentment in pity, knowing that their daughters' daughters will in time reproach their daughters. There was just such a Janus-headed duality among the traitors who gave evidence against their kind in the courts-martial. (They appeared not so often in the civil cases, because the civil authorities, more experienced and apt in legal matters than the service authorities, used such tainted evidence as little as possible.) While they swore away their comrades' lives they seemed just as pitiless as they seemed pitiful when their comrades swore away their lives; and in most trials involving prisoners of war there were disclosed circumstances which showed the man in the dock as subjected to such coldly and cleverly planned temptation that the heart bled for him. But in another place White established his claim to be a victim, piteous as Rose, for his own trial was to take place some months later. He was then to look small and young sitting on a kitchen chair in one of the drawing-rooms of a great house, rolling his solemn yet trivial eyes up to the plaster doves that floated on medallions on the ceiling, to the carved vases of fruit and flowers on the panelled walls which were not covered by the plywood shields, to the treetops of Hyde Park, seen as a green blur through windows varnished against blast. Here, in White, one saw a sad, small effect mourning beside one of its causes. For in this great house Sir Edward Carson and Lord Birkenhead had rashly made their threats of armed resistance to Home Rule which had encouraged the Germans to believe it a good moment to attack Great Britain in 1914; and in this house Ribbentrop had been so hospitably received that he reported to Hitler that the governing classes of England would never permit a war to be made on Germany.

Now the house was handed over to the military, and seven officers sat beside a trestle table spread with army blankets and deliberated the case of John White. He told a story which cannot be doubted because it so closely corresponds to stories which were told by other prisoners with whom he had no contact. He had been taken out of the camp and was working in a small saw-mill in a country district. His particular job was to work quite alone in the chamber which received the sawdust. One day there came to him Martha, the young daughter of the miller, who made advances to him, putting her arms round him and drawing him close to her. He resisted but, he said, in the end "I gave in to her". Soon afterwards Gestapo men seized him and he was taken before Schaper, who told him he could be shot for having sexual relations with a German woman and would be if he did not buy his safety by working as an informer.

The army required White to refuse to buy his life at that price, and this demand was not past reason, for many men in like circumstances found themselves able to make that refusal, and most of them were not killed. But White was not forthright, and he wavered. He was taken to a new place, where there was a prisoner-of-war camp, and a hut outside it for informers. Among a half-dozen informers living there were Martin and Galaher, who took the new boy in charge. They got him down by wisecracking about him. He recalled with smarting irritation that after Martin had brought him into the hut Galaher asked Martin what the new arrival was like and Martin had answered, "He may look dumb but might be honest". White also mentioned, obviously as a powerful seduction, that at his first meal in the hut he was given three eggs. After supper Galaher talked to him seriously about the sound future which would be open to him if he became an informer, saying that he himself looked on it as a business like any other. But White was very reluctant to make the irrevocable decision. So presently Schaper took him and Galaher to stay in a comfortable house in the neighbourhood. It is quite apparent from what happened there that his unit of the Intelligence organization had got completely out of hand, that it was no longer supervised by any sane authority, and that Schaper was using his position to indulge his peculiar fantasies. But at the same time those fantasies were so peculiar that, it must be admitted, they helped Schaper to secure the ends for which he was working in his capacity of Intelligence officer.

Schaper and he shared a bedroom with twin beds. After they had settled down for the night Martha came in and tried to get White to take her into his bed. While Martha was making her assaults on White's virtue Schaper did not leave the room, and White felt nothing but disgust. Finally Schaper took Martha into his bed and she remained there for the night. In the morning Schaper and White were in the garden, and Martha and another girl came up and talked to them. Schaper had intercourse with the other girl on the lawn, in the presence of White and Martha. Not long afterwards some Gestapo men came in and told Schaper that they were arresting him and ordered him to take off his uniform and put on a civilian suit which they had brought with them. White was apparently almost as much shocked because Schaper changed his clothes out in the garden in front of the two girls as he was by his extraordinary sexual indecencies. Stunned, White went back to the informers' hut with Galaher, who ingeniously devised a new way of tormenting him. He spread among his friends the story that Schaper had told him that White had had sexual intercourse with Martha seven times during the night, and they teased the boy about it. He complained in his statement that this made a laughing-stock of him, and he consented to become an informer. Possibly he thought that this would mean going away to various camps, and in this he was partially right, though he was always being sent back to the company of Galaher and Martin and Schaper, who was not long out of favour.

The story of White's entrance into the sphere of espionage was not actually to his credit as the story of Rose's entrance was to him. But it is a pitiful and comprehensible story. The spectacle of Schaper's vast varicosed and bandaged limbs tossing in spasm must have been horrible to a young boy who had obviously been

242

brought up in a respectable provincial home. But he did not suggest there was such a defence for himself when he gave his evidence against Rose, towards whom, as was alleged at his own trial, he had professed friendship, and whom he had advised to become an informer, acting on the instructions of Schaper. He told the same unconvincing stories as Galaher and Martin concerning radar and Portsmouth, and said that Rose had told him that he was giving information "to get his freedom and some money", words which were unlikely to have been uttered by this lachrymose child in view of the circumstances connected with Williams's escape, which the prosecution had admitted had brought him into Schaper's power. But he then began to tell the truth, which was clearly defined as such by its unpredictability. Some time about the middle of 1944, when Rose made a last unsuccessful attempt to be sent back to a prisoner-of-war camp, Schaper took White and Rose to Frankfurt-on-Main, where they all got into the Paris express. After they had crossed the border into France a squadron of R.A.F. planes appeared and bombed the train and they had to climb out of the carriage and run into a wood, which they found swarming with German soldiers taking cover. At the end of the raid they came out of the wood and found only the wreckage of the train. Schaper handed his two captives over to some of the soldiers to be guarded until he had found an automobile. He introduced Rose to these soldiers as "his adopted son". When White repeated these words he fluted his harelip and looked down his eyelashes.

Schaper came back and took White and Rose to Châlons-sur-Marne, a town which in peace-time was specially memorable for a hotel called the High Mother of God which served a very good still champagne as part of its market-day lunch. It was not possible to judge how far White and Rose carried out their instructions. It can quite safely be assumed that they contributed the barest minimum which would be accepted, and that they palmed off as much false information as they could. But they certainly went through the motions of gathering information, and certainly they must from time to time have produced a little genuine information to avert the threat of Buchenwald or shooting. In any case a certain Sergeant Norman who was among the prisoners came to the conclusion that they were informers. After some weeks, probably when Sergeant Norman's convictions became widely known among the prisoners, White and Rose were taken out of the camp at Châlons-sur-Marne and sent back to an informers' hut outside a camp at Luckenwald, south of Berlin, where they had been before, and where they met Galaher again. He testified that Rose brought back with him from France a quantity of powder, perfume, silk stockings, and what he pudently called "other silk articles". Apparently the Nazis worked as assiduously on informers as on members of the British Free Corps to demoralize them with liquor and prostitutes, and Schaper would have thoroughly enjoyed the carrying out of this policy. But it is remarkable that Schaper worked so hard on this boy, whose languor, lack of intellectual equipment, and reluctance must have made him a poor instrument.

Some time afterwards White and Rose were sent to a castle near Coblenz where a number of British and Americans were imprisoned, and were put in amongst them to do their work. But, as White related with a smarting sense of grievance, there was a hitch in the proceedings. Hardly had they settled in when an American colonel came "stamping into the hall and told everyone to keep their mouths shut". It was evident from White's tone that the American colonel seemed to him a low fellow who was not playing the game, a fault he shared with Sergeant Norman, who had so far broken the rules as to have been sent to this castle from the camp at Châlons-sur-Marne. Later White and Rose were summoned to a meeting with Sergeant Norman, who, White complained, "slied out on them" and tricked them into entering a room where they stepped into a spotlight cast by an electric lamp lying bulb outwards on a table. In the darkness behind the lamp stood some people whom they could not see but who announced themselves as four British officers and four American officers, assembled to question them as spies. Rose danced about in the spotlight shouting that he was willing to fight anyone who called him a spy. This was a curious action for a lethargic and worried young man. At this point White's story became confused and he simply stated that after a great deal of talk the officers let them go. It may be deduced that White and Rose left the castle by giving the guards the pass-word by which they could always gain release from a camp when they had an urgent matter to bring before the Intelligence officers. But what bewildered White, so much so that he would plainly have liked the court's opinion on it, was that when they reported the incident to Schaper he seemed pleased at what had happened. And, indeed, examination of the incident made it very hard to believe that it could be an accident. When informers were sent from camp to camp the German authorities must have exercised the greatest care to see that they made contact with an entirely fresh set of prisoners each time. It is odd that this system broke down over a prisoner who had a personal reason for certainty that these two men were spies, and that the German Intelligence officer responsible for the break-down should show, instead of annoyance, something like pleasure.

But there were many mysteries in this case: the most profound, a matter of a name. When the informers were put into the camps they always assumed false names. Rose worked as Johnson and Müller and Jones, but the name which he chose for himself and in which he seemed to take a special pride was Aylmer. There was never a more puzzling juxtaposition of names in a law case.

> Ah, what avails the sceptred race!
> Ah, what the form divine!
> What every virtue, every grace!
> Rose Aylmer, all were thine.

> Rose Aylmer, whom these wakeful eyes
> May weep, but never see,
> A night of memories and of sighs
> I consecrate to thee.

It is one of those poems which will not lie down on the paper after they have been written, but which ramble on, living their own life in the continuance of literature. Walter Savage Landor wrote it and the great classical scholar Walter Headlam translated it into elegiacs; and the greater classical scholar von Wilamowitz-Möllendorff meditated over the Greek version with that degree of appreciation which ranks as a creative art, and declared that if it had been found on a papyrus it would have been counted one of the jewels in the *Greek Anthology*. And a stoker called

Rose, choosing a fake name, chooses, with marked interest and excitement, the name of Aylmer. This might be a coincidence, or it might be that when he drove a coal-cart round Portsmouth he sometimes descended from the driver's seat to converse with someone of imagination and literary taste, whom it amused to remember verses concerned with the name of Rose. That we shall never know, any more than we shall know why Schaper introduced Rose to a German soldier as his adopted son, or why, if he did not, White said that he did, or why Schaper contrived quite without profit to himself a nightmare for the boy, while he stood naked in his shame under a bright light before his fellows, who were clad in their honour, or why Schaper laughed when he heard of it.

For Schaper was not called to give evidence. Instead there appeared an underling of his called Richard Wigge, to whom all persons in the court, sinking the marked division between them, alluded as Mr. Wiggy. He was one of those fleshless dust-coloured Germans with pale but fervid eyes who are perhaps as disagreeable as any other of their nation, and though he had been styled an interpreter in the German Army, he had been employed in briefing the informers and arranging for their pay and their pleasures. He was a perfect example of the unassimilability of the German. He was a man of forty-eight who had spent all his youth in England, from the age of two till twenty-one, and he had lived with us for another year in his maturity and visited us half a dozen times; and we had not made the slightest impression on him. We had not demoralized him by our come-day-go-day slovenliness. When he was asked about a department of the German Army he knew its origin and its function; when he was asked about a prisoner he knew exactly where he had been at any given moment; when he was asked about a document which had been in his charge he remembered its every detail. His particularity was repulsive, an affront to charity. Asked what clothes Rose had been wearing when he first saw him, he answered, "A blue suit, a pink shirt, I don't remember the colour of his tie, black shoes". He had not the faintest inkling that it would be better not to observe a human being so closely unless one was prepared to like him, just a little.

Quietly and efficiently Mr. Wigge damned Stoker Rose. He explained that he had put him to the task of questioning prisoners about their occupations, which was ostensibly a preliminary to the formation of working parties, but it was a blind for getting information. He described how, before putting Galaher and White and Rose into a camp, he had shown to them a questionnaire which indicated what information they were to seek; it told them to ask the prisoners about aircraft factories, jet planes, radar, rustless steel, synthetic rubber, and the like. This questionnaire, he said, had been of little use, because most of the prisoners knew nothing; behind his drab speech there glittered for an instant a sneer at the idiot Allied armies, which had not deserved to win. Rose, he said, had certainly been shown this questionnaire, but had for long turned in no specific reports. The spectators stirred with pleasure, but were still again when he went on to say that in November 1944 Rose had given him a written statement concerning information which he had extracted from a man who before he was called up to the army was in a fort connected with the boom defence of Portsmouth. He himself had translated it into German and typed it. The little man's evidence became more and more distasteful. He said that to his certain knowledge Rose had a post-office savings-bank account with between nineteen and twenty-one hundred marks all earned by good treachery, and that Rose and White and Galaher talked to him about eight thousand dollars which was waiting in a Berlin bank for their use after the war, and he described with his odious particularity a contract which Rose had signed with representatives of German G.H.Q. before he went to work in France. Nothing could have been less desirable than to hear this evidence from his lips; for he was as unrepentant a Nazi as still draws breath. When he used the initials O.H.K. and the court asked him to explain what they meant, he held his head and rolled out the words with awe—O.H.K.—Oberste Heeres Kommandantur. If there was anything he regretted about the war, it was the losing of it. But having lost it, he was willing to please those who had won it. He was anxious to load the dice against Rose, and this could not be from any personal animus, for he was too thrifty to spend emotion on a person who could be of no material consequence to him. If he had been honest in his patriotism, and honest in his evidence, he should have felt grateful to Rose for the work he had done for Germany. So he must have aimed at pleasing the government which had flown him over to give evidence at this trial. With a careful air of impartiality he said that the Germans had never used threats to make Rose act as an informer. He carried out the work, said Mr. Wigge, and gave the impression that he was interested in it, and certainly never refused to do it. He expressed the opinion that Rose could have escaped if he had really wanted to, on quite a number of occasions, when he and Rose had gone for walks together. Asked if he had not always carried a gun on these walks he agreed that he had, but, asked if he would have shot Rose in the event of an escape, said that he would not. Nazis, apparently, never used guns to shoot people.

He was a persistent Nazi, and had the Nazi's charm and worth, but there was still another reason why his evidence gave pain. It appeared in a reply of his which revealed the flaw that is nearly always found in the performance of the virtuosic linguist. His English was perfect, but it had been crystallized at the age in which he learned it. Since those days he had shed no obsolete idiom and acquired no modern one. When he was talking of the liberty the informers had enjoyed he said that when any of them failed to return by midnight he assumed that they were "on the spree", a phrase descriptive of dissipation which has been outmoded for twenty years. It was as if a bad old gentleman were leering at one out of Mr. Wigge's words. But had he spoken in the purest classical English his evidence would have offended. Though certain Englishmen had sold their brothers for liquor and prostitutes, it would have been preferable not to hear their commerce reported with cool scorn in an English law court by the Nazi who was their pimp. By hearing this witness the trial was injecting itself with the offence which it was its intention to purge. For what is treachery? It is the betrayal of familiars to strangers, of those who are near to those who are far, of those to whom one is bound by real interest to those who, being foreign, will treat one as a foreigner and maybe, in the end, turn against one. To this dangerous error the court inclined itself by hearing Mr. Wigge, no matter if they called him Mr. Wiggy.

The truth is that it is the business of the army and the navy to fight upon land and sea and deal with the consequences of their wars and keep themselves well disciplined; but not to deal with serious crime at leisure. They have not the technique, and they have not the cold patience which makes for long views. The army is better than the navy, because it lives side by side with the law on land. The navy cultivates an intense wisdom about the sea and the ways of men in the isolation of ships which has necessarily to be counterbalanced by intense ignorance about the land and the ways of men in relation to the community as a whole. This court-martial of Stoker Rose shared certain vices with the army courts-martial of the traitors. It is the custom of the law not readily to accept evidence against a person accused of a crime from witnesses convicted or suspected of complicity in that crime, unless it is corroborated by the evidence of reputable witnesses. This rule was followed in most of the traitors' trials in the civil courts, with a few exceptions, but it has been violated in many courts-martial; and never so flagrantly as at the trial of Stoker Rose. When Martin had been tried on a charge of betraying to the Germans the position of a secret radio set in a prisoner-of-war camp, one of the prisoners who had been in control of the radio set gave evidence against him. But there were no such respectable witnesses called by the prosecution in the case of Stoker Rose. If Rose had left Marlag-Milag Nord not under compulsion but voluntarily, it was odd that no British Confidence officer came to speak of his departure. If Rose had collected information from British and American soldiers, it was odd that none of them were brought to Portsmouth to say so. Where was Sergeant Norman? Where were the eight officers that had stood behind the lamp in the castle near Coblenz? Where was the man from whom he had extracted information about the boom defence of Portsmouth Harbour? Those men could certainly have been traced. But it would have been a trouble to trace them. Some lawyer in Whitehall had known quite well that the navy would not know enough about the law to recognize the inadvisability of using tainted witnesses and had saved himself this trouble by using Martin, Galaher, White, and Wigge.

This malpractice was not censured by the court, which was oddly amateurish. In some ways it was a very gracious tribunal. It was pleasant to see the Deputy Judge-Advocate thank each of the witnesses for giving their evidence. They were the worst of men, but they were paying for their crimes, and he was not there to judge them. All that concerned him was that they should answer the questions that were asked them, and that they did. So to each he gave a friendly smile and said, "Thank you very much", and for a second restored them to their original value. But in other respects the court was unhappy. It was obvious that the naval officers trusted the Prosecuting Officer, because he spoke slowly in what seemed to them creditable contrast with the professional lawyers' suspicious fluency, but under cover of his sober delivery he was talking fantastically. He maintained that Mr. Wigge was a model of all that a witness should be: that in looking after the traitors he had simply been doing his duty as a good German, and that, having committed no crime against German law, he must be regarded not as a criminal but as a perfectly respectable person. But a man who goes about with a gun controlling the movements of a prisoner of war who has been removed from a prisoner-of-war camp against his will in order that he should collect information for his captors (and it was not disputed that this had happened) has violated Article 5 of Section II of the Geneva Convention relative to the treatment of prisoners of war, which deals with their molestation.

There was another point, not referring to the credibility of the witnesses but to the charge itself, in which the Prosecuting Officer seemed to move without the care that would have been imposed on him in a civilian court. It had become clear that any information about radar given by Rose must have been false because he knew nothing; but the Prosecuting Officer maintained that this did not make Rose any less of a traitor. For, he said, the indictment charged him with giving "intelligence" to the enemy, and the dictionary definition of "intelligence" was information, with nothing added to say whether it mattered that this information was true or false. Now it is true that prisoners of war are warned against giving false information: a lie may be very dangerous. It might draw the fire of the enemy from a spot where a military objective of a certain importance is situated to another spot where a military objective of still greater importance is situated. It might lead to a sudden outburst by the interrogating officer, who, detecting a lie, might bully the prisoner into a state of confusion in which he might give anything away. It might betray a vein of knowledge in the prisoner which would betray the existence of certain inventions or tactics. But Stoker Rose had never been warned of this danger, because, as his commanding officer had told the court, he was never given any security instruction; and he was certainly unable to work out the existence of this danger for himself. It was true, moreover, that no fixed rule could be based on the existence of this danger, for in practice many English and Americans working with the resistance movement in France and elsewhere used to give false information when they were captured in order to give their friends time to cover their tracks. These were points the judge in a civil court would have taken up with the lawyer who presented the case which, put forward by the Prosecuting Officer, this court accepted in silence.

The embarrassments of Stoker Rose were, however, not to last long after he returned from the singular visit to the castle of Coblenz, so far as the giving of information was concerned. For this was early in 1945. The informers' life had become more and more grim. As soon as White and Rose had come into the orbit of treachery Galaher and Martin had tormented them by a gloomy cynicism that was part of their tough-guy outfit: the sort of debunkedness that is heard in small and shabby saloons where men sit and congratulate themselves on having been hard-boiled enough to see through deceptions which, in fact, life never troubled to practise on them. "If you're doing this for a woman, it's not worth it." "Well, well, if you men will sign your own death warrants . . ." Such was their small talk. Galaher had had a considerable reverse. He had joined a working party of prisoners of war and had been recognized as an informer. The scars on his hands which had so perplexed the court at Portsmouth were left by the wounds he then received. Also, his face was left a bleeding jelly and several of his ribs were broken. He planned to escape in company with Rose, but was too drunken and nerve-rotten to keep his tryst on the appointed evening. Rose cut the barbed wire round their compound, but turned back when Galaher did not join him, and when the guards found the gap did not confess but let the whole camp take the blame. They drank, they quarrelled, they were lecherous and sentimental; Rose grew greatly excited about one of the whores the Germans had purveyed for the informers. But the real inflaming interest of their lives was the map of Europe, on which the Allies were tracing such invincible paths. They asked each other what they should do, and never answered. They implored the Germans to put them into a prison camp where they would not be known; and it was the ultimate baseness of the Germans that they refused to show this mercy to these men whom they had corrupted and exploited. According to White, Rose believed until the last moment that the German authorities were going to send him by plane to Sweden. But the bullies fell silent and fled, then the guards went; White and Rose found themselves their own masters and in mortal terror. They stole bicycles and rode towards the advancing Allied troops through deliquescent Germany, and at Munich they joined a working party of genuine prisoners of war. During this time Rose constantly asked White not to tell the authorities when he was repatriated that he had known him. On the 27th of February 1945 American troops inflicted on them the liberation they had dreaded. White and Rose were separated, the one having been in the army and the other in the navy, and for at least a time Rose must have believed that all was going to turn out better than he had hoped. In May he was sent back to England and he rejoined the navy. In August he was visited at Portsmouth Barracks by two of the great contemporary figures at Scotland Yard, J. M. C. Davis and Percy Edwards.

These are formidable people. Both of them are clean and neat in the manner of battleships, and they conceive of themselves as bringing the earth up to battleship standards. They stand for justice and not for mercy, and mercy is the better of the two; but the pleasures of mercy can be indulged in only behind the shelter of justice erected by such as Joe Davis and Percy Edwards. When they came to see Stoker Rose they knew a great deal about him. For White, as soon as the reports from the Confidence officers in the prisoner-of-war camps came in and the authorities showed signs of interest in him, had told everything he knew, and had provided a full and annotated list of all the persons with whom he had been associated during his life as an informer. To his prim and self-satisfied character it would not seem that thereby he showed himself a rogue ratting on his fellow-rogue. He would see himself as a respectable young man who, under duress, had been compelled into co-operation with a gang of criminals and naturally hastened to denounce them to the police the first moment he was free. In the list of persons he prepared for the authorities he included, obviously on the assumption that they were as criminal in coercing the prisoners of war to become informers as the prisoners of war were in becoming informers, Schaper and Mr. Wigge; and in that, common sense and international law were with him.

Armed with the knowledge derived from White, the two inspectors said to Rose, "Have you been to Luckenwalde?" He answered, "No, I've never been there." They asked him if he had been at Lamsdorff, and he denied that he had been there too, and told them a fake story of sojourns in other camps which in fact he had never visited, and of a period of hiding in France. He was asked if he had ever used the names of Johnson, Müller, Jones, and Aylmer, and he answered, "You've got me mixed up with someone else." He was asked if he knew Galaher and Martin and White, and he said that he had never heard of them. Then he was asked if he knew Schaper, and that appalling name was too much for him. He asked for time to think. Then he said, "What I've been telling you is lies. I did work for the Germans, but I only did it so that I could escape." He was still lying. He had worked with the Germans not so that he should escape, but so that he should go on living. In his continued agony he dictated a statement which was apparently insanely and unnecessarily incriminating and unusual in its abjection. But neither before his trial nor after would he consent to obey the request of the authorities and give evidence against Galaher, Martin, or White.

But when Stoker Rose's statement was brought forward by the prosecution it was disallowed. It is forbidden by the code known as the Judges' Rulings that the police should take a statement from an accused person by means of question and answer. In practice this is interpreted as a prohibition of leading questions: of questions, that is, which are so framed as to suggest or force certain answers. It cannot be carried out to the letter because an illiterate, temperamentally inarticulate person will often find it difficult to tell a story without being brought back to the point. Joe Davis and Percy Edwards are experienced officers and are perfectly aware of the required practice and faithful to it. But when they took this statement from Stoker Rose they were acting not as police officers but as Intelligence officers attached to the War Office, working on a matter in the "top secret" category, and they had not been so careful as usual to observe the conventions. The King's Counsel who appeared for Stoker Rose was glad and taxed them with having taken the statement by question and answer, and they at once admitted it. It might have been doubted whether this departure from the letter of the Judges' Rulings amounted to a violation of the Judges' Rulings as they are usually interpreted, but the court accepted the claim that the Judges' Rulings had been violated absolutely, and pronounced the statement inadmissible. The effect on Joe Davis and Percy Edwards was catastrophic. They had been taking statements for something not far under twenty years, and I doubt if in all that time they had had one pronounced inadmissible. For a minute it appeared as an intoxicating possibility that they would arrest the entire court-martial. There were visibly present in the court not merely two conflicting elements, the navy and civil law, there was a third—there was the police administration. The court was abashed at this. It wondered if it was handling the matter properly, and lost confidence; thereafter the court passed into a phase of wrangling over this and other legal formalities which needlessly extended the trial. Stoker Rose kept on breathing heavily and holding his mouth open in a little square, drawing his lips outward from the teeth as people do when they feel sick. Courts-martial always drag out longer than a comparable civil trial; and for him this was the dragging end of a prolonged ordeal, for five months had elapsed between his interview with the police and his arrest, and three more months had passed since then.

This court, being uneasy, did not take the opportunity, as a judge in a civil court would have done, to throw out at the earliest possible moment the two indictments which charged Stoker Rose with giving the Germans intelligence concerning radar equipment and the defences of Portsmouth. This was a pity, for if the case could have been purged of any of its offence the navy would have drawn its breath more easily. For, it is true, many men can form a single being, and that single being can grieve. The life of the barracks was usually hidden from us visitors, for we went in and out of the court-martial at times when the naval personnel was about its business, save for a few dark figures halting at the end of remote perspectives and looking towards the court-house to see what they could. But one day the court rose for lunch at an hour when the men were in their quarters, and from every window a row of intent and unsmiling faces, crowded towards the side from which they could see best, like beads pushed along the wire of an abacus, were looking down at the door of the court-martial house and waiting to see Stoker Rose brought out. There must have been hundreds of them, and none was speaking. The silence was absolute.

Not only that giant body, apprehensive lest it had lost its virtue, which it required as much as strength if it were to be strong, would have been relieved if the proper legal course had been followed; the whole town of Portsmouth would have breathed more easily. One night a young woman standing behind the bar of a Portsmouth hotel expressed herself in a monologue of which, in the opinion of two who heard her, this is an accurate enough transcription: "If he gave anything away about Portsmouth, and him a Portsmouth man, I hope they shoot him. Look what the Germans did to us. We kept that pub at the next corner, you've passed it every day going up to Dockyard, and it was just before the Christmas of 1940 we got ours. I shan't ever forget it. I was in the lounge, talking to a chap and a girl who were sitting at a table, and I was resting one hand on the table, and we were saying that surely we heard gunfire far away, and suddenly all the lights went out, and the silly thing was that I blamed it on my dad. To make the place a bit festive, he'd hung a line of fairy lights round the wall in and out among the pictures, and he'd been fidgeting about with them, and three times he'd fused the lights. So when it went dark I called out to him, 'Dad, you've been and gone and done it again'. And he came out of the bar and stood in the doorway quite close to me, and he said, 'Honest, I haven't touched the things since yesterday', and then it came down on us. The chap and the girl kept on calling to me, but my father never said another word. I put out my hand to him, and I could just touch the hem of his trousers, and I kept on trying to wriggle closer and closer to him, so that I could give him a real good nip and get some sort of a sound out of him. It never struck me he was dead, but of course he was, and so were the chap and the girl by the time they got us dug out. They took five and a half hours to get at us, and it seemed for ever. I could see the fireplace tilted forward and the fire still burning, and I said to myself, 'Sooner or later that'll set the place alight, and we'll all be burned alive', but it never did, and presently the fire went out. Then the rescue squad made a little window in the rubble and passed a cup of tea to me, but I couldn't get it up to my mouth, there was all sorts of rubbish and stuff round my face. Then they scraped away some more, and got my face clear, but I couldn't hold the cup right, the tea spilled down my dress, and I said, 'This isn't any use, give me a cigarette', and someone said, 'Bill, give her a cigarette', and someone else said, 'Give her a cigarette nothing, don't you know there's a gas escape round here?' So I just gave up, and the next thing I was on a stretcher rolled up in blankets, and I beat off the blankets. I said to them, 'I want to be free'. They took me off to hospital, and I went to sleep, and when I woke up the next morning I realized I hadn't a father, I hadn't the pub, I hadn't a stick of furniture or a rag of clothes, for of course what I was wearing when the bomb fell was in ribbons. Even the nightgown I was wearing wasn't my own. Then I went up to my brother's in Scotland, but after two months I said, 'I'm going home, I'm going back to Portsmouth'. He said, 'You're mad', and I said, 'I may be, but I won't be happy till I go back'. So I came back and I did war work in the harbour, and I stuck it to the end, but I was frightened all the time, and even now I sometimes wake up in the night feeling I want to beat away the blackness. But that's an improvement, for I used to have a light all night. So what I say is that if that little blackguard had anything to do with the bombing of Portsmouth, and him coming from the place, being like one of us, I'd like to get my hands on him."

Our schools give perfunctory instruction in patriotism; and this woman belonged to a sceptical generation which, however little was taught, distrusted it all. Her culture also did not put these words into her mouth; her favourite reading was *Picture Post*, without regional sentiment save for the Parks of Rest and Culture in the U.S.S.R. Her nature had without prompting sorrowed for her birthplace when it was wounded, and knew it the supreme misfortune of her tribe if a tribesman had procured its other misfortunes. It appeared that Stoker Rose had the same disposition to feel, under ordeal, emotions often alleged to be artificially fostered by the bourgeoisie, when it was time for him to give evidence. The tall lad, who was indeed old enough to be called a man but could not be so described without inexactitude, stood there more like than ever to a plant in need of staking. His fairness changed from negative to positive according to the light; now he was mouse-coloured, now he was golden. His nervousness, which was extreme, might have been charming to some. It must have given Schaper great pleasure to see this boy grow pale and droop at a threat of pain and revive at a promise of mercy. A sadist could hardly hope for more delicate meat.

He muttered that he had done nothing against his country. He repeated the story of how he had switched identities with Williams, and had then been taken out of his camp. It appeared that the agent who had been sent to fetch him was the odious Galaher, who had been described to him by the guards as a Gestapo agent. Galaher had taken him to Schaper, who had put him in a cell and later had come to him and said, "You know what the penalties are for helping people to escape. Nobody knows your identity now—you would never be missed if you disappeared". He kept on, Rose said, "threatening to have me done away with". Then he was turned out into a hut to live with Galaher and Martin and White, who picked a quarrel with him and tried to fight him. This nightmare had subdued him. He talked of it drowsily. Again it was in Shakespeare. Emilia asks Desdemona, after Othello has been raging at her, how she does; and Desdemona says, "Why, half asleep". It was natural enough, however, that the Royal Navy should fail to appreciate a stoker who resembled Desdemona. He confirmed the stories of the traitors that he had struggled in the net. He spoke of interviews with superior officials at which he had begged and prayed to be put back in a prisoner-of-war camp, and he swore that, though these efforts had been fruitless, he had not been a traitor. Had he signed a dossier concerning the defences of Portsmouth? Absolutely no. Had he ever had a post-office savings-bank account in Germany? Absolutely no. Had he ever signed a contract to work for the German High Command?

Absolutely no. He spoke without pride, not claiming, as Galaher and Martin and White had done, that he had been serving England. Simply he sighed that he had not betrayed her.

At last, when all specific charges had been denied, his examination ceased, and the Investigating Officer began to cross-examine him. The boy cringed before this man who wore the uniform of the service which he knew he had disgraced, and agreed with him whenever he could. Though he persisted that he had never been instructed not to tell the Germans anything but his name, rank, and number, he accepted the far-fetched suggestion that he should have deduced this instruction from the "Careless Talk Costs Lives" which he had seen on English walls before he sailed; and meekly he admitted that, although it was true that Schaper had threatened him, it was also true that he had never put these threats to the test; and that he had never made a determined attempt to escape. Nor did he lose his patience when the Investigating Officer sternly taxed him with inconsistency because he had once described as "moonshine" the bottle of spirits which Schaper gave him at one of his interrogations and at another time had described it as cognac. The cross-examination was interrupted by one of those unpleasant incidents which are bound to crop up when a trial is held in unsuitable premises. The statement taken by Joe Davis and Percy Edwards had been pronounced inadmissible. That is, the court was supposed never to know what confessions he had made in the course of that statement. But when the Investigating Officer asked Stoker Rose certain questions he consulted and read from a document which, as the courtroom was so small, could be clearly recognized by the President and the rest of the court as Stoker Rose's statement. It then became perfectly obvious what had been in the statement, and it was as much a part of the court proceedings as if it had been admitted. The King's Counsel, who was defending Rose, steamed with a sense of injustice, and the gentle Deputy Judge-Advocate, his left hand combing his hair with his spectacles and his right hand jerking free his sword, which kept on getting wedged against the leg of his chair, provided a picture of a good man who has got mixed up in something he does not feel happy about, which would have been recognized anywhere. But Stoker Rose drooped in the dock, unresentful of injustice, borne down by noise. He was ensphered in a certain resolution. He had been a coward in Germany. He was determined not to be a coward in England. He was not going to lie to save his skin; and in excess of abnegation bent his neck beneath the yoke of what this man told him was the truth. In his examination he had denied that he knew anything of a sum of eight thousand dollars he and Galaher and White were supposed to have to their credit in a Berlin bank. But now some recollection of the traitors' trade babble came back to him, and he stuttered, with desperate accuracy, that he remembered taking part in talk of some such sum. His efforts at accuracy, made in the confusion of abject fear and its counter-blast of suicidal courage, were further complicated because he had accepted the Investigating Officer's extreme theory of the equal criminality of giving the enemy false and true information, and he spoke continually, and with an air of shame, of communications he had made to the Germans which were in fact nonsense. At last, when he had covered himself with a web, the Investigating Officer said to him, "I suggest to you that right from the start you knew that what you were doing was wrong. Is that not so?" The boy did not answer for a long time. His face became greenish-white, then the discoloration cleared and left it steadfast, though still languid. "Yes, sir," he said. It was the truth, and he told it when he was being cross-examined on a capital charge.

The moment was, from his point of view, satisfactory. He had always known that he should have resisted the Germans to the point of death, and he felt cleansed by this confession of long-standing cowardice, which was of the sort that is more usually made to a priest or a parent than to a lawyer in court. Plainly he felt about this Investigating Officer as young Kenneth Edward had felt about Captain Notman. So deep did this confession mine in the young man's nature that it satisfied the demands of art; on its revelation a writer could have founded a novel. That revelation was touching; his confession pleased by its desperate candour. But that the spectator knew because Stoker Rose knew it. He had said, "I am inferior to the Investigating Officer because I did not uphold the values that he has always upheld". He had gone down into the depths of his nature, he came up again elated because he had dared to do so. A minute later his own counsel asked him, "Did you do what you did with the purpose of betraying your country?" He answered, with a new strength, "Absolutely no, sir". "Why did you do it?" asked his counsel. He answered, "I had no alternative", and added with a little laugh, "I was frightened to death". "You mean," said the counsel with a smile, "you were frightened of your life." They were both eased, because the exact truth, as the boy saw it, had been told.

That ended the third day of the trial. On the morning of the fourth day Rose was called back into the witness-box to answer two questions put by the President of the Court. He was asked if on repatriation he had reported the activities of Galaher, Martin, and White. He answered that he had not, because he knew he had been mixed up with unscrupulous characters. This was not a very sensible question, for a man in Rose's position could hardly be expected to volunteer a statement which would certainly incriminate him. Then the President asked, "While a prisoner of war, did you at any time represent your particular case to anyone in authority in the Allied Forces?" and Rose answered, "No, I was too frightened". Again, this question was not so sensible as it sounded. The case of Kenneth Edward had shown that British Confidence officers in the same camp from which Rose was abducted had been utterly unable to help an unhappy boy who had been caught in the web of treachery, and had even thought it wiser not to mention his name to the German authorities. Then Rose went back into the dock, and was succeeded by people who spoke of the innocence which coexisted in him with his guilt. The first was a petty officer named Ellenore, a sturdy young naval officer who had been in camp with Rose when he was first captured. He remembered very well how Rose had switched identities with Williams, and how this had been discovered, how the German guards had said that a Gestapo agent was coming, how Galaher had arrived and taken Rose away with him. When he had not returned, Ellenore asked what had become of him, and for that was at once thrown into a cell. "What happened to you then?" asked Rose's attorney. "I was beaten into unconsciousness", said Ellenore. He smiled as he said it, holding his round head high and straightening his short spine, unaffected by the memory. Again, as at all the treason trials, the injustice of nature was apparent. It was not fair that Ellenore should have a compact and controllable body through which his blood coursed at a good sensible speed, not rushing at every fear from his face to his heart and back again, to the total confusion of his thought, while Rose should have this lank body, difficult to mobilize by the will, a long hiding-ground for his timid life. Ellenore himself spoke of this difference with the direct unsentimental sympathy of a realist, and told how he had several times taken Rose to the sick bay because he had fainted. There was a B.B.C. monitor to say that there had been no broadcast from London about a raid on Portsmouth such as Galaher had spoken of in his testimony. Two witnesses came to tell how well behaved a lad he had been in earlier days. Rose's father, Jack Rose, former stoker in the Royal Navy, son of a naval rating, grandson of a soldier in Queen Victoria's army, was as pitifully spruce, as closely shaven, as the fathers of accused persons not previously in trouble are apt to be. He said that he had never had any trouble with his son at all. "He has always been a very good boy to his mother", he said. Last came an old man with thick white hair, a city councillor, the coal merchant who had employed both Roses, father and son, to drive his lorries. He spoke in the deep, slow accents of the West Country, and his voice was burdened with the woefulness the old feel when they fear that the story which they hoped was going to end peacefully is to be disrupted by one of those catastrophes they hoped they had outlived. He said that he had known young Rose ever since he was born, and his character was "wonderful good". He had never known him to refuse duty, and if the foreman was up a tree, all he had to do was to ask the boy to lend a hand. This evidence was plainly true. Stoker Rose was a most biddable lad. Every time he had coughed in court—and he had quite a troublesome cough—he had been mindful to raise his hand and cover his mouth, as he had been taught when he was a child. Again, the injustice of the world was manifest. It was iniquitous that these prim and decent men should have been put to live in this wild world, where there was war and fear and lust and grief.

The court adjourned to give its verdict. Outside, the town passed the time quickly enough for those who cared to take a stroll. It seemed sometimes less like a town than the setting of a ballet, because of the troops of nimble sailors. Over the main street a low bridge runs to the railway station, and across it coursed a party of bluejackets, carrying their long blue-grey kit-bags that look as if each might hold a swaddled girl: a leaping, bounding frieze of figures, large and dark against the sky, free from care now, yet still not free from the mark of discipline. The pillars of the great Guildhall now surround nothingness; behind its hollow menace there is a cosy public park, set thick with memorials to naval campaigns and disasters erected by the survivors in the days when campaigns kept their distance, disaster confined itself to moderate figures. One memorial bore a testy inscription: "This monument was removed from Town Hall Square at the request of the survivors". There must have been a godalmighty row, but it happened in the early 'nineties, nobody will ever know the truth of it now. A Wren officer, handsome and middle-aged, confided to a stranger: "I have to leave the Wrens in a few weeks. I am so miserable. I do not know what to do. I have no family life, and I will have to look for a room, and God knows where I shall find it. And when I do, I shall be so lonely. Here, when I come in at night, there are always people I like, but in a room of my own I shall have nobody, and I am too old to make new friends." In a cage there was a marmoset, very engaging with its fine black guide-hairs rising from its downy yellow-brown pelt. Some boys were giving it little ice-cream cones, and it licked up the first, and it licked up the second, but the third it did not eat. Very gravely it looked from face to face of those who were standing in front of the cage, like an old yogi in search of an apt pupil. Suddenly it sent the ice-cream cone flying over our clothes, shrieked in joy and turned a somer-sault, in salutation of the spring that was pushing the blue scillas through the black earth in the beds near by. A gate led out to the ruined district by the harbour. A walk between chestnut trees looked as if it went to a church, and indeed at the end of it was a high house which had an air of hieratic difference from an ordinary dwelling, which might have been a presbytery when it had windows or floors or a roof, and beside it the long grass grew to the edge of a pavement of coloured marbles. It kept its past a secret as blitzed buildings do not often do. It was impossible to find where the altar had been, or the pulpit, or the font. This

262

was disturbing, like looking at a clock-face and finding it was inscribed with some unknown measure of time. A woman setting out her baby in a pram to sleep in the spring sunshine said that it had been, not a church, but a synagogue. Such differences are there between minute and minute and between acre and acre. A man who is kept to the same square yard or so of a cell and has his time artificially drained of variation must miss them sadly.

But, by a curious custom, all the witnesses at a court-martial are set in the front rows of the court to hear the verdict. The expert on radar sat between Mr. Wigge and little White, who pursed his mouth as if he would like to whistle, just to show that he did not care what anybody thought of him. Percy Edwards and Joe Davis, who, since the rejection of their statement, had been looking on the proceedings with the melancholy disdain of aristocrats painted by Van Dyke, sat on each side of Martin and Galaher, who were divided by the captain of the boat on which Rose had served. At the end of the row sat the B.B.C. monitor, and then Jack Rose and the white-haired old coal merchant. These men's faces were as distinct as notes of a scale; in a row they made a phrase of wild music. They had their eyes fixed on the prisoner, who was drooping in the dock, the Master-at-Arms' naked sword a bright erect line behind his head. He did not return their gaze, his face was twitching, his too-mobile blood was there and went and came again. The President of the Court announced that the court had found him guilty of the first charge, which related to treacherous correspondence with the enemy, but innocent of the two charges relating to the communication of intelligence concerning radar and the defences of Portsmouth. The boy's head rolled forward and he swayed. Then he was taken from the dock, and the court was cleared, for, by a raw cruelty of procedure, a court-martial pronounces its verdict, then retires again and deliberates on the sentence. Where there is a jury and one judge, the jury brings in the verdict; if it be "guilty", evidence regarding the prisoner's character is given, and the judge makes up his mind on the spot; but where there are several judges who are also the jury, as is the case in a court-martial, they have necessarily to retire before they can pronounce sentence. That this delay is made inevitable by the form of the court does not make it any easier for the prisoner to bear. Stoker Rose had been found guilty of a capital charge. He might have been sentenced to be shot and he had to wait for nearly an hour before he knew that that was not the intention of the court; and he must have suspected, as we all did, that such a delay meant that some of the court had been in favour of shooting him. Then the witnesses were led again into the front row. They sat in a different order this time, though Jack Rose and the old coal merchant were careful still to sit together. They did indeed need each other's company. For the president announced that the court had sentenced Stoker Rose to sixteen years' penal servitude.

The announcement stunned and horrified and, at the same time, amused, for the severity of the sentence entailed a certain drollness; a man who puts too much of his strength into a swinging blow falls over. The seven men in gold lace and blue serge sitting at the long table now seemed absurdly naïve. That side of the courtroom was like a magnified scene from a Punch and Judy show, while the other side, where the pale and awkward boy quailed under the respite from death which was too harshly conditional to be a relief, was like a scene from a school play representing a martyrdom, perhaps because he was now too exhausted to feel anything more than remote and clouded emotion. A more lively despair was made manifest on the face of White, though his expression had but slightly changed. He had yet to be tried, and now knew what he might expect, and was in any case being at this time horribly savaged by the demon which takes charge of the services in their relations with the law. This demon, which means no harm, was taking enormous trouble to protect White's dignity, during his presence at Rose's trial, by backing the truck which brought him to and from his jail so that nobody should see him as he crossed the pavement, and by preventing anybody from meeting him in the corridors. But it was shutting him up throughout the trial (and he was obliged to attend it every day) in a small room with Galaher and Martin, against whom he had given evidence, who, as all parties knew, were to give evidence against him. According to his testimony at that trial they told him they were going to "fix him". Whether these words were spoken or not, the act of enferming persons joined in this horrible relationship for four days in a small room is of a sort that might well be left to the jail authorities in Hell.

As the boy moved dreamily out of the dock and was led away by the man who held a naked sword, we were left in confusion. For an immediate discredit fell on the total protest a humane person would wish to feel against a sentence which sent a man to prison from the time he was twenty-three till he was thirty-nine for an act committed under the dread of extreme violence. It was certainly an excessive sentence compared with the standards set by the civil courts, which had been sending people of a like degree of culpability to prison for periods varying from three to seven years. But about one pressed in men with stern though sometimes very young faces, who pitied Stoker Rose yet wanted no gentler justice for him than he had received. They said various things, but what they all meant was that members of the fighting forces should, owing to the extreme temptations by which they are beset, be protected by stronger deterrents than civilians, for the sake of both the individual and the services. Without passion these men and boys explained their special need for penalty, as scientists who work on atomic energy might explain their special need for cumbersome protective uniforms. As for the argument that it is harsh to call a man to account for what he does under the threat of death, all of us knew the graves, in land or under water, which answer it. Certainly these men and boys had the right to the last word. There was therefore no opportunity for the bland, relaxing happiness of mercy, no escape from the boundless horror of a heroic age.

Yet, after some months, the sentence was reduced. The Sea Lords brought it down to five years: perhaps because justice, like everything else, cannot be overstrained, and the severity of sixteen years retained its drollness under scrutiny; perhaps because the trial had been so rich in irregularities such as the indiscreet visibility of the inadmissible statement. It was young White who, in the end, was to be given the larger sentence. None of his kin came to the great house in Park Lane where he was tried early that summer. Sitting on the kitchen chair in the fine room under the high gilt-and-plaster ceiling, he looked a tired wisp. He had been nearly a year in custody. His neatness and the careful combing of his strange upright palisade of wavy hair made a claim to self-respect. The evidence of the Intelligence officer who had first examined him showed that, like young Kenneth Edward and Stoker Rose, he had believed absolutely in the standards he had violated. He had felt shame before this man as Kenneth Edward had felt it before Captain Notman, as Stoker Rose had felt it before the Investigating Officer. Galaher and Martin gave their odious testimony, odious as his had been, and he looked primly past them. After the court had brought in a verdict of guilty he walked alone down the great staircase, his small, canny face—grave with self-exhortation to take the inevitable sensibly—floating in many places on the walls, in the drowned distances of the old mirrors. In the hall waited his guards to take him back to prison, where he was to spend several weeks, according to the barbarous custom of military trials, before he learned that he had been sentenced to ten years' imprisonment. By comparison with Stoker Rose's five years his sentence was as heavy as it would have seemed light if the Admiralty authorities had upheld Stoker Rose's original sentence of sixteen years. Sentences cannot, in any system of jurisprudence, be standardized, because guilt is not standardized; but this is an irregularity beyond reason. Furthermore, after some time, White was pardoned and released. It is impossible to imagine a civilian prisoner being subjected to such an agony of suspense who was so mildly dyed with offence that his release after such a brief imprisonment could be contemplated. Such disharmonies as these show that the court-martial is a very wild garden indeed.

But it was not the penalties suffered by Stoker Rose and White which make them so notably pathetic; it was the futility of their sufferings. The whole elaborate drama had been completely pointless. What they had done had seemed at least to have had the justification of serving the Germans' purposes; but it had no such effect. Mr. Wigge had been very naïve when he said that the traitors' activities had been useless because the silly Allied prisoners had known nothing. For it was not with the traitors as he, and they, thought. The predominant condition of their lives must have seemed to them loneliness. When they spoke of themselves they sounded solitary as one had not thought men still alive could be. Galaher told of a Christmas party they had held in their hut: the Germans had given them some extra rations, cake and wine and brandy, and had allowed them to ask their favourite prostitutes. (The ill luck which dogged Stoker Rose was faithful to him here: his girl-friend could not come.) No explorers among Arctic snows, no shipwrecked sailors on a desert island, could have been so far from human fellowship as these wretched creatures, who were not only physically but spiritually divided from all people they had ever known except a few of their enemies. So they believed; but were mistaken, for at the same time they were bathed in a strong light which they themselves could not see. Hundreds of thousands of men, of several nations, had been instructed in their names, all details of their appearances, and their designs. Their fame had run from lip to lip, as if they were great statesmen or soldiers or comedians. For complete descriptions of all the informers, at a very early stage in their operations, had been sent through the channel of communications which was, by means not yet revealed, maintained throughout the war between the prisoner-of-war camps and England, and were circulated among all persons likely to become prisoners of war. So the degradation of Stoker Rose and his fellows had served no purpose, not even an evil one. It was sheer waste. There was no answer to that sum but zero.

III

CHILDREN sometimes go away with strangers who offer them cakes and sweets; and the ending of that story is not usually happy. Whoever loves a child will leave it with its natural protectors unless they are false to their trust, and then the loving stranger buys the child, if he can, but does not steal it. Stealing is not the way of love. It is, however, the way of lust, and of crime seeking an accomplice; and once the child has submitted to the act of lust, once it has crept through the narrow window and opened the door from within, it becomes a tedious burden and a potential betrayer. It may even inspire fear simply by being what it is. A child, seen in twilight by a person with disordered nerves, may be mistaken for a malignant dwarf; and crime is a dusk, and criminals often overtax their own serenity.

The children who go from their homes with strangers because they have been given cakes and sweets are unsustained by pride when the unkindness falls on them. They know well that they have done wrong. A person should be loyal to his father and mother, to his brothers and sisters, to his friends, to his town or village, to his province, to his country; and a person should do nothing for a bribe, even if it takes the form of a promise that he should live instead of die. This is the faith which such children hold: to which they feel they must be true, if they are to be saved, if they are to be loved, by others or by themselves. When Kenneth Edward came face to face with the jovial serenity of Captain Notman, when Stoker Rose was asked by the Investigating Officer if he had not known what he was doing was wrong; when White sat down with the Intelligence officer and told him all he had done, opening his breast to him with surgical honesty: it was apparent that this was the faith in which they believed, that they felt themselves lost because they had betrayed it, and that they looked up to these men who had been true to it as, according to ancient cosmogonies, the damned look up at the happy in heaven. This attitude was clearly distinguishable from regret for having been on the losing side, and it was not feigned; the rush of blood from the cheek after the shameful admission, the greenish swaying sickness of repentance, are inimitable. It is not an attitude which has been taught them by an exploiting class. They were born into a tongue-tied age, and neither their school-teachers nor the culture within their reach had given them such positive instruction. The judgment they passed on their own disloyalty and the loyalty of others was a spontaneous reaction to experience. Those who would call them foolish to suffer for having violated a faith so local, so provincial, so national, should consider what satisfaction they derived from their international ties: with Plack, who did not answer letters; with vigilant Mr. Wigge; with the playful Herr Oberleutnant Schaper, rolling on the grass. Their parents were kinder to them: with whom they can never be as they were, since with the natural parental love there now coexists a natural consternation, a natural horror.

IV

THE NEW PHASE

I

WITHIN two years of the end of the Second World War the stream of prosecutions of British persons charged with treacherous relations with the enemy became a trickle and dried up. The Emergency Powers (Defence) Act, 1939, was allowed to expire on February 24, 1946. It is true that after this date an Englishman was tried for broadcasting in occupied Paris, and that his case was taken to the Court of Appeal and to the House of Lords; but the space he covers in the law reports was not due to any special desire of the law to punish him, but to the need for discovering whether the words "the expiry of this Act shall not affect the operation thereof as respects things previously done or omitted to be done" could be interpreted as meaning that a prosecution could be validly launched after the Act had lapsed on account of acts committed while it was in force. It was hideously appropriate that this particular defendant should have been the occasion for this orgy of word-chopping, for he was one of the most famous litigants of the past half-century. A man of exceptional gifts, much beloved by his family, he had offered up his life in martyrdom to an idea connected with insurance finance. He and his wife were caught at the outbreak of the war in Germany, and a series of horrible misfortunes then engulfed them and their children, to whom he was devoted. This most unhappy man was typical of the company in whose wake he travelled, the persons accused of acting in concert with the Germans, in that what he had done could plainly connect with nothing in the future. He and the rest had all been hobbled by some constraining factor, which had prevented them from running away in time when the great rocks of the Nazi cataclysm had dropped down the cliff of history. Their tragedies were linked to that particular event. Whether they were alive or dead, that particular catastrophe could never happen to them again or to anybody else; and the flavour of their other trials was already as definitely dated as a Victorian breach-of-promise case or an eighteenth-century impeachment.

But treachery was not a peculiar product of the war between Great Britain and Germany. It is a business which has been carried on since the beginning of history. Faint cries from the past tell us how the Illyrians were ashamed when those of their blood without pride worked for Rome, and how Central Europe blushed over the renegades who joined the yellow barbarian hordes; and the Republic of Venice entered on its books the figures of its competition in the traitor-market on the Mediterranean coasts with the great corrupter, Islam, who for centuries made aliens like William Joyce beys and pashas and tutors to the children of its great, and picked the Islam Free Corps from the galley-slaves. The traitors who stood in the dock in the Old Bailey were enduring their two-hundredth incarnation or so, allowing three generations to a century and putting the first complicated civilization in the fourth millennium before Christ. There is always loyalty, for men love life and could not survive if they did not faithfully gather together to protect themselves from the uncaring universe. So there is always treachery, since there is the instinct to die as well as the instinct to live, hatred as well as love; and as loyalty changes to meet the new threat against survival which is brought by every age, so treachery changes also.

Six months after the hanging of William Joyce, the most remarkable representative of the phase of treachery which ended with the defeat of Germany, there followed him into the dock at the Old Bailey Dr. Alan Nunn May, Lecturer on Physics in the University of London, who represented the new phase of treachery. The community condemned in the person of William Joyce the extrovert who sought to find in politics what in other ages he would have found in religion, and made his search on the field of fascism, with its marches, its bands, its shouting, its bright colours, its blows, its violence. Dr. Alan Nunn May was the personification of the introvert who makes the same transference but is better pleased by the secrecy and drabness of communism: which is fascism with a glandular and geographical difference. He was a scientist, and in that was as representative of his breed of fascism as Joyce had been of his. For the New Fascists, the new traitors, who stepped forward after the war to carry on the old business under a different label, were, in England, under scientific domination. It had been the claim of the violent men who formed the Nazi-Fascist movement that they should be entrusted with power because they were endowed with a greater amount of physical strength and vitality than the mass of the population: an amount which would enable them to seize that power if it were denied them. It was now the claim of the scientists who formed so influential a part of the Communist-Fascist movement that they were endowed with a greater amount of special technical knowledge than the mass of the population: an amount which would enable them to seize that power if it were denied them. There is a similarity between the claims of the Nazi-Fascists and the Communist-Fascists, and no less similarity between the methods of putting them forward. The claims depend on an unsound assumption that the man who possesses a special gift will possess also a universal wisdom, which will enable him to impose an order on the state superior to that contrived by the consultative system known as democracy: which will enable him, in fact, to know other people's business better than they do themselves.

If this assumption seems less patently absurd when it is applied to a scientist, the reason is simply the dizzy novelty of science. The study of physics or chemistry is no more likely than the study of harmony or counterpoint to develop social omniscience in the student; nor have these or any other branches of science made any contributions to the technique of government which would give them any right to intervene as experts. It frequently happens that the B.B.C. asks certain Communist scientists to speak about the age we live in, and they are all remarkable for the vanity with which they claim that the advance of science has at last made it possible for man to contemplate a planned and abundant economy for the world. But modern science has, in fact, done almost nothing to give man the precognizance necessary for planning, and still less to guarantee any kind of useful abundance. It cannot foretell or control the foundation of all economy, which is weather. It has not yet found a way of providing cheap houses, or a cheap and convenient source of light and heat and energy, or a cheap and reliable food supply. The groundless boasts were, like the equally groundless boasts of the Nazi-Fascists, covers for a threat. Mussolini and Hitler, when they said that they and their followers could govern because of their physical strength and ruthlessness, meant that they and their followers had enough physical strength and ruthlessness to beat and shoot anyone who refused to be governed by them. The Communist scientists, who say that they and their associates could govern because of their technical knowledge, mean that they and their associates play a sufficient part in the development of modern processes used in modern war and industry to be able to blackmail society if it will not accept their dictation. The one demand is as absurd as the other. Obviously any fragile doctor or research worker has as much right as any brawny Fascist to have his say in the conduct of the community; and obviously any teacher, or any factory hand, or any house-wife, is as necessary to the state as a scientist and has as much right to self-government. If it is asked why scientists, who of necessity must have a certain amount of intelligence, should be Communist-Fascists, it can be answered that the British and American scientists come from a group which has been deprived of its defences against absurdity, and especially against totalitarian absurdity, by their social origins.

II

BRITISH and American scientists are drawn from the intellectuals of their two countries: that is, from a section of the English middle classes, or from American groups profoundly influenced by the culture of that section. Intellectuals may be defined as persons whose natural endowments and education give them the power to acquire experiences of a rich and varied order, usually linked in some degree or other with learning and the arts, and, furthermore, to analyse their experiences and to base generalizations on the results of the analyses conducted by them and their fellows. They are essentially gregarious. They pool their experiences, they conform in their conclusions, nobody can be an intellectual all by himself. That is why William Joyce, though he had an intellect capable of passing exacting academic tests, could never be called an intellectual. His Anglo-Irish loyalist tradition and his early Irish background made it impossible for him to fit into the conventional groove. Intellectuals are thrown up for the most part by the middle classes. Though there have been notable exceptions, such as Bertrand Russell, the old landowning class bound its young too closely to the services and to politics and to estate management to give them much time for the life of debate; and the industrialists have always been too busy. Intellectuals thrown up from the lower classes immediately pass, in this country, into the middle classes.

It is the function of intellectuals to enable society to adapt itself to changing conditions: which is, indeed, to attack the essential problem of politics. But while there are few functions so important, there are few so constantly subject to degeneration. A lazy intellectual, or an intellectual who has adopted the vocation with insufficient equipment, can pretend that he is discharging that function simply by attacking the *status quo*, without regard for justice, and without giving any indication of what he proposes to substitute for it. This actually gives him an advantage over the constructive intellectual, for in destruction wit and irony can more easily come into play. He will often have dynamic force behind his wit, because the intellectual who had not a religious sense of the duty of selflessness burned till recently with the grievance that unless he was a man of fortune he could not gain a position of power. He felt this more and more as the nineteenth century went on, for the industrial revolution had created a new field of power other than that which had been cultivated by the landed aristocracy. There is an immense ominousness in Matthew Arnold, with his rage against the Philistinism of the manufacturing classes, which was defiling the English mind as the smoke from their factories' chimneys was defiling the English sky, and his anguished, nostalgic love of the traditional English culture based on classical studies, and therefore on the existence of a leisured class under no compulsion to follow utilitarian studies. He rightly supposed that there were far more aristocrats than manufacturers who could understand and value him. It was most sinister, though it seemed most innocent, that in his distress he looked for comfort to a country other than his own: to Germany, which in that age was the country from which there had come the Prince Consort, Christmas trees, the music of Mendelssohn.

Every decade of the nineteenth century was to produce more

and more Matthew Arnolds, who were to feel furiously that by all traditional standards they formed the superior class of the community, the sages and the prophets, and that they were wholly disregarded by a rising class of industrial tyrants. They dealt with their fury in two ways. Either they clung to the old landowning aristocracy, with something often difficult to distinguish from snobbery but actually concerned with deeper matters. For an example of that form of adaptation we can turn to an alien who, when his discontent took the usual form of looking to another country for salvation, looked to ours. The English landowning aristocracy, transplanted to America, had found it physically impossible to cover the vast and ever-expanding terrain, and was a weakly growth except in certain localities, whereas the industrial revolution had been, as gardeners say, a good grower, and its flowers of Philistinism were lush. Henry James simply turned his back on the distressing scene and went to England and basked in the sunshine which still, though with diminishing strength, warmed the terraces of the great houses. His correspondence illustrates the curious historical fact that the nineteenth century, which knew few vestiges of the system of patronage, can show many more respectful letters from intellectuals to aristocrats than the eighteenth century, when peers were really patrons.

But if the intellectual chanced to be neither a rich American, nor a writer successful enough to be lionized, nor a scholar holding authority in a public school or university, he could not range himself with the landed aristocracy, because he would be too obscure to attract its attention. Friendless, he would rage alike against the old class which had held power and the new class which was taking it from them; and he would find relief in attacking the capitalist system which maintained them both. In this enterprise he found certain important allies. Chief among them were the humanitarian members of all classes who were becoming revolted by the cruelties inflicted by capitalism on those who were unable, for one reason or another, to share in the benefits it was conferring on the country as a whole, and the industrial workers who were gathering together to demand a larger share of the profits which industry was creating. This meant that the intellectuals joined the procession which was formed by a union between the humanitarian section of the Liberal Party and the idealistic but legitimately acquisitive Labour Party. They were, however, not entirely contented. The Liberal Party consisted largely of Whig aristocrats and Philistine industrialists, who carried more weight than the humanitarians and took no notice of their intellectual friends; and the Labour Party was dominated by industrial workers who had a deep distrust of intellectuals and thought them just another type of toff. English intellectuals might have become as purely academic and politically ineffective as their French colleagues at this period, had they not found exceptional leaders in Sidney and Beatrice Webb.

Both these gifted people were animated by a special discontent. Sidney Webb had a deep understanding of the administrative problems of the modern state; and it was most unlikely that he would ever be in a position where he could communicate this understanding to society, because he belonged to the lower middle class, and though he had many endearing qualities lacked the social charms which opened the doors of great houses. Beatrice Webb had talents of the same sort to an unusual degree, and they burned with a fiery brilliance because they had been set alight by a fierce resentment. Her diaries frankly confess what she was: a member of the wealthy industrialist class, bitterly jealous of the landowning aristocracy which had a longer title to power and often failed to conceal that they looked on her class as intruders. She despised the proletariat. Few people have written of the rank-and-file Socialist more savagely than she did. But even more did she dislike people who lived in houses with useless parks round them, people who gave their little boys ponies, people who had their own private libraries and picture galleries. Now she and her husband recognized that the modern state was becoming so complicated that it would have to be governed by a bureaucracy of experts, and they embarked on a long campaign to form the young intellectuals of their day into an army of experts which should be the cadre of this bureaucracy, while at the same time they influenced the policy of the Labour Party so that it would call this army into action as soon as possible. They were, in fact, planning to pick up power when it fell from the hands of the industrialists as it had fallen from the hands of the landowners.

They were aided by the support of the two most interesting young writers of their time, Wells and Shaw, who also were animated by discontent. Wells was full of justified proletarian resentments. His mother was the housekeeper in a great house, and he knew the agreeable life from which those without property were excluded. He had been phthisical in his youth and had suffered a grave internal injury when playing football, and had felt the panic realization of insecurity which was then the lot of the sick poor. Worst of all, he had an exceptional intelligence and had to fight to get it trained. He was also to know the intellectual's sense of impotence in the form most relevant to the special case of the Communist-scientist. By a miracle of courage and persistence he wrested from society a degree in science, and with his quick, glancing mind grasped sooner than most of his colleagues what innumerable windows, looking on what fantastic views, were going to be opened by modern scientific discovery. He was therefore repelled by the lack of imagination shown by the non-scientific minds of the age, who were, indeed, quite strangely blind to both the threats and the promises which were being held out to society by science, even when they might themselves have derived profit and security from examining them. It is staggering to realize for how long British industry grudged spending money on research, and how the need for mechanization of our armed forces was worked out on paper not many years after the South African War, though professional soldiers were still resisting it till quite a late date after the First World War. Wells had, therefore, a number of legitimate grievances against society, and so had Shaw, though his were fewer, less searing, and more drily historical. He was the son of a poor gentleman, and was in his youth so literally penniless that he often lacked clothes fit to be worn in the street; he was also Anglo-Irish, member of one of the ascendancy families whose ascendant days were numbered. He was white-hot, and Wells was red-hot, and they were as good as a combined firework and bonfire show for drawing sightseers, who, as they gaped at the astonishing brightness, necessarily drew into their lungs much of the political atmosphere of the group.

The Webbs were not successful in some of their dearest enterprises. Their army of experts was apparently not trained on quite the right lines, and furnished few of the contemporary leaders of the Labour Party. It might almost be said that Dr. Hugh Dalton is the only rose-bush which has sprung from the Webbs' grave. But the Webbs did much positive work. Till they set up in business our local government system was an uncharted jungle, and they took it over as if they were a highly efficient Woods and Forests Department. It would be incautious to ascribe to the influence of the Webbs any great part in the making of the Beveridge Report on which our present welfare state is founded, but it must be remembered that Lord Beveridge was for many years Director of the London School of Economics, which the Webbs brought into being, and no one could direct that mighty engine of research without being in some degree also directed by it. The Webbs also urged their followers to whip up their energies and follow all sorts of political activities, including standing for local government offices; and for that reason the English Left Wing has been preserved from the lack of practical experience which makes the Northern Liberalism of the United States so sterile. They were positive indeed, and so, following different paths, were their literary supporters. Wells revolted against them, partly because he found any form of co-operation impossible, partly because he was fundamentally demo-cratic and saw that the logical consequence of their bureaucratic theories was dictatorship. Ruddy with excitement over life, he went his own way, alone in his time dreaming dreams of the future which matched its strangeness when it came, bringing to life characters rich as life itself makes them, spilling over into history and theology, and by the use of the technique of free thinking coming to an oddly Christian conclusion: that there is a glory, and that man by himself cannot lay hold on it, and that man and the glory ought to meet, for man is lovable. Shaw, just as excited but pale, went on with his life-work of injecting the tired English prose of the late nineteenth century with the genius of eighteenth-century prose, which had been laid up, not in lavender, but some more pungent herb, over in Ireland. He refused to follow the fashion set by the Victorian and Edwardian playwrights and look at man through the wrong end of the opera-glasses; his plays showed characters not merely as involved in social and sexual imbroglios but as making choice between salvation and damnation. Many of the rank and file of the Webbs' followers were positive in their own lesser ways, as civil servants, teachers, doctors, lawyers, bringing a certain new initiative and conscientiousness to their work. The women among them were moved to much usefulness; many of the voluntary institutions for the care of mother and children which were taken over by the National Health Service were founded and carried on by such women. But positive as both the leaders and followers were, they lived in an atmosphere of negativism. The foundation of their creed was the assumption that there was nothing in the existing structure of society which did not deserve to be razed to the ground, and that all would be well if it were replaced by something as different as possible. They were to do it quietly, of course; but the replacement was to be absolute. To them the past was only of value in so far as it gave indications of how to annul the present and create a future which had no relation to it.

The condition of these people's children was paradoxical. They were brought up in a state of complete immunity from any form of physical want. They not only never suffered from hunger or cold or lack of clothing, they lived in a society from which such deprivations were being eliminated more quickly and more thoroughly than ever before. They were surrounded from birth by the affection and extreme conscientious care of their mothers and fathers, who took parenthood very seriously indeed. They were exempt from fear of war as we now know it, for the airplane was still a toy, the British navy was the supreme munition of the world, and it was an article of faith in this group that all foreigners (except, for some reason, the French) were pacifists. These children were, in fact, more fortunate than any groups which had ever existed previously, save certain scattered patricians, during periods when the wind blew war away from their cities and trade was good; and even over them these English children had a huge advantage so far as freedom from violence and disease is concerned. Yet they were taught and believed that they were living in the worst of all possible worlds but that they need not despair, as it would be the easiest thing they and their parents ever did to tear it down and make a better one.

They lived in cheerful homes that would recommend to them all that they were taught therein. Victorian frowstiness had been turned out of doors. The walls were distempered in light colours, the furniture was made of unstained wood which could be scrubbed, the curtains were of bright washable materials. Behind this simplicity there was an ideological complexity. The furnishing annulled the eighteenth and nineteenth centuries, it cancelled the immediate past which had produced the people who were using it. It had gone back to peasant art, because it was held that all that was true and beautiful lay so near the surface that primitive peoples had possessed it completely and it was only wicked recent civilization which had perversely lost it. Clothes were peasanty too, rough tweeds for the men, hand-embroidered smocks for the women, and never orthodox evening dress; and the abundant, carefully prepared, simple, often vegetarian food was served on peasant pottery. The ideological complex came out into the open in the books lying about in their homes, of which the most treasured were the green volumes, tooled with gold lettering, which contained the plays of George Bernard Shaw. The prefaces of these were prized more highly than the plays, for they were battlefields where the values of our traditional culture made their last stand and bled and died, all except altruism and truthfulness and austerity, of which he and they thought well and claimed the monopoly, believing that they, and they alone, were the saviours of society. Of the other virtues patriotism, it is to be remarked, was the first to get its dismissal. It was naïve for a man to feel any conviction that his own country was the best, or even as good as any other country; just as it was naïve to believe that the soldier of any foreign army committed atrocities, or to doubt that any English soldier or sailor or colonial administrator failed to do so. The difference between the Webb-minded group and Joyce can be judged from the letter he wrote to the University of London Committee for Military Education when he was a lad and was seeking admission to the Officers' Training Corps. No boy or girl in that group could possibly have written with a straight face of loyalty to the Crown or professed a desire to draw the sword for beloved England. Many were to learn better and prove it with their lives, in 1914 and 1939; but earlier their attitude was anti-patriotic. Here the whole group, adult and juvenile, were agreed; but there was a point on which the rank and file went further than their leaders. Both Shaw and Wells wrote books on religion which showed that they were neither atheists nor even agnostics but heretics. Most of these households, however, had adopted materialism, but not at all tragically, like the mid-nineteenth-century sceptics which Mrs. Humphry Ward describes in *Robert Elsmere*. On the contrary, it braced them like a cold bath.

This society had its own brightness and charm and virtue. But the position of its children was very difficult indeed. Not only were they taught to think of themselves as living in a miserable capitalist world when in actual fact they and most of their neighbours were not miserable at all; they were also taught to think of their parents and themselves as a courageous minority who were attacking the impregnable fortress of capitalism against fearful odds, and this also was not true. The capitalist system as these people knew it was about to collapse, not in consequence of their attack, but because it could not operate confidently (and confidence was necessary to its efficiency) except on an expanding market, and the rising ability of the Americans and the East to satisfy their own needs was contracting the market at the very same time that the system was having to meet the cost of the social services and of the rearmament made necessary by the threat of emergent Germany. England would have had to socialize itself during the last half-century even if there had not been a single Socialist alive; and though it would have discovered socialism for itself, it welcomed every Socialist who would save it that trouble. It therefore happened that few, if any, Socialist intellectuals ever suffered a pennyworth of inconvenience owing to their faith, and that, indeed, an ambitious young man or young woman might find it a considerable material advantage to hold that faith.

Thus the children of this group were doubly sealed in fantasy, and were bound to be discomforted by the passage of time. There is nothing spiritually easier than being in opposition, and those suddenly translated from that ease to the ordeal of responsibility must feel like oysters suddenly prised from their shells. That was the condition of these children when they became adult and found a socialized state forming itself round them. They no longer could feel brave in demanding that coal should be nationalized, for all-party action had granted that long ago; now they had to go on the Coal Board, and face the consumers and the trade unionists, who had arrived at the favourable position of being in opposition to state power. Many of these children were strong enough to find no difficulty in facing this reality in their adult years, but some were not, and sought to go on playing the rebellious part for which their parents had cast them, even when the times were not safe for play-acting. Some of these were lucky and were able to continue the pretence that they were rebels by ascribing a rebellious quality to actions which were, in fact, the pink of conformity. Such people feel that they habitually show courage in reading a Left-wing weekly, though there has been a Left-wing government for five years, and there cannot be imagined any safer occupation on this globe than reading or writing this publication. But other people cannot buy their fantasy so cheaply. They are conscientious and feel that if they were taught to be rebels, then they must go on being, truly and effectively, rebels. The faith that inspired their fathers and mothers to rebellion was socialism, and since that is now the established practice of their land they must find another dissident faith. It is obvious that such minds, at once fantasy-bound and literal, will turn happily to communism. It is on the Left, where they learned in their infancy salvation lay. It has a materialistic basis, and one of its first claims is that it transcends the claims of patriotism, which, if one has been brought up to believe that patriotism existed only to have its claim transcended, gives it the authority of a fulfilment of the prophets. Thus communism can, alone of all the parties, truly gratify nostalgia. The Conservatives cannot re-create the great days of colonial expansion, the Liberals cannot re-create the smoky but glowing dawn when manufacturers and factory hands alike knew that the expansion of industry gave power into their hands, the Labour Party cannot put itself back into the glorious drunkenness of opposition, but the Communist Party can still put people further Left than anyone else. That is to say, they can carry their converts back to the golden days when the flowering almonds along the avenues of the Hampstead Garden Suburb were saplings, and revolutionary activities could be carried on serenely in the lee of an unthreatened British navy. This is especially magical for those who were not born until those almond trees were tall and sturdy, and have only their elders' reminiscences to tell them how delightful it was to follow a gallant liberal line in the midst of a stable conservative community. Thus communism offers a haven to the infantilist; and since it is perfectly possible for a highly gifted intellectual to be an infantilist, it appeared not surprising that a prominent English scientist should be a Communist, and therefore, since every Communist is bound to regard treachery as one of his Party duties, a traitor.

III

IN many ways the trials of William Joyce and Dr. Alan Nunn May were as different as black and white. Both prisoners were poorly built; but Joyce had made himself a little knuckleduster of a man by hard exercise, whereas Dr. Nunn May had plainly never noticed that he had muscles. When Joyce was in the dock the court was full of his simple and forthright and ungifted followers, open in their grief. When Dr. Nunn May stood in the same dock his complicated and secretive and able associates were discreetly absent, because only the Party was of importance. It had been the singularity of Joyce's case that it depended entirely on evidence regarding matters of fact and law, which he could have neither confirmed nor disproved since he was unaware of them until the time of his trial. His destiny had depended on outward events. But there was no evidence at all against Dr. Alan Nunn May, except his own statement, which set down facts convicting him of guilt which were known only to himself. Here we confront an unrevealed mystery.

In 1948, in a Philadelphia bar, during the Progressive Party Convention which adopted Henry Wallace as a Presidential candidate, a Russian forgot, and talked. He said: "In England, now that the war is over and espionage trials take place in open court, persons detected in espionage on behalf of the Soviet Union are instructed by whichever of our organizations it is which has been using them, to plead guilty and to admit to the police their participation in the particular crime of which he is accused, and nothing more. In the United States, such persons are at present instructed to proceed in precisely the opposite way, and to deny everything. This is a compliment to England. It is felt that British legal procedure is so efficient that if a false plea of not guilty is entered, it will be detected by the lawyers, the judge, the jury, and the press, and other matters may be stirred up which will extend the scope of the inquiry into the doings of the Communists. It is probable too that the case will be settled so quickly and will take such a clear form that the public will see what is going on, and it is therefore best to limit the matters disclosed. In the United States, where legal proceedings are likely to be prolonged and confused, and all sorts of considerations may prevent the truth from appearing, it is worth while putting up a plea of Not Guilty, no matter how absurd this may be in view of the real facts. This policy would, however, be altered and would fall into line with the policy advised for English suspects if courts in the United States became more vigilant, as altered circumstances may make them at any time."

It is true that in the only two such cases which have been tried in England both the accused persons have pleaded guilty, and that until recently it has been remarkable that in all such cases tried in America the accused persons have denied everything, often on such a wholesale scale that they have got themselves into unnecessary trouble by denying minor points which the prosecution was able to establish with ease, thus throwing doubt on their credibility. But there is nothing to suggest that Dr. Alan Nunn May had received such instructions, when he told the story of his misdoings, which were indeed deplorable. He had voluntarily entered the service of the British Government during the war, as the senior member of the nuclear physics division in the unit devoted to research on the atomic bomb, and had gone to Canada to work under Sir John Cockcroft in the Atomic Energy Project, as a group leader in the Montreal Laboratory of the National Research Council. During the course of these proceedings, he signed a statement acknowledging his liabilities under the Official Secrets Act. He then used his position to collect information and hand it over to a Russian agent who forwarded it to Moscow. Later he and his friends claimed that he took this step because he had come to the conclusion that his researches were contributing to create a situation dangerous to mankind unless steps were taken to ensure that the development of atomic energy was not confined to America. This is the line his defenders have followed, but it is not an honest account of the situation. It omits the important factor that other members of the Communist Party had long recognized him as one of themselves, working underground. During the war the English Communist Party carried on a singularly disingenuous campaign for deep bomb-proof shelters, which contributed no single valid idea to the sum of our knowledge of defence, and neither achieved nor proposed any untried method which if it had been adopted would have saved a single life, but which fulfilled its real intention by spreading distrust of the shelters provided by the authorities and suggesting that the Communists alone were taking thought for the safety of the public. Douglas Hyde, who was then news editor of the *Daily Worker,* describes this campaign as "led by our scientist-members, among whom was Dr. Nunn May". It must be remembered that a member of the Communist Party is obliged to act on all instructions originating from the authority in charge of the section to which he belongs, and would have had to hand over to any person named in those instructions any material directed, no matter what relevance his action had to the dissemination of scientific knowledge.

Nor would his attitude to that problem explain why, as he himself confessed, he gave information about quite other matters. As well as handing over notes regarding atomic energy, of what scope and nature is unknown, and two samples of uranium, he also gave information regarding electronic shells. This last was conveyed to Moscow in a telegram from Colonel Zabotin, the Military Attaché in Ottawa, which read thus: "On our task Alek [the code name for Dr. Alan Nunn May] has reported brief data concerning electronic shells. In particular these are being used by the American Navy against Japanese suicide-fliers. There is in the shell a small radio-transmitter with one electronic tube, and it is fed by dry batteries. The body of the shell is the antenna. The bomb explodes in the proximity of an aeroplane, from the action of the reflected waves from the aeroplane on the transmitter. The basic difficulties were the preparation of a tube and batteries which could withstand the discharge of the shell and the determination of a rotation speed of the shell which would not require special adaption in the preparation of the shell. The Americans have achieved this result, but apparently have not handed this over to the English. The Americans have used a plastic covering for the battery which withstands the force of pressure during the motion of the shell." It would be interesting to know if Dr. Alan Nunn May's passion for the universal dissemination of scientific knowledge led him to take steps to break down the barrier which he described existing between the Americans and the English in this matter.

Furthermore, Dr. Alan Nunn May rendered the Soviet authorities yet another service which it is extremely difficult to interpret as springing from a desire for the dissemination of scientific knowledge. There came to Canada in 1945 an Englishman in his middle twenties, one Norman Veal, a flower nurtured in the parterre of the Hendon branch of the Young Communists' League. He had worked in the Meteorological Service of the Air Ministry in England from 1939 till the end of 1941, when he was transferred to the Atomic Energy Project in England, working there until January 1943, when he was sent to the Atomic Energy Project in Canada as an instrument-designer. After two years he approached the Soviet authorities, anxious to help. Interviewed later by the Canadian Royal Commission he explained that his political views changed from day to day, but if he had met a Russian agent, and the agent had asked him to turn over to him information which he (Mr. Veal) had gained while working in the National Research Council and which was secret—well, it would naturally depend on the circumstances and the situation at the time, and he would certainly not have done it in the last year or so, because he thought he could put an end to secrecy in scientific work by supporting the United Nations and its work for international scientific co-operation, but yes, "prior to that period", if he had felt anything he could do would help to shorten the war, he might possibly have done it, and in spite of signing the declaration regarding the Official Secrets Act, "I think I can honestly say I might have given that information, assuming that I had any information that was worth having". The Russians, however, were struck by a certain artlessness about him. They consulted Dr. Alan Nunn May, who gave them what information he had about him, stating that "Veal occupies a fairly low position and knows very little", and pronouncing him "inclined to be careless", as he had begun a conversation with Dr. Nunn May on conspiratorial matters in the presence of a third person. This really cannot be disguised as activity designed to enfranchise science from lowly bonds.

In any case, it is difficult to understand why these scruples about the illegitimacy of engaging in researches which were not to be published did not occur to him when the post was first offered to him, as he was then made fully aware of the nature and conditions of the work he was to do; nor why, when these scruples did arise in his mind, he did not take the obvious step of resigning from his post, which would have caused serious inconvenience to the authorities, and explaining his reasons to his fellow-scientists and to the general public. The one thing he could not do from any point of view was what he did: to disclose the result of his researches in spite of the understanding between him and the government that he was to be bound by the requirements of the Official Secrets Act. No society, whether capitalist, socialist, or communist, can survive for ten minutes if it abandons the principle that a contract is sacred. It has subsequently been pretended that Dr. Alan Nunn May forgot this elementary social principle in his desire to give help to the U.S.S.R. so that it might the better defend itself against Germany and Japan. But he made no such claim in his own statement, and indeed it is patently absurd. He handed over the samples of uranium and his information about the theory of atomic energy in the early days of August 1945, three months after VE-day, and some days after the atomic bomb had been used at Hiroshima, when the defeat of Japan was quite certain. The telegram sent by Colonel Zabotin to Moscow regarding the information received from Dr. Nunn May later fell into Canadian hands. It contains a specific reference to the Hiroshima explosion. Dr. Nunn May cannot have thought the U.S.S.R. would use the information he had given it except against the United States and Great Britain.

To the very end, to the moment when the sentences were delivered, the contrast between the two trials was maintained in its acuteness. The guilt of William Joyce was over and done with; the guilt of Dr. Nunn May was a continuing force. By

the time Joyce came to trial it was impossible that what he had
done could harm anyone. He had tried to do evil and had failed.
But the samples of uranium and the notes Dr. Nunn May gave the
Russian agent threw such light on the research into atomic energy
that they were immediately flown to Russia on a flight undertaken
solely for the purpose; and if ever Russia drops an atom bomb on
Great Britain or America, the blame for the death and blindness
and the sores it scatters must rest largely on this gifted and frivolous man. But whereas nobody in court at Joyce's trial except
his kin and friends was greatly moved when the sentence of death
was passed on him, the spectators were plainly appalled when
the judge passed sentence of ten years' imprisonment on Dr. Nunn
May, though none of them was his follower. The Attorney-
General, Sir Hartley Shawcross, showed that he was heavy-
hearted under the necessity of making the prosecuting speech,
and he waited for the sentence with an apprehension rarely shown
even by a defending counsel. It was the light about Dr. Nunn
May's head which made the thought of his imprisonment intolerable: the sense of a network of perceptions and associations and
interpretations, which made the Nazi-Fascists seem like hogs
rooting among the simple unimproved beechmast of the world.
William Joyce had great courage; but though it is a terrible
thing not to have courage, to be courageous carries a man out
of that terror but not a step further, unless he has other qualities
to transport him. Millions of men have been brave, but have
been nothing more, and the brute creation also is brave. Dr.
Alan Nunn May was precious to us as Joyce was not, because
he was something which man must be and is not yet, save here
and there, and with great difficulty. They were actually on a
perfect parity in the dock. They had even been on the same side
in 1939 and 1940 when the Stalin-Hitler pact was signed and put
an end to the pretence that there is any real difference between
fascism and communism. But the kind of mind possessed by
Dr. Nunn May had seemed to hold out a promise, which, it
could now be seen, was not to be fulfilled.

THE conviction of Dr. Alan Nunn May was followed by an active campaign for the remission of his sentence. In so far as this was conducted by those bound to him by ties of blood and friendship it was of course above criticism. But other and less commendable elements were involved in it. A number of scientists gave their support to the demand for his release on the ground that his offence was negligible. Of these scientists, some would hardly have cared to argue the case. It would be very natural for a man to feel great horror at the thought of a comrade, with whom he had probably had pleasant social relations, being sent to prison for ten years, particularly such a gifted comrade. It would also be unpleasant not to join in such a demand in a laboratory where the feeling was running strongly in favour of Dr. Nunn May, and abstinence would be taken as a sign of inhumanity or reactionary views. There were also some scientists who were so genuinely distressed by the imposition of secrecy on scientific workers by the government, which had been weighing on them more and more heavily since the beginning of the war, that they envisaged Dr. Nunn May's treachery simply as a protest against that secrecy. There is much to be said for the principle here involved. It is ridiculous to think of small groups of persons with rare gifts working on related facts of high importance to our species, at points dotted over the globe, and failing to pool their discoveries. But the universe is constantly forcing us to do ridiculous things for the sake of our survival. It is ridiculous for a man to crawl along the ground on his stomach when he has two legs and can walk, but if an enemy is looking for him he will be very foolish if he does not. It is very hard, however, to believe that these scientists held the principle that research must never be secret to be absolute, as they pretended. They did not demand that the scientists of England, including the German Jewish refugees, should smuggle the results of their labours over to German scientists during the war. Nor have they burst into cheers on any of the occasions since the war when it has become manifest that the Nazi scientists who escaped from Germany at the end of the war imparted many of their secrets, particularly regarding the construction of jet planes, to the government of President Peron in Argentine, though that broke down one national barrier at least, which is no more than Dr. Nunn May could have claimed to do. There is something genuine in this scientific attitude, but a great deal that is humbug.

The real motivation of this campaign was twofold. A large number of those who took part in it were animated by a feeling, for which psychiatrists have a name, that they formed an elect class which should be allowed to do as they liked. Their real argument for the release of Dr. Nunn May was quite simply that he was a scientist, and that therefore it was ridiculous to consider that he should have been bound by the undertaking he had signed regarding the Official Secrets Act, and that if he thought it right to give away the results of his researches to a foreign power, it was disgraceful that a society which consisted in the main of non-scientific inferiors should call him to account. This is an attitude which had already been detectable in various writings by scientists on the subject of atom-bomb policy, in which it is assumed that it should be left entirely in scientific hands. The claim that because scientists had invented the atomic bomb they should be given the right to decide what should be done with it, and the claim that because Dr. Nunn May was a scientist he should be allowed to break the law without paying the penalty, rest on the assumption that because a man has scientific gifts he is likely to be superior to his fellows in all intellectual respects, including that kind of general far-seeing ability, tender towards the future of the individual and the race, which we call wisdom. This assumption is based on no evidence whatsoever. Modern science has been a recognizable entity for some considerable period, but no community has yet registered its joyous certainty that it can always look for wise counsel to its scientists. This cannot simply be because the scientists have always been done down by the wicked industrialists and financiers; for if it were so the people who were fighting the industrialists and financiers would have been glad to hail the existence of a force of wise counsellors on their side. But nowhere is this recorded. All our experience suggests that, though special gifts rarely appear in individuals below a certain level of general ability, that level is not very high, and gifted individuals may appear anywhere in the scale above it; and quite obviously the possession of special gifts, such as scientific or musical aptitude, which demand technical training beginning at an early age and a long and exhausting working day, will prevent the possessor from developing his general ability. The very fact that a man took a leading part in perfecting the atom bomb might unfit him for forming an opinion as to what should be done with it; and Dr. Nunn May must surely have been too busy in his laboratory to have worked out a social cement which could replace the idea of contract.

The second strand in this campaign was, of course, Communist. Few of the scientists concerned with it in its more dignified manifestations were Communists, and few of the well-known Communist scientists took a prominent part in organizing it in any way that would take the eye. But there was often a sense of Communist influence guiding a hand which without doubt thought itself writing of its own and innocent free will. An appeal to the Home Secretary urging him to reduce the sentence passed on Dr. Nunn May may seem strange at first reading, as it contains statements about the convicted man's offences which could not possibly soften the Home Secretary's heart, as the files would show him that these statements were wholly untrue. But it becomes an intelligible document if, and only if, it be recognized that the person who wrote this appeal had been naïve enough to accept direct or indirect suggestions from some other persons who did not care a button about Dr. Nunn May, but who were extremely anxious to whitewash a criminal known to the public as Communist, and thus deceive it regarding the essential nature of the Communist Party. The same spectacle of enthusiasm for a friend and for science being exploited as Communist propaganda was manifest in the demand of various branches of a certain association that Dr. Nunn May should be released on grounds as wide of the mark as the claim that "the information divulged was of a purely scientific character, unconnected with the manufacture of the atom bomb, or other form of weapon". There was also a certain amount of open and undiluted Communist propaganda which maintained quite starkly that Dr. Nunn May should be regarded as innocent because his treachery had benefited the U.S.S.R., which as one propagandist stated, "had torn out the guts of the German army practically single-handed". Such persons could not envisage the act of handing over to Russia a defence secret possessed by Great Britain as a crime at all, because Great Britain had no right to defend herself against Russia. Among this sort of fanatic the idea that Dr. Nunn May had handed over the information about the atom bomb before and not after the defeat of the Nazis was widespread; and it is not possible that all those who spread it so widely could have been ignorant that this was a lie. But what was interesting about all grades of these campaigners was their ingenuous readiness to show that, if they were for the dissemination of truth in science, they were all against it in the press. Fierce efforts were made to prevent the publication of the true facts of the Nunn May case, whether in a newspaper or in a book.

The public, indeed, had the greatest difficulty in learning those facts; and some other facts which made the case much more disturbing by showing that Dr. Nunn May was not an individual working in isolation but a cog in a complicated machine. For in 1946 the world was still in a state of disorder, travel was impossible except for those who pleaded a special mission, and the transmission of news was almost as gravely impeded, by lack of newsprint, the eating up of space by items dealing with the peace, and the concentration of correspondents in the war areas. Hence it happened that for long there did not reach Great Britain in any easily assimilable form the story of the Canadian Spy Ring, of which Dr. Nunn May had been a member. One night in September 1945 a Russian cipher clerk named Igor Gouzenko, employed in the Soviet Embassy at Ottawa on the staff of the Military Attaché, snatched an armful of documents from his files which would bear witness to the existence in Canada of a treasonable conspiracy, organized from the Soviet Embassy and working through a group of Canadian and British citizens, and went out into the city with the intention of handing over these documents to some responsible person connected with the Canadian Government and of seeking asylum for himself and his wife and his child. By this action he put himself into the position of the German refugees who aided the Allies against the Axis, and laid himself open to the charge of treachery. He had an answer to that charge, as they had. Allegiance is given only in exchange for protection, and he felt that Stalin gives his people as little protection as the German refugees felt that Hitler gave his. It is true that British and American Communists would claim that their governments also did not give their peoples protection. That is, indeed, the essence of the contention between the Communist Party and the states of the world.

It might well have happened that Mr. Gouzenko's actions had no consequence, except for him and his wife and child. For although he spent part of that night and the whole of the next day visiting newspaper offices and Ministries and police stations he found nobody who appeared to take the slightest interest in him or his documents. Actually the police were sufficiently interested in his story to shadow him, but not as closely as he could have wished. In the evening he returned home to his flat entirely discouraged and in great fear; and he approached his neighbours and asked them to take charge of his child in case he and his wife were murdered. The neighbours responded sensibly and kindly, and took in the whole family, but might have thought him a lunatic or a liar, had not the Russians, with that peculiar gift for blundering which is a far greater protection for the West than any Western merit of character or intelligence, sent along the Second Secretary of the U.S.S.R. Embassy, a member of the staff of the Military Attaché, the Military Attaché of the Russian Air Force, and a cipher clerk. These four gentlemen proceeded to enter the Gouzenkos' flat by breaking in the front door, and when the police were called in to stop this crass burglary and asked the burglars to produce their identification cards, they produced their own quite genuine ones. No more convincing proof of Mr. Gouzenko's story could have been provided; and indeed it is hard to imagine what other proof could have been provided.

The material filched from the Soviet Embassy by Mr. Gouzenko was finally investigated by a Royal Commission appointed for that purpose by the Canadian Government; and its report is the most complete picture of Communist treachery that we possess. It is hardly necessary to say that it cast no discredit on the U.S.S.R. whatsoever. Not till the Earthly Paradise is established and man regains his innocence, can a power which has ever been at war be blamed if it accepts information regarding the military strength of another power, however this may be obtained; and of course it can be blamed least of all if the information comes to it from traitors, for then it is likely to touch on the truly secret. There is no need to blame any but the Britons and Canadians who formed this Spy Ring because they regarded their allegiance to the Communist Party as annulling their allegiances to their own countries and to the ordinary moral obligations of society, and who therefore felt no qualms whatsoever, but great pride and pleasure, in handing over to the representatives of the Soviet Union any information it required of them, no matter how brutally this treachery might conflict with their duty to their employers, public or private, nor what dangers it might bring down on their fellow-countrymen. This group cannot have been actuated by the desire to enfranchise science, for it included others than scientists and dealt with matters which could not possibly be regarded as scientific. Nor can it have been inspired by hatred of fascism, for the nucleus of the group was in being before the war, and during the Stalin-Hitler Pact the Canadian Communist Party showed peculiar gusto in co-operating with the Nazis. Miss Kathleen Mary Willsher, for example, was a graduate of the London School of Economics who was the trusted assistant registrar in the Ottawa office of the High Commissioner for the United Kingdom. From 1935, with no discernible breach on account of the Hitler-Stalin Pact, she handed over to a Communist agent information which she obtained during the course of her day's work in the High Commissioner's office, such as a complete account of the size and functions and organization of his staff, and a report of Lord Keynes' confidential conversations in Ottawa in 1944 on the subject of post-war credits. It can hardly be maintained that information on either of these subjects can have helped the U.S.S.R. to fight Hitler.

But it is true that the bulk of the members of the group, so far as the Gouzenko papers enable us to identify them, were scientists, and that their proceedings were alarming. Prominent among them was Dr. Nunn May; and nobody who has read the Canadian Commission's Report can visualize him as an individual engaged in a solitary battle with his conscience over the question of secrecy in science, so plainly do the extracts from

Gouzenko's files and their confirmation in his own statement show him as a Communist snugly working among his Communist fellows under Party discipline. But even more conspicuous and alarming was Dr. Raymond Boyer, a French-Canadian of forty, a handsome, popular, spoiled, sulky millionaire, the foremost chemist in Canada, one of the foremost chemists in the world. He had for some time been a subscriber to the funds of the Communist Party, and he gave before the Royal Commission just the type of evidence which the Russian at Philadelphia indicated that Communist headquarters advise persons to give who are standing trial for Communist activities before a vigilant and competently conducted tribunal. It appeared in the files brought in by Gouzenko that he had given the Soviet agents the formula of a new method of producing an explosive known as RDX. He made a full confession of his guilt: of how he had handed over to a Soviet agent the formula of a new method of producing an explosive known as RDX. Alike in his laboratory and as a witness he showed exceptional ability.

This restraint was in marked contrast with the loquacity which had evidently characterized Dr. Boyer and his friends at all other times. These scientists talked and talked and talked. Dr. Boyer had talked about RDX. Dr. Nunn May had talked about his own work on atomic energy and about the great experimental plant at Chalk River, Ontario. Their friends talked about radar; they talked about the anti-submarine device known as Asdic; they talked about all the explosive propellants that were being developed and improved; they talked about the V.T. fuse, which knocked the Japanese Air Force out of the air; they talked about the locations of research stations and production plants; they talked about everything they knew, with a freedom which amounted to what psychologists name "total recall". It might even be termed gabbiness. Now this strange disease did not affect all scientists working in Canada. The afflicted group formed only a small proportion of the whole. But it was large enough to have a great quantity of valuable information to give away, and though the mass of its members and supporters were drawn mainly from the lower grade of scientific worker it contained some men of outstanding ability, even allowing for the extent to which Communists in every walk of life, and particularly in science, deliberately inflate the reputation of their fellow-members. But what was really remarkable was that this epidemic of gabbiness was spreading amongst scientists all over the world.

Everywhere, it is true, the mass of scientists proved immune to it. They adhered to the normal pattern of behaviour and, in some cases at the bidding of their consciences and in others from fear of the police, did not consider themselves free to communicate to a foreign power, or to a political party which was an agent of a foreign power, information which they had acquired in the course of their employment and which they had undertaken not to divulge. But it is equally true that all over the globe there sprang up these groups of scientists which, in the middle of the war, claimed the right to publish as they thought fit all information arising out of their labours without either consulting their own governments or informing them afterwards. In Great Britain this group had little opportunity to manifest itself during the war, but it was organized to become richly vocal as soon as peace was achieved. In America it was peculiarly happy and carefree. During the war Communist influences romped round the war-time Atomic Project at the radiation laboratory of the University of California at Berkeley, and a group of young scientists kindly formed what was practically a dining club to offer hospitality to Soviet agents. Never before has treachery been so sunny and light-hearted, presenting itself not as Judas, conscious of the last suspension from the elder-tree, but as some innocent little figure in straw hat and sailor suit. Typical of this new dispensation is a figure who was cleared of guilt, a Californian scientist who dined at a restaurant in San Francisco with a Russian official on the eve of his departure for home, and talked so loudly about his work that he was clearly overheard by two officers of the Federal Bureau of Investigation who were dining at an adjacent table; and who, when he had to appear before the Committee on un-American Activities some years later, to explain this incident, made little jokes about his violin-playing. His conversation was not deemed criminal; but the gaiety with which he faced suspicion of treachery gives some indication of the curious mental climate in which he and his associates had their being, a climate most dangerous to the general weather of the world. Few of these people were experienced in the ways of the world, and a number revealed themselves in evidence as even simple-minded when they left their own field. They would of course have gladly handed over their secrets to the Nazis during the Stalin-Hitler Pact; it is a startling proof of the extreme inefficiency of the German Intelligence Service under the Nazis that their secrets did not reach Berlin just the same after the Pact was ended, for these simpletons would certainly not have been able to tell a Nazi agent from a Soviet agent if he had cared to impersonate one. It is to be noted that some of the information regarding non-scientific matters which was handed over by members of the Canadian Spy Ring could have inspired the unscrupulous to successful financial speculation. But what might have happened or actually happened in the past is of small moment compared to our present situation: wherein, at a time when munitions have become more deadly than ever before, the task of designing the deadliest of them inevitably falls into the hands of a group of specialists peculiarly subject to the temptation to hand over their designs to our only potential enemy, Communist Russia.

V

THE Canadian Spy Ring made it quite apparent that Dr. Nunn May was merely one of a close corporation of the most inconvenient kind of traitors any community had ever had to fear. This was no matter of members of a negativist generation in England finding a new and picturesque way of falling out with their neighbours, these were not mere dilettanti of revolution, who made trouble on the scientific field if they happened to be scientists. These were revolutionaries who meant to shoot to kill, and though their origins were certainly in the middle-class Left-wing society moulded by the Webbs, their present practice was determined by their way of life as scientists. It became necessary, therefore, to examine more closely than before the reasons, apart from their social background, why scientists should be specially attracted to communism.

There would seem to be an obvious cause in the underpayment of scientists, who, with a very few exceptions in the employment of exceptionally well-endowed universities or imaginative industrial corporations, are paid far below their deserts. A first-class scientist, who, if he were a pianist, would be on the level of Solomon, and if he were a financier would be a partner in an important bank, will be lucky to have a salary of two thousand or fifteen hundred pounds a year. A number of men with gifts far above the average earn, not merely at the beginning of their working lives but in their middle and closing years, salaries ranging between six and twelve hundred a year. But this meanness of reward, though it is an ungracious folly on the part of the community, probably plays less part in the scientist's mind than the lack of political power, which is what the men of our age want, even more urgently than money. It may play a greater part in America where the relative underpayment is at once more marked and has more relation to power than in England. An American employed in any grade of industry is apt to be much richer than his English equivalent, but an American scientific worker is not infrequently paid no better than an English scientific worker and is sometimes actually paid worse. The average salary of a scientist employed by a university is under $5,000, by the government just over $6,000, and by industrial corporations just over $7,000. Moreover, learning still has a prestige in England which it lacks in certain communities in America. The situation, therefore, is embittering. One of the less fortunate American scientists, working in a university in an industrial town, will not be able to afford to buy a new car, though an old car is the recognized symbol of outer and even inner failure; his wife will not be able to hire domestic help or a baby-sitter because she will be outbid by the wives of the executives and operatives in the neighbouring factories; he will be conscious that he has no incontestable claim to the respect of the community whose heroes are Ford and Kaiser. It would be strange if in these circumstances the desire to find compensation in political power did not spring up with a special irate urgency.

There is a peculiar reason why scientists should feel this desire for political power with a strength unusual even by the standards of this age. A scientist knows that he can understand a great many things which are mysterious to the non-scientific man. A great scientist knows that he can understand a great many things which are mysterious to lesser scientists. He would have to possess the gift of humility in very full measure, were it not to occur to him that maybe he could solve the economic and social problems which have so long perplexed non-scientific men. He is the more prone to form this opinion, because the long years of his training and the long hours of his working-day restrict the scope of his experience, and prevent him realizing the disorderly quality of economic and social problems. He is apt, too, to live in the company of his fellow-scientists without meeting men of affairs and thus learning appreciation of their special talents and virtues. It must be very tempting for any scientist to think that he can solve any major political conundrum, say the housing problem, by applying to it the same methods he uses in his laboratory: by assembling the necessary apparatus, handling his material with dexterous and economical movements, observing accurately all the changes set up in that material, and subjecting his observations to a process of logical analysis. But, in fact, houses come into being on quite another plane of creation. Any house not built by a tyrant with unlimited power to draw at will on materials and slave labour must represent a struggle between conflicting interests, only to be resolved by frequent compromises of a sort which would never be called for in the course of a scientific experiment. There is an initial conflict between the person who is going to live in the house and the person who is going to pay for it, which exists even when these are the same person, sometimes to the extent of making it impossible for him to live in it when it is finished, because he has spent so much on it that he has nothing left for upkeep. This conflict becomes more bitter in the hard times when housing becomes a major political problem (which are the only times when scientists would wish to emerge from their laboratories and solve it) because the landlord, who is often a hybrid composed of the state and a local government body, is therefore at war with himself as well as with his tenant, who also often is at war with himself, because he is also a hybrid composed of a subsidized pet who is paying less than the economic rent of his house, and a taxpayer and rate-payer who is paying the subsidy and keeping himself as a pet. Moreover, as building is rationalized and more and more of the component parts of every house are made by specialist firms, and more and more people than the actual labourers who work on the site are involved in its construction, each of them acts as a brake on its rise from the sod. For though these people's demand for higher profits and wages may be controlled, their not less natural demand for more leisure and less tension cannot be so controlled, and their refusal to work long hours or over-strain themselves slows down the speed of building and adds to its cost by amounts which may not be less than those involved by a spectacular rise in wages and interest, and must always be less convenient for actuarial handling, since they are indirect and highly variable and often unpredictable. The authorities who are building the house must attempt to counter this tendency by encouraging the firms which are least affected by it, but with-out forgetting their concern with efficiency or the accepted principles of industrial welfare. Bricks and mortar cannot meet and marry until there have been countless wrangles of this com-plicated sort; and it may well happen that an administrator responsible for a housing project may be uttering a worthy *apologia pro vita sua* when he says to himself, "Well, I am building these houses very badly indeed. If you judge them with the conception of a house as 'a machine to live in' at the back of your mind, they are all wrong from the foundations to the chimney cowls. But I am building them, they are going up, soon people will be able to shelter in them, and thank God for that." This is not an *apologia* which is permitted to either the artist or the scientist, who must build his work of art or his research right, and let the people seek their shelter where they can find it. The martyrdom of the man of action is that he must take pride in botched work; the martyrdom of the man of science and the artist is that they must never take pride in botched work.

Much more is demanded from the scientist and artist than from the man of action, and much less. Each has to be acquainted with the view of the universe created by the predecessors working in the same medium, and he has to have command of the technique they have developed. He has, in fact, to master by his individual powers the experiences accumulated by generations. But all the same a scientist does not have to conduct an experiment on material with a will of its own which is distracted by an ambivalent attitude to the experiment, nor with apparatus which has its own and respectable reasons for exercising a delaying force on the speed with which his body and mind can work, nor does he have constantly to modify his research, even to the point of making it nonsensical and no credit to him, because of a consideration which outweighs his and all other experiments. Nor does he have to compromise. It is falsely held that compromise is the easy way, but few things come harder to the type of mind which is drawn towards creation. Ibsen's *Brand* is the portrait of an intellectually lazy man. In a sense, Einstein is doing something much more difficult than what is done by the chairman of the Housing Committee of any Urban or Rural District Council. But it must also be recognized that he is doing something much easier. There is as little reason to suppose that Einstein could do the work of the chairman of a Housing Committee as there is to suppose that the chairman could do the work of Einstein. But the human lot is so hard that human beings could not keep going unless they pretended that they were more than human. Therefore scientists are apt to think that they could discharge the duties of politicians as successfully as they discharge their own.

It happens that throughout the nineteenth century and the early years of the twentieth century the Russian mind was strongly attracted to science. This was due in part to the experimental nature of the Slav; it is significant that the practice of artificial insemination was invented by the illiterate horsemen of the steppes and was developed to a very high pitch of efficiency by the not too literate masters of the stables of the Tsars and their nobles. It is also significant that Peter the Great believed in nothing but what the Americans call "know-how", that Catherine the Great was injected by the French philosophers with faith in all kinds of learning, including the physical sciences, and during the nineteenth century the German people, having begun to manifest their terrible genius for producing a vast excess of the very best specimens of the white-collar class, exported a number of them, including many scientists, to Russia. Consequently an understanding of the scientific character is one of the Russian traits which were profound enough to survive the

Revolution and pass unaltered into the U.S.S.R. Hence the Bolsheviks have steadily pursued a policy based on their awareness of the occupational risk to which the scientist is subject, this temptation to believe that he is called to wear a double crown, and surpass Caesar as well as Archimedes. The U.S.S.R. has therefore posed to the scientists of the world as the one country which gives their tribe real power. In point of fact, as Nazi Germany showed, a totalitarian state must keep art and science in strict subjection, since it claims that its creed represents the finality of wisdom, and it cannot permit artists and scientists to set forth on researches from which they may bring back disconcerting revelations of reality quite inconsistent with that creed. It is significant that the word "objectivity", which to all free artists and scientists means a necessary precondition of their work, meant in Nazi Germany and means in the U.S.S.R. a vice implying disloyalty to the state. But foreign scientists are invited on flattering and delightful visits to the state which give them experiences bound to be uniquely intoxicating. When a certain prominent English scientist visits Moscow he is always accorded the rare privilege of being received by Stalin. It is impossible to imagine him being granted a similar favour by the King of England or by the President of the United States or France. There is a good reason for this. It is unlikely that the King of England or the President of the United States or France, geared to their administrative duties as they are, would have anything interesting to say to him, geared as he is to his highly specialized scientific duties. It is even more unlikely that Stalin, geared to a highly specialized type of administrative duty, and wholly alien from the West, should find any basis for an intellectually profitable exchange. But though the adult self of the scientist would learn nothing from the interview, his childish self, that wishes to live more than his life, would rejoice at being raised by a ruler to be his companion.

At home too there is the same elevation into another sphere, the same promise that ordinary human limitations are to be transcended and the Communist scientist shall discharge two functions and live two lives. During the past quarter of a century, both in England and in France, there have been conspicuous examples of Communist scientists who, though far from brilliant or even sensible outside their own fields, have been carefully built up into popular political oracles. It is hard to think of any agency which would so transform the destinies of their non-Communist colleagues. It cannot be charged too heavily against the scientists that they are self-seeking in accepting these benefits from Russian sources or that they show themselves blind to the suffering of the millions who are incompetently governed by the Bolsheviks. For it must be remembered that they believe that political problems should be solved by the same method as scientific problems, and that if it is impossible to build a new house without a struggle between conflicting interests unless the builder is a tyrant with unlimited power to draw at will on material and slave labour, they will consider the U.S.S.R. sensible in becoming such a tyrant, and will feel there is no degradation in receiving presents at its hands.

It is argued, in any case, that this movement towards comradeship with the U.S.S.R. can lead to no harm, since scientists can never go far wrong, because they are scientists. Shortly after Hiroshima, a scientist, not a Communist but very much of the Webb-determined world, was talking with horror of the efforts that the soldiers of America and Britain were making to get the control of atomic energy into their hands. It should, he maintained, be left with the scientists to whom the world owed the knowledge of atomic energy. One of his hearers (thinking, as it happened, of an American scientist who was not Communist but Fascist in his sympathies) asked what guarantee there was that, if scientists controlled atomic energy, extremists among them might not hand over their secrets to the most aggressive of soldiers. He, the least arrogant of men, replied by a simple claim that he and all his kind were born without sin. "How can you suppose that any scientist would do such a thing?" he asked, his spectacles shining with anger. "Science is reason. Why should people who live by reason suddenly become its enemy?" He put into words an implication which often can be recognized when Communist scientists write on other than technical matters, although even from their own point of view it appears archaic. Psychology is considered by the strict to be a bastard science, wandering too often from the verifiable, but it has certainly collected a great deal of material which suggests that it is difficult to be sure when reason is reason and when it is unreason wearing logic as a disguise. Sometimes we use our inductive and deductive powers on the material brought us by our sense, and make decisions based on our examination of the results in the light of our experience; but often we merely pretend to use our inductive and deductive powers on material we merely pretend is brought us by our sense, in order to justify decisions to which we are impelled by a dream, an appetite, a fear. Our political decisions are well within the field which is liable to be invaded by this pretence.

Of course reason often operates in a high degree of purity. The late nineteenth and early twentieth centuries covered a period as fecund in political and economic thought as the late eighteenth and early nineteenth centuries in music. Of course these children of the Webb-minded group often speak of politics and economics directly and reasonably, in truth subjecting political and economic material to their inductive and deductive powers, and judging the results with objectivity; and of course a number of them are captivated on intellectual grounds by the vigorous genius of Marx. Since they are human, fantasy must play some part in their lives, but it would be profitless to treat them as if they were governed by it. Nevertheless there are others in whom we can recognize the mechanism which gave us some of the Fascists. No persons and no people can get rid of religion by becoming atheist. The troubling ideas in the depths of man's mind, which religions try to formulate and clarify, do not suddenly cease to trouble when these attempts are abandoned. All that happens is that men continue to debate them in terms borrowed from the dominant art or science of their time, and swear that it is of this art or science that they speak. Because politics and economics preoccupy us today, we carry on that discussion in political and economic terms. Joyce and his type of Fascist conducted their part of it in vague and general terms, seeking to find in political activity the kind of recognition of their individualities which could more appropriately have been sought in religion. But among intellectuals not only the problems set by the pious but the solutions they found persist in recognizable form.

The capitalist system is evil and must be destroyed, not one

305

stone may be left upon another. So it has been prophesied regarding the kingdom of the flesh, ever since the first of the prophets. There will be a revolution and then the state will be governed by us. The pious tell us that the Day of Judgment approaches when it shall be declared who are the sheep and who are the goats, and we shall be raised to sit on his right hand. All existing political arrangements are regarded with loathing; it is cowardly to argue that they may be the best which can be contrived at present, for approval must be withheld from every social prescription except those written by the masters of perfection, by the Webbs, by the T.U.C., by the Bevan group, by Lenin, by Stalin. What the faithful must believe has been decided at the Councils of the Church. All industries must be nationalized, it is not enough to suggest that some industries might do better if nationalized, and to nationalize them if the accumulation of evidence gives promise that they will do better if nationalized. The principle of right in the universe demands nationalization, as God demands that the faithful partake of the sacraments. There is the church, a house not made with hands, founded in eternity and enduring till eternity; there are schisms, there are heresies, of which it was said, If any man preach any other gospel unto you than that ye have received let him be accursed. Do not look now, but that is the I.L.P. platform over there, the furthest from Marble Arch; do not take that leaflet, the woman who is giving it away is a Trotskyite.

The resemblance between Left-wing politics and the religious field is often so close that it must distress those who take seriously the tradition of materialism. That is, perhaps, one reason for the tolerance given by non-Communist Left-wingers to Communist scientists. They stand for materialist hands across the sea, for the export of atheism from the U.S.S.R. Some who were not actually Communists must have found grounds for satisfaction rather than dismay in the treachery of Alan Nunn May, because it was an intellectual conviction of the rightness of Communism which had led him to disregard all other considerations. Here was the new man who had driven out the old (yet the Evangelical preachers used to say that) and could build a future which would have nothing in it of the past (alas, another echo, for he saw a new heaven and a new earth, for the first heaven and the first earth were passed away). The heavens must have been laughing when, four years after the trial of Dr. Nunn May, in the beginning of 1950, there followed him into the Old Bailey dock a Communist scientist traitor beside whom he was a timid amateur, and that this new traitor should plainly have derived the strength of his treachery from a transplanted heresy. The sternest orthodoxy would allow Quakerism its special grace, and it is a shame that any shadow should fall on it. But it is only the truth that Dr. Klaus Emil Fuchs was born in a Quaker home, and that, materialist though he was, he was inspired to his breach of faith with England, which had sheltered him as a refugee, by his memory of the doctrine of the Inner Light.

VI

IN 1874 in the little industrial town of Beerfelden in the Odenwald, that district of wooded hills which lies between Darmstadt and Heidelberg, there was born a child named Emil Fuchs. He grew into a man who had a great effect on his fellow-men: though short and full-faced he had great physical charm, he could speak in private and in public with burning intensity, he was inflexible in his courage and single-mindedness, he never ceased to seek the truth, and in the opinion of some of the people who liked him best he was not very intelligent. He became a Lutheran pastor and held ministries in various places until 1918, when he settled down in the industrial centre of Eisenach. His functions must have altered, for he joined the Society of Friends in 1925, but he remained in Eisenach until 1931, when he became professor of religious science at an academy for the training of teachers in Kiel. He was politically very active and was the first pastor to join the Social Democratic Party. After 1921 he became very well known throughout Germany as a speaker for a group known as the Religious Socialists. He married young and had several sons and daughters. His family life was remarkable for its simplicity and its gaiety. There were few homes in which parents and children seemed to live on a smoother plane of happy equality.

As the Nazi threat grew stronger in the late 'twenties and the early 'thirties Dr. Fuchs considered what he should do and decided that it was his duty as a Christian to oppose Hitler. Throughout the whole of the Nazi regime, in peace and in war, he stood by this decision without making the smallest compromise, though he was cruelly persecuted. Meanwhile his youngest son, Klaus Emil Fuchs, who had been born in 1911, was helping to create the situation for which his father was preparing himself by prayer. He was a university student, first at Leipzig and then at Kiel, and at both places he was involved in the useless and silly and violent political activities by which German undergraduates have done so much to destroy the civil order and social coherence of their country. He joined the students' group of the Social Democratic Party, but quarrelled with them because they supported a policy of naval rearmament and he had been brought up to be a pacifist, but then he quarrelled with his father's pacifism, and joined the Reichsbanner, a semi-military organization composed of young members of the Social Democratic and the Democratic Parties (as it might be here, the Labour and the Liberal Parties). Then he went to Kiel, where he transferred to the University branch of the Social Democratic Party, but quarrelled with the Party when it decided to support Hindenburg as Reichspräsident for fear that if they ran their own candidate they would split the anti-Nazi vote and Hitler would be elected. He offered himself as a speaker to the Communist Party, and at the same time joined an organization, frowned upon by the Social Democratic Party, in which members of the Social Democratic and Communist Parties attempted to convert those members of the Nazi Party whom they believed to be sincere and open to appeals to their better feelings. Then, when Hindenburg had been elected, Papen was made Reichskanzler and he dismissed the elected Prussian Government and put in the Reichsstatthalter, as a kept government. Klaus Emil Fuchs ran along to the Communist Party headquarters and joined it because the Social Democratic Party was doing nothing effective. What had happened was that the Communists had been attacking the Social Democratic Party instead of the Nazis, telling all the young idiots like Klaus Emil Fuchs that it was Codlin who was their friend, not Short; and the Social Democratic Party was in consequence so weakened that it could do nothing. This had been the intention of the

Communists, who desired Hitler to come to power because they believed that he would soon fall and they would then come to power. Hence the doom of Germany, and all of us.

Klaus Fuchs then became busy and happy, in the suicidal way of Germans, in carrying on a silly and mischief-making campaign regarding the internal affairs of Kiel University. The Nazi students had started an agitation protesting against the high fees; and the organization composed of Social Democratic Communists, of which Klaus Fuchs had now become chairman, decided to call their bluff, and started negotiations with the Nazi students, proposing that they should join to carry on a campaign for lower fees and should organize a strike of the students. The Nazi students hedged, and after a few weeks Klaus Emil Fuchs issued a leaflet describing the negotiations and pointing out how little the Nazis had been in earnest. Then the Nazis, to get back their prestige, used some dispute between the faculty and the students as an excuse to call a strike against the Rector of the University. By this time Hitler had been made Reichskanzler and the Nazi students were able to enlist the support of the S.A., who demonstrated in front of the University. Klaus Emil Fuchs was physically weedy, with a large head and a narrow rickety body, but he had inherited his father's courage, and every day he walked up and down in front of the S.A. to challenge his Nazi fellow-students to do their worst. On one occasion they threatened him with violence but he escaped. Then, on his way to an illegal conference of anti-Nazi students held in Berlin, he read of the burning of the Reichstag in the newspaper and realized that the Communist Party would have to go underground, and he took the badge of the hammer and sickle from his coat-lapel, and prepared to go underground.

For some time he hid. Then the Communist Party arranged for him to go abroad as a refugee, telling him that he must continue his studies, because there would come a time, after there had been a revolution in Germany, when people with technical knowledge would be required to build up the new Communist Germany. The Communist Party had a finger in every pie during that period. They had not fought Hitler, they had only fought the Social Democratic Party, but they gained a large measure of control over the organizations distributing the offerings of good-will which were made by the liberals of the world to the victims of the Nazis. Klaus Emil Fuchs was first sent to France and then to England, where he was befriended by the Society for the Protection of Science and Learning, and sent to Bristol University, to get his doctorate of philosophy in mathematics and physics. Afterwards he got a scholarship at Edinburgh University and there took his doctorate of science, afterwards being given a Carnegie Research Fellowship. He carried on the work it enabled him to do after the war broke out, for he went before an Aliens Tribunal and pointed to his membership of the Communist Party as proof that he was anti-Nazi. But in May of 1940 the Nazis invaded the Low Countries and France, and it became necessary for the British to intern all aliens, for the safety of all parties. He was one of a group of alien scientists who were taken to Canada and placed in a camp on the Heights of Abraham outside Quebec. There was a strong and open Communist section in this camp, led by Hans Kahle, a veteran of the Spanish Civil War, who is described in Douglas Hyde's *I Believed* and in Mrs. Haldane's *Truth Will Out*. He is now Police Chief in Mecklenburg in the Eastern Zone of Germany. Fuchs was his recognized second in command.

In 1942 he was allowed to return to Great Britain, and he went to Glasgow University to continue his researches. Very soon Professor Rudolf Peierls, a young and very eminent German-born physicist who was working at Birmingham University on atomic research for the British Government, asked for his assistance. So he went to Birmingham and in June signed the usual security undertaking and in July applied for naturalization as a British subject, in due course taking the oath of allegiance to his Majesty the King. At about the same time he decided to inform the U.S.S.R. about the work he was doing, and he established contact with another member of the Communist Party. For the following eight years he maintained continuous contact with persons who were personally unknown to him but whom he knew to be charged with the duty of transmitting to Russia all the information he gave them; and he told them all he could about his work, without hesitation. For some months he worked happily with Professor Peierls, making his home with him and his family in Edgbaston. In 1943 Professor Peierls went to

America and worked on the American Atomic Project for three years, and so did Klaus Emil, the British Government guaranteeing his loyalty. When they returned Klaus Emil was made head of the theoretical physics division of the Atomic Energy Establishment at Harwell, and he held this post, regularly communicating to Soviet agents information regarding the researches carried on in the establishment, until he was arrested in February 1950.

Meanwhile his father was treading a stony path with great courage and endurance. When Hitler came to power, Dr. Fuchs was deprived of his professorship at Kiel, and later was imprisoned in a concentration camp for nine months. He was not singled out for punishment owing to any act of his own, he was taken in a blanket catch of dissenting ministers. But he did nothing to ward off his fate, though he was invited by the Ministry of Education to come into the Nazi Party on easy terms, and as soon as he was released, though he was under surveillance by the Gestapo, he and two of his sons started a car hire service which was a cover for an escape route for refugees. After three years the cars were confiscated. At various times his sons fled the country, and a daughter of his, who was a painter, became subject to recurrent mania after she had helped her young husband to escape, and finally threw herself off a moving train and was killed. In complete loneliness, except for his motherless grandson of four, Dr. Fuchs lived through the war-years, maintaining his opposition to the regime, and performing such courageous acts as addressing disaffected Nazis gathered together in private houses.

When the war came to an end his life brightened. He was reunited with his scattered children, and though he was now over seventy, he embarked on an active life as a Quaker preacher and teacher, travelling all over Germany to find and reassemble the remnants of the Society of Friends, and to welcome those who wished to join it. In 1948 he went for a year to lecture at the American Quaker Centre, Pendle Hill, and then returned to Germany to take up his work again, which was lying more and more among the members of the German branch of the body known as the Fellowship of Reconciliation. None of these associations is suspicious. The Quaker movement has been subjected to many attempts at Communist infiltration, but these

L

have been checked by wise and hard-headed leadership. It is possible that the professed Quaker who makes propaganda aimed at weakening the defences of Great Britain or America is a disguised Communist, but it would be unlikely that a Communist would be able to carry on any agitation useful to his cause inside the Quaker organization. Some of the members of the Fellowship of Reconciliation had dubious political antecedents, but investigation shows that most of these were due to family connections which it would have been hard to waive. But it so happened that from 1947 Dr. Fuchs and his followers had had one overmastering desire, and this certainly looked suspicious when the activities of Klaus Emil were exposed; for what they wished was that Dr. Fuchs should go and live and work in the Eastern Zone of Germany. This was, however, not because he and his followers liked the Russians, but because they did not. They saw Soviet rule as an extreme example of sinful man's tendency to bring suffering into the world by violating what is holy; and it was Dr. Fuchs' intention to save oppressed and oppressors alike by meeting the Russians with love and recalling them to peaceful ways by reminding them of Christ. When Dr. Fuchs became professor of ethics and religion in the University of Leipzig, his followers did not conceive this as a release into Utopia, but as a descent into Hell.

There could hardly be a more striking example of the difficulty of applying security tests to people above a certain level of mental complexity. On the face of it Dr. Fuchs' desire to go into the Eastern Zone, and the readiness of the Soviet authorities to give him a professorship, look as if the old gentleman must be a full member of the Communist Party. But investigation was bound to show that he regarded himself as Daniel about to enter the lions' den, and that the Soviet authorities were employing him as they will employ anyone of good repute who is willing to associate with them. When that conclusion was reached, it would inevitably happen not only that no black mark was inscribed against the head of the theoretical physics division at Harwell, but that it was less likely that a black mark would be inscribed against him afterwards. If somebody had conceived a suspicion that Klaus Emil might be a Communist it would be examined with the reflection that after all there would probably be nothing in it, since he came from a quietist family which extended its tolerance to Communists not because they were Communists but because they were human. It would obviously not be within the scope of a security officer to conduct his investigations on a plane likely to reveal that in the quietism of the father there was a strain which might, to his amazement and distress, emerge in the son as Communist treachery, though it was logical enough. A glimpse into Dr. Fuchs' mind is given by a remarkable pamphlet he wrote, called "Christ in Catastrophe", which has been widely distributed by the Quakers in America and England.

It is an eloquent pamphlet, which is beautiful in its description of the joy felt by the mystic when he is aware of the presence of God. But it is also egotistical and smug and curiously unsympathetic towards the sorrows and achievements of others. It lays stress on the Divine favours that were showered on Dr. Fuchs, and the mission which Christ gave him to carry on in stricken Germany. "Was it imagination that enabled people like me to know, from the beginning of all propaganda, that the spirit of Hitler was not God?" he asks. "Why did so many, very clever and orthodox theological thinkers, scholars, pastors and leaders of churches not recognize evil?" He goes on to taunt those who "had Christianity as doctrine, very elaborate, very refined, very traditional", but "had not that experience in which the living Christ, the risen Lord, gives his call and task for this day and this time". There is not one word of praise to be spared for, say, the German Catholics, though the heroism of many of them was exemplary. There is also an unengaging passage in which he describes how when he came back to Germany from a six weeks' visit to his son in Switzerland in 1947, he saw the faces of the people in the street with a new sharpness, and he describes them with singular lack of pity. He admits that "sometimes" he sees a face "in which it is written that this man, this woman, overcame suffering and despair, that behind the face is serenity, a conscience at rest and yet awake to love, truth, helpfulness", but concerning the rest he permits himself to make assumptions which, considering the time and the place, seem remarkably disagreeable. It also seems a pity, when describing the reactions of American newspaper-readers to "the lynching of a Negro in an unknown township in the South", to say, "they read, shudder a little, and forget". A number of Americans, when they read of a lynching, shudder but do not forget; and engage in activities of a most purposeful kind to prevent another one happening. The slow recession of the hatred between black and white in the Southern States is due to individual decisions of a moment which every human being must respect.

There is also a curious lack of shrewdness in the pamphlet. At one point Dr. Fuchs recounts how, after he had given a talk in a German town, a man of about fifty had come to him and told him, with tears in his eyes, that he longed to go to church and acknowledge God, but he could not because every time he came near the church he saw standing by the door the field chaplain attached to his regiment in the First World War, and heard him saying, as he said then, "Shoot them, beat them, kill them, win the attack!", and was therefore prevented from entering the church. On inquiry Dr. Fuchs found that the man was chairman of the Communist Party of that district. He regrets that the man has rejected Christianity and attributes his rejection to the fault of the chaplain in not understanding that a Christian must be a pacifist. But he does not remind the man that it is inconsistent for one who leaves the church because it is not pacifist to go over to the Communists, who rejoice in the exploits of the Red Army. Indeed, he seems himself to forget the existence of the Red Army, for he talks of the Communist Party as promising a "world of justice, peace, and love". But at the same time he deplores that this man should have been so disillusioned by hearing the warlike utterances by the chaplain that he accepted it as proven that man will always fight, and therefore all of us have not only the right but the duty to fight in the same way for their ideals. If that were the man's own conclusion, it was illogical of him, and uncharitable, to feel such bitterness against the chaplain because he had come to the same conclusion. The emotional force behind this passage, its air of moral authority, and its incoherence, make a painful impression.

It was information received from America which led the British security organization to turn its attention to Klaus Emil Fuchs in 1950. It was strange that they had not been actively interested in him long ago. He had made no secret of his Communist sympathies when he came before the Aliens Tribunal which granted him temporary exemption from internment at the beginning of the war, and his fellow-internees have never doubted but that he was an active Party member: but though the Americans actually gave the information which touched off the fuse, their record was not more creditable than the British. The existence of a courier system transmitting information to Soviet headquarters in the United States had been notified to the Federal Bureau of Investigation by an ex-Communist spy named Elizabeth Bentley who had repented and made a voluntary confession of all her activities in the autumn of 1945. Had her evidence been followed up it would have led to Fuchs. No fewer than three of the couriers appeared in 1947 before a Federal Grand Jury summoned to investigate espionage, and cleared themselves by what now seem oddly unconvincing stories. In May 1949 Elizabeth Bentley again disclosed particulars of the courier system before a committee on Immigration and Naturalization which is a sub-committee of the Senate Judiciary Committee. In the United States, as in Great Britain, the weakness of security is not that it does not collect information but that the information it collects is not used. It is interesting to note that Alger Hiss was first accused of espionage in 1939, and that no effort was made to conduct an official investigation into the charges until 1948. This was equally unfortunate whether he was innocent or guilty.

The arrest of Klaus Emil Fuchs on February 2, 1950, and his appearances at Bow Street on February 10 and at the Old Bailey on March 1 told the world that a new page had been turned in the book of history. On that page were written two facts. First, Great Britain and America had lost most of the protection they thought they enjoyed against their only potential enemy, the U.S.S.R., in their monopoly of knowledge concerning the atomic bomb. Thanks to Klaus Emil Fuchs and Alan Nunn May, its theoretical basis must be known to the Russians. It may be remarked that, although it is often maintained that nuclear physicists all over the world have so much knowledge in common that it is only a matter of time before all of them rediscover that theoretical basis for themselves, and therefore there is no point in keeping secret any work done by British and American nuclear physicists, many non-Communist scientists do not agree. They point out that, though many scientific discoveries have been made by different people working independently at about the same time, many more have been unique achievements, and that in this field especially the individuality of a single scientist may determine the direction of a complex research. They find significance in the circumstance that British and American and German scientists went into the war with a common stock of knowledge, and that the British and Americans came out of the war knowing a great deal about atomic energy and very little about rockets, while the Germans came out knowing almost nothing about atomic energy and a great deal about rockets. If we had now no other advantage than lay in our knowledge of the practical problems concerning the manufacture of atomic bombs, and our superior industrial equipment, then we enjoyed no protection which the Russians might not destroy by further spying of a sort which they evidently found easy to command, and by the concentration of their resources, on a scale that a totalitarian state finds far easier than a democracy; and the blame lay on these Communist scientists. And the second fact written on this page of history was the complete unmanageability of the Communist scientist. This was an even stranger animal than we had imagined.

When Klaus Emil Fuchs was approached by the security officers, he began to talk in a manner which cannot exactly be called light-minded, for indeed one might as well call *The Sorrows of Werther* light-minded, but which was not what could have been expected from a man charged with his particular offence. It is to be conceded that he had been found out, and that he must have been extremely disconcerted. It also has to be conceded that his statement was typically German in the way that English people find most difficult to understand. He spoke with the subjectivity left to the German people as a legacy from its romantic movement, which makes them pass round their emotions as if they were nosegays which give out perfume; and he showed that obsessive interest in political activities of the more violent sort combined with a complete lack of political sense which has put Germany where it is today. If this is remembered, it seems less strange that he should have begun by assuring the security officers that he had had a very happy childhood, a matter concerning which they could not have expressed any anxiety; that he should have gone on to recall, as a doomed man might like to recall some spirited act of his early innocence, how, when all his school-fellows wore Imperial badges on the anniversary of the Weimar Republic, he alone put on a Republican badge and had it torn off; and that he recited in pitiless detail all the political fatuities of himself and his friends and his enemies in Leipzig and Kiel Universities, with a respectfulness that no Englishman of thirty-eight would extend to his own doings at the age of twenty. But, even after making all allowances for his plight and for differences of national characteristics, his statement is odd and displeasing.

It is the work of a man who has never emerged from adolescence, and who on matters outside his special province could not even be considered as an intelligent adolescent. It has a confessional quality. He was speaking to the representatives of the state, whose business it is to consider the interests of all, but he importuned them with particulars of the phases of his spiritual condition, to which nobody could give attention unless they were representatives of a God who has infinite time and love to bestow on the totality of each individuality. It also appears that he shrank from no responsibility whatsoever, he believed that he could solve any problem; it was as if he believed himself to be Sophia, heavenly wisdom. Though sometimes conscious of sin, this did not affect his confidence in himself, and he makes it plain that he regards it as his part to forgive, not to seek forgiveness. He also shows extreme inhumanity.

It was in the political sphere that he had made his great decision of treachery; but he showed unusual political ignorance. It is well known that in the early 'thirties, when the German Communists accused the Social Democrats of not opposing Hitler, they were doing so to draw anti-Nazi enthusiasts away from the Social Democratic Party, and thus split the Popular Front, so that Hitler had to come to power. Their intelligence service and their political sense were so weak that they believed that Hitler's regime would last for only a short time and that they would make a revolution and build a Communist Germany on its ruins. This interpretation of these events is so generally accepted that it would be virtually impossible for a non-Communist to write of them without alluding to it, and for a Communist to write of them without attacking it. But it is plain that Fuchs has never heard of this interpretation. He writes of these events as naïvely as if he were still twenty. He goes on to bare his breast concerning the origin of the readiness to deceive which, from first to last, is the only aspect of his own character that seems doubtful to him. At Kiel University the Left- wing organization he had led, which had pretended to co-operate with the Nazi students in propaganda against the high fees, had proposed to them that they should jointly organize a strike of students, well knowing that the Nazis would turn tail when it came to the point. After the negotiations had gone on for some time Fuchs suddenly issued a leaflet explaining that the negotiations had been going on for some time and had only proved that the Nazis were not in earnest. He had been highly praised for taking this step at the conference he attended in Berlin just after the burning of the Reichstag, but it had been an unfair thing to do. He should first have warned the Nazis that he would issue such a leaflet if they failed to take action by such and such a date. "I omitted", he said, "to resolve in my mind" this point, and perhaps he thought that it was then that he had begun to accept the Communist view that scruples "of this kind are prejudices which are weaknesses and which you must fight against".

He went on to describe how he went first to England when he "tried to make a serious study of the basic Marxist philosophy". He describes this study in terms of the most startling banality. "The idea which gripped me most was the belief that in the past man has been unable to understand his own history and the forces which lead to the further development of human society; that now for the first time man understands the historical forces and he is able to control them and that therefore for the first time he will be really free. I carried this idea over into the personal sphere and believed that I could understand myself and that I could make myself into what I believed I should be." This would not be considered good at the least distinguished Youth Congress. He goes on to relate respectfully the ill-informed and elementary opinions he had held concerning foreign affairs up till the time he was interned, and then suggests that it was a pity that the internees were for a long time not allowed any newspapers. The practical consideration that, if newspaper reading had been encouraged and the war had gone against us for any length of time, it might have been difficult for the guards to keep discipline, and even to protect the non-Nazi internees against the Nazi internees, does not occur to him. "I felt no bitterness at the internment because I could understand that it was necessary and at that time England could not spare good people to look after the internees, but it did deprive me of the chance of learning more about the real character of the British people." It is implied that he might have spared them if he had known more about them. It never crosses his mind that it was not for him to spite them or spare them, nor that at any time it might be right for him to submit to lawful authority and not to transcend it. The Lutheran right to private judgment in spiritual matters had been magnified to the right of private judgment to supersede public judgment in all fields, and it was claimed with a confidence which has only been equalled in those devotees who believe that divinity enters into them and illuminates them.

It is the heavy task of the heretic who rejects the authority of the Church to rediscover the whole spiritual cosmos by his own unaided efforts. In describing what happened after he began to work at Harwell and hand over the results achieved by himself and other scientists to the Soviet authorities, he said:

In the course of this work I began naturally to form bonds of personal friendship and I had to conceal from them my inner thoughts. I used my Marxist philosophy to establish in my mind two separate compartments. One compartment in which I allowed myself to make friendships, to have personal relations, to help people and to be in all personal ways the kind of man I wanted to be and the kind of man which, in a personal way, I had been before with my friends in or near the Communist Party. I could be free and easy and happy with other people without fear of disclosing myself because I knew that the other compartment would step in if I approached the danger point. I could forget the other compartment and still rely on it. It appeared to me at the time that I had become a "free man" because I had succeeded in the other compartment to establish myself completely independent of the surrounding forces of society. Looking back at it now the best way of expressing it seems to be to call it a controlled schizophrenia.

In fact, he had rediscovered the fact that it is possible to lie and cheat and deceive: nothing more than that. Later, in an equally muddled passage he tells us that he rediscovered that to lie and cheat and deceive is wrong, destructive to oneself and to one's environment. Many quite stupid little children would have told him as much, and although they had learned it by rote, it would still have been worth his while to listen to them. But his enormous vanity was too great for him to entertain the idea of ever listening. It was for him to be listened to. Perhaps the most terrifying sentence in his statement was this:

> In the post-war period I began again to have my doubts about Russian policy. It is impossible to give definite incidents because now the control mechanism acted against me also in keeping away from me facts which I could not look in the face, but they did penetrate and eventually I came to a point where I knew that I disapproved of many actions of the Russian Government and of the Communist Party, but I still believed that they would build a new world and that one day I would take part in it and that on that day I would also have to stand up and say to them that there are things which they are doing wrongly.

He had decided that the Western World was unfit to survive and had betrayed it to the Soviet Government; but the Soviet Government also was not worthy, he would have to correct it in its turn. George Fox believed that he was filled with the Inner Light and that he then "knew nothing but pureness, innocency, and righteousness". He was followed by James Nayler, whose followers called him Jesus and "the dear and precious Son of Zion, whose mother is a virgin and whose birth is immortal". The materialist in Klaus Emil rejected omniscience as impossible; but it firmly claimed omniscience, and it was willing to manifest omnipotence as the occasion arose. It happened to be the atom bomb of which he had disposal; but if it had been some weapon approaching still nearer to the absolute

320

of destructive power he would have disposed of it as blithely. He was unrestrained by any tenderness. He makes no mention of the sufferings of his family under the Nazi regime, he expresses no concern about the horrors of atomic warfare which, owing to his action, henceforward threaten Great Britain and Western Europe. Though he says that what he has done may "endanger" his friends, he apparently means merely that he might endanger their prospects of continued employment at Harwell. Though he admits that he recognizes his deceitfulness as wrong, he is unabashed, as Madame Guyon was when she had to sign what amounted to a retractation of her quietist doctrines. She had previously explained that it never seemed necessary for her to find a defence for her conduct "for I no longer have a conduct, and yet I act infallibly".

The trial of Klaus Emil Fuchs before the Lord Chief Justice at the Old Bailey on March 1, 1950, had the reticent quality which appertains to trials of Russian agents anywhere. The authorities would prefer it if nobody saw anything. They want to lift the cloth that hangs over the cage just long enough for the judge and jury to see the kind of bird which is inside, and sentence it accordingly, and pop back the cloth. It was all over in ninety minutes. Klaus Emil came into the dock, a pale neat young man, like innumerable middle-class Germans, with a bulging forehead and glasses, not much of a chin, and a weakly body. He was charged under the Official Secrets Act on an indictment comprising four counts: that on a day in 1943 in the city of Birmingham for a purpose prejudicial to the safety or interests of the state he communicated to a person unknown information relating to atomic research which was calculated to be, or might have been or was intended to be, directly or indirectly useful to an enemy, and that he had committed similar offences on a day unknown between December 31, 1943, and August 1, 1944, in the city of New York, and on a day unknown in February 1945, at Boston, Massachusetts, and on a day unknown in 1947 in Berkshire. His plea of guilty was entered. The Attorney-General opened for the prosecution and read passages from Klaus Emil's statement. A security officer gave evidence that he had taken down the statement, and he made the same assertion that was made at the trial of Dr. Alan Nunn May that before he took down the prisoner's statement there was no evidence upon which he could have been prosecuted. Now, this must be technically true. But all the same there must have been substantial reasons why the security officers had ever given Dr. Alan Nunn May or Klaus Emil opportunity to make their statements, and it is a pity to create an impression that here were two honest souls who confessed when they had no need. Fuchs' counsel made the debatable point that as the first three offences were committed during the time that Russia was fighting as an ally of Britain, it would be difficult to see how giving information to Russian agents could be interpreted as prejudicial to the safety or interests of the state; and he pointed out, too justly, that the authorities had bought this betrayal with their eyes wide open, for Klaus Emil had not concealed his Communist convictions when he appeared before the Aliens Tribunal. Then the Lord Chief Justice asked Klaus Emil if he had anything to say before sentence was passed on him, and he answered by a last flare-up of his celestial impudence. Complacently he complimented the court on having given him a fair trial. When the thin pipe of his voice was no longer heard, the Lord Chief Justice went on to deliver judgment. He enumerated the four main consequences of Klaus Emil's crime. He had imperilled the right of asylum which had extended to political refugees; he had not only betrayed the work he himself had done, which was the property of his employers, he had handed over the work of other scientists, who might therefore have fallen under unjust suspicion; he had imperilled the good relations between Great Britain and the United States by betraying work done in an American project; and he may have brought the irreparable ruin of atomic warfare on Great Britain and the United States. He then sentenced Klaus Emil to fourteen years' imprisonment, not for the sake of punishment, but to safeguard the country. "How can I be sure that a man of your mentality, as shown in that statement you have made," he asked, "may not at any other minute allow some curious working in your mind to lead you further to betray secrets of the greatest possible value and importance to this land?" It was the maximum sentence that could be given under the Official Secrets Act. It was much less than the sentence which the astonishing fact of Klaus Emil's existence passed on the human race. If he was one of the most gifted physicists in the world, then none of us, not even Communist scientists, could ever feel quite safe again. We could not be sure that some other genius would not arise, just a little sillier, just a little crazier, who would decide to set fire to all the world in order to please the dematerialized Red Indian who was his spiritualist aunt's control, or the holy men in Mars that he knew were waiting for the signal of the flames to come down and bring us salvation. It cannot be argued that no laboratory worker could have the power to initiate a holocaust. For an individual can contrive vast destructive results by such simple means as the sabotaging of his own results in such a way as to leave his employer defenceless before an enemy; or he can gather collaborators by a pretence of a saner mission. These are but two devices which might prove that other things than love can find a way.

VII

THE Communists made no protest against the sentence passed at the time of the trial or afterwards. The only observable consequence was one which follows any event which draws attention to the criminal proceedings of the Communist Party: in Great Britain and the United States a number of prominent Communists expressed disapproval of the Party policy, and dissociated themselves from it. This creates an illusion that the Communist Party is weakening, and that these particular people have become innocuous. But some resentment was expressed by those dissidents who, though not themselves Communist, have been persuaded that it is reactionary to punish a Communist for even the most unlawful act. An American radio commentator, assuming that look of country shrewdness which has unfortunately been bequeathed by Abraham Lincoln to inheritors often too urban to wear it appropriately, said: "I always heard that your British justice was the fairest in the world, but anybody could see that your Lord Chief Justice came into court with his mind made up about the case. Why, the minute Fuchs had stopped speaking he started right off with his judgment." It was explained to him that the Lord Chief Justice would certainly have read Klaus Emil's statement beforehand, as it had been admitted

323

without challenge before the examining magistrate, and would probably have been told that a plea of guilty was to be entered. But it was no use: the American came from a generation conditioned to grumble at authority, and it was as unprofitable to argue with him as it would have been to try and staunch by logic the flow of saliva that dribbled from the jaws of Pavlov's dogs when they heard the dinner-bell.

Others likened Klaus Emil's statement to the confessions so monotonously proffered by persons tried in Soviet courts for offences against the state. They were moved by a desire to prove that the confessions proffered in the Soviet courts were as freely given as it was known that Klaus Emil's statement had been. But the analogy does not hold good. The confessions in the Soviet courts are cut in the same pattern and astonish by their incompatibility with all that has been previously known about the persons who make them. But Klaus Emil's speech could not have been made by anybody who had not been a student in a German university in the early 'thirties, who had not read English Left-wing weeklies and newspapers in the late 'thirties, who had not a quietist background. It had traces of adherence to a pattern.

He remarked that when he accepted the position offered him in the Atomic Project "at first I thought that all I would do would be to inform the Russian authorities that work upon the atomic bomb was going on". It is a curious coincidence that in the propaganda distributed for the purpose of getting people to petition for the immediate release of Dr. Alan Nunn May, it was stated that "the real significance of his action was to inform Russia of the *existence* of the vast atomic energy programme". It is a strange echo. But for the most part the statement was highly individual. Then towards the end of May there was announced the arrest in Philadelphia of an American citizen named Harry Gold on a charge of espionage, based on allegations that he had acted as a courier for Dr. Fuchs, receiving from him written and oral information about the work in Los Alamos Atom Project and handing it over to a Soviet official. It was believed in London that Gold's arrest was due to information given by Klaus Emil, but this was not so. He talked, and talked with great profit to the authorities, but not until after Gold had been arrested.

This was the first of a series of arrests made in connection with this particular American spy service. Within six months they numbered eight. Most of them illustrated a tropism which few historians would have predicted. Their parents had left Russia to avoid persecution and had been received handsomely in the United States. They themselves had been nourished by the swelling abundance of the last half-century as America had known it; none was poor by European standards. They all had had good educations, most had graduated from universities, all had gone out to steady employment on a high level. At the first opportunity they set to working, year in year out with great pains and at great risk, in order to betray the United States to Russia. It is not easy to find out what moved them, for most of them refused to testify on their own behalf. The Party direction had changed now that the eyes of the world were on such cases, and there were no longer the protestations of innocence, the attacks on the probity of the courts, the barracking of spectators, and all the elaborate procedure which had been part of the standard American Communist drill till then. Now the direction to American Communists was, as it long had been to English Communists, to get these trials over as quickly and quietly as possible. But there were two among the accused who broke away from the Party while they were under arrest, and talked. One was a young soldier, David Greenglass, who in 1945 had come back to his post in New Mexico from leave in New York with a bit of cardboard in his pocket, the top half of a box of jelly-cubes, cut across in zigzags. Later Harry Gold had come down to New Mexico with the other half of that box-top, and the soldier had matched his with it and had known that this was the man to whom he was to hand certain information he had learned in the course of his work on the atom bomb project. After arrest this young man soon threw in his hand, and gladly testified against his sister and her husband, Ethel and Julius Rosenberg, who had got him into this trouble. The other accused person who became a Government witness was Harry Gold.

He carried the apotheosis of the new traitor a stage further. He was a little dark man, so swollen with good living that he lost fifty pounds during the first six months of his detention. He was born in Switzerland in 1910, of Russian parents named

Golodnitsky, who brought him to America three years later. Through his adolescence he worked in a laboratory by day and at night studied for a course at Pennsylvania and New York Universities. Finally he took his Baccalaureate of Science, Summa cum Laude, at Xavier University, a small but old and renowned Jesuit College in Ohio. From then on he held well-paid and interesting research posts. But from 1935 to 1946, which included his undergraduate years at Xavier University, he was a Communist agent, specializing in courier work. It might have been expected that, when he came to tell of this work, the most interesting part of his story must deal with his relationship to Klaus Emil Fuchs. But his account of this told us few new facts, other than that there had been a meeting between them at Santa Fé, which is not among those mentioned in the indictment brought forward at his trial, either because it never took place, or because it was not known to the authorities at that time. This alleged meeting, by an extravagant irony, took place on the 19th of September 1945, the very same day that the less fortunate William Joyce was sentenced to death for treason at the Old Bailey. One item in the conversation which Gold reported as having taken place at this meeting did, indeed, have its startling aspect. Fuchs had, it appeared, expressed anxiety to Gold because the British and not the Russians had taken Kiel, explaining that the Kiel Gestapo had a very complete dossier on him, and that he was afraid lest British Intelligence would find it and "become aware of his very strong Communist background and ties". It was surprising to hear this from Harry Gold's lips in March 1951, since in March 1950 Mr. Attlee had told the House of Commons that he objected to "loose talk in the press suggesting inefficiency on the part of security services. I entirely deny that. Not long after this man [Fuchs] came into this country— that was in 1933—it was said that he was a Communist. The source of that information was the Gestapo. At that time the Gestapo accused everybody of being a Communist. When the matter was looked into there was no support for it whatever." That was a strange remark, in view of the fact that Mr. Attlee must recently have read Klaus Emil's own statement with its abundant particulars of his Communist youth. But Mr. Attlee went on to paint the lily by saying that "from that time onwards there was no support", which in view of Klaus Emil's close association with the well-known Communist, Hans Kahle, in the internment camp on the Heights of Abraham, under the nose of a notably capable security officer, was stranger still. The security services cannot be held responsible for this astonishing pronouncement, for they would obviously have been unlikely to put out anything so incompatible with Klaus Emil's statement or with facts known to numerous internees; nor could they have approved a form of words which might have spread abroad the false suggestion that the British Government in the 'thirties was in the habit of discussing the eligibility of German refugees with the Gestapo. The muddle must have been made nearer Mr. Attlee, and it proves how little the subject of Soviet espionage has been mastered by persons in authority in this country. It also may explain why of late the United States Government has shown a certain reluctance to share atomic energy information with the British.

More novel was Gold's account of his exploits in the field of industrial espionage. Most of this work was done with another of the persons arrested in the summer of 1950, a man a couple of years younger than himself, named Abraham Brothman, who had taken a degree in chemical engineering at Columbia University in New York and was working in the Republic Steel Corporation. From 1941 Brothman had steadily handed over to Gold blue-prints and drawings of various industrial processes relating to high-octane gasolene, turbine-type airplanes, chemical production, and synthetic rubber, which the other handed over to Amtorg, the Soviet trading agency, which rapidly photographed them, and gave them back to Gold, so that he could return them to Brothman after a few hours. There was a sordid commercial side to this. Some of the documents, such as the blue-prints of the "kettles" or vats used in chemical processes, were the property of the Republic Steel Corporation, which was paying Brothman well for his work; and the Soviet authorities could have bought these vats by the simple process of paying for them. It would take a great deal of ingenuity to read international idealism into this.

But this happy relationship broke down in 1945, when Gouzenko gave the papers referring to the atom bomb spy ring to the Canadian Government. The Soviet authorities then dispersed for the time being all agents who had been concerned in any way with this ring, sending the Russians among them back to Russia, and telling the non-Russians to find some innocent occupation. Harry Gold then went to work in the laboratory owned by the firm of consulting engineers belonging to Brothman, which was contrary to the iron rule that Communist agents never associate publicly with one another, but it was a ruse designed to avert suspicion in these special circumstances. If investigators should become aware of the previous association Gold would be able to say that he had been seeing Brothman in order to arrange his transfer to Brothman's firm. In 1947 the confession of Elizabeth Bentley led to the appearance of both Harry Gold and Abraham Brothman before a grand jury which had been impanelled to investigate espionage, on well-founded charges of industrial espionage, but they lied their way out on this prearranged story of common business interests arising out of Brothman's employment of Gold. According to Harry Gold's own statement, he appears to have operated as a Communist agent until he was arrested in May 1950. He was then engaged in research on chemical conditions associated with certain cardiac diseases in the Philadelphia General Hospital.

In Klaus Emil's statement it had become apparent that his rejection of England and his treachery towards it only represented an intermediate stage; he was already preparing to reject Soviet Russia after he had helped it to conquer England, and to rebel. Harry Gold was able to enjoy an immediate realization of similar intentions as a result of his arrest. Though he had been a Communist agent for eleven years, he had never joined the Party. He did not like it. He regarded the Party members as "a lot of wacked-up Bohemians". He associated with them reluctantly, simply because he had to have somebody to conspire with against the United States. It appeared possible at first that his expressions of repugnance for Communists might be a directed attempt to make him seem detached from the Party, so that public condemnation of him should not fall on the Party also, like the attempt to present Dr. Nunn May as a scientist and not as a Communist. For he trotted out some of the orthodox Party propaganda, declaring that he "felt as an ally I was only helping the Soviet Union obtain certain information that I thought it was entitled to", a poor excuse for spying that went back to 1935. But he proved his sincerity when he gave evidence against Abraham Brothman and a defendant who was charged with him, a woman of thirty-five named Miriam Moskowitz, who had been his private secretary and later was a partner in his engineering firm, as well as owning her own cosmetic factory. These two were prosecuted on a charge of obstructing justice, in connection with the occasion when Gold and Brothman had been summoned before the grand jury in 1947 and had committed perjury. There could be no doubting the genuineness of the gusto with which Gold gave evidence to support these charges. He described with unsparing humour how Brothman, who was long-faced and serious and simple, had fetched and carried for him, and how he had played a joke on him when he had complained that his services had not been sufficiently recognized. Gold had taken the chief Russian spy in America, Semen Semenov, to see Brothman and thank him, assuring him that Semenov (who actually worked in Amtorg and lived in New York) had come all the way from Russia specially to express the gratitude of the Soviet Government. Merciless, Gold described how Brothman had, choking with emotion, described this as "one of the most wonderful experiences of my life".

Gold described how, before their appearance before the grand jury in 1947, they had paced the streets of New York all night, getting their perjured stories consistent, rehearsing the right convincing accents. He recalled later a scene conveying the very essence of his association with these people: after he had made his appearance before the grand jury he went to see Brothman and Miss Moskowitz and tell them how he had fared. He described how he had succeeded in getting the grand jury to see him as "a small, timid, frightened man, who in some manner was involved on the fringe of espionage and who now was completely aghast at what he was on the brink of". They had all laughed together in delight. They were then a group that had split off from society. Now the group itself had split. There was laughter again, after this second fission made by the dividing force. It was heard in Harry Gold's voice as he mocked at his friends, and Miss Moskowitz grinned across the court an answering mockery. But there was no more laughter heard on April 5, 1951, when Ethel Rosenberg and her husband Julius were sentenced to death for espionage committed in time of war, as the result of testimony given against them by her brother, David Greenglass, who thus saved his life at the cost of theirs. These were people far cleverer than John Amery or Alfred Vivian or Herbert George or Stoker Rose; but not even Galaher or Martin had come within touching distance of that infamy. They had started on the way to it, but they were artless pioneers. They had not foreseen this climax of faithlessness where treachery was eclipsed by new treachery, but eclipsed that too. The Rosenbergs' trafficking in atom secrets had been immense. Like Fuchs and Nunn May, they may yet number their victims by millions. Yet this small matter of brother and sister, this hostile twin to incest, this seduction of a brother into peril by an ideologically inflamed sister, this selling of that sister's heated flesh by a brother chilled with fear, kills quantity of horror by its quality. Still, millions of victims are millions. It was no wonder the photographs of the Rosenbergs show that their faces, formed by nature to express natural emotions, resigned the expressive function, and became blank as if they had made the final resignation of that function which is death. For the living to look like the dead is, as the book of Leviticus says about a bizarre but really not so important a matter, confusion. But such are the children of internationalism, which was to cast out the dark blunder, men's love of their own country, by a white radiance of universal charity.

EPILOGUE

THE trouble about man is twofold. He cannot learn truths which are too complicated; he forgets truths which are too simple.

Today we have forgotten that we live outwards from the centre of a circle and that what is nearest to the centre is most real to us. If a man cut his hand, it hurts him more than if he cuts some other man's hand, therefore he is more careful to guard his own. Even if he spend his whole life in teaching himself that we are all of one body, and that therefore his neighbour's pain is his also, he will still suffer more when his own hand is hurt, for the message then runs straight from his palm and fingers to his brain, travelling at a speed faster than the messengers, which bear the news of others' accidents. Throughout his life it remains true that what is nearest to his body is of greatest interest to his mind. When a baby is given food and held warmly by a certain woman, he grows up to feel a closer concern for her than for other women of her generation, and at her death will feel greatly disturbed. Should he be institution-bred and have no woman as his particular slave and tyrant, grievance will sour him till his last day.

If in his maturity he should live with a woman for any considerable period of time, he and she are apt, unless they are overtaken by certain obviously disagreeable circumstances, to behave as though there were a complete community of interest between them. There must have been some instinctive liking between them or they would never have been drawn together in the first place; they became involved in each other's prosperity; experience has taught each how the other will behave in most eventualities. Therefore they do better by one another than strangers would. Should he have children by this or any other woman, they will have great power over him, while other children will have little or none. He will know so much more about them. The veiled moment of their conception is his secret, and resemblances to him, to a familiar woman, or to his kin, enable him to trace their inner lives, disguised though they be first by their inarticulateness and then by their articulateness. He can read them by the light of his own nature, and read his own nature by their light, and will have a sense of fusion between himself and those who are so inextricably tangled with that self.

If that man live in a house during the days of his childhood, he will know it better than any house he lives in later, though it shelter him forty years longer; and though the staircase wind as deviously as any in the world he will find his way down it in the darkness as surely as if it were straight. All his life long, when he hears talk of woods, he shall see beech-woods if he come from a Buckinghamshire village, and a castle to him shall stand on Castle Rock if Edinburgh was his home; and in the one case he shall know Southern English country-folk, and in the other Lowland Scottish townsfolk, better than other Britons. Born and bred in England, he will find it easier to understand the English than the rest of men, not for any mystical reason, but because their language is his, because he is fully acquainted with their customs, and because he is the product of their common history. So also each continent enjoys a vague unity of self-comprehension, and is divided from the others by a sharp disunity; and even those who profess the closest familiarity with the next world speak with more robust certainty of this world and seem not to want to leave it.

This is not to say that a man loves what is nearest to him. He may hate his parents, his wife, and his children. Millions have done so. On the tables of the Law it was written, "Honour thy father and thy mother, as the Lord thy God hath commanded thee; that thy days may be prolonged, and that it may go well with thee, in the land which the Lord thy God giveth thee", and it is advice of almost gross practicality aimed at preventing the faithful from abandoning themselves to their natural impulses and wasting all their force on family rows. St. Paul, that great artist who perpetually betrayed his art because he was also a great man of action, and constantly abandoned the search for truth to seek instead a myth to inspire vigorous action, tried to gild the bondage of man to the familiar. "So ought men to love their wives as their own bodies", he says. "He that loveth his wife loveth himself. For no man ever yet hated his own flesh; but nourisheth and cherisheth it, even as the Lord the Church." But countless men have hated their own flesh. Everywhere and at all times men have carried such hatred to the point of slaying it, and still more have persecuted it by abstinence and mortification and debauchery. But it has a value to them far above their loathing or their liking. It is their own flesh and they can have no direct experience of any other. Not with all the gold in the world or by incessant prayer can we obtain another instrument case, packed with these our only instruments, the five senses, by which alone we can irradiate the universe that is a black void around us, and build a small irradiated platform in that darkness. A wife is someone who has stood on that irradiated platform long enough to be fully examined and to add the testimony of her own senses as to the nature of that encircling mystery. She may be loved or hated, or loved and hated, and still serve in that research.

A child knows that what is near is easier for him to handle than what is far. All men took it for granted till recent times, when it was challenged, together with some other traditional assumptions, not because they had proved unsound, but because a number of urbanized populations from which the intellectual classes were largely drawn had lost their sense of spiritual as well as material process. They had lost their sense of material process owing to the development of the machine; goods which had formerly been produced by simple and comprehensible processes, often carried on where they could be witnessed by the consumer, were now produced by elaborate process, not to be grasped by people without mechanical training, and carried on in the privacy of the large factories.

The reason for their ignorance of spiritual process was the urban lack of the long memory and the omniscient gossip enjoyed by the village. The townsman is surrounded by people whose circumstances he does not know and whose heredities are the secrets of other districts; and he is apt to take their dissimulating faces and their clothed bodies as the sum of them. People began to think of each other in a new way; as being simple, with a simplicity in reality unknown in organic life. They ignored the metabolism of human nature, by which some experiences are absorbed into the mind and magically converted into personality, while others are rejected, all in the interests of love or hate, good or evil, life or death, according to the inhabiting daemon, whose reasons are never given. Man conceived himself as living

335

reasonably under the instruction of the five senses, which tell him to seek pleasure and avoid pain.

The first effect of this rational conception of life was cheerful vulgarity; and there are worse things than that. Man might well have felt this view of his destiny as a relief after the Christian philosophy, which abased his origin to criminality, and started him so low only to elevate him to the height—even more disagreeable to most people—of company with godhead, after dragging him through all sorts of unpalatable experiences, including participation in a violent and apparently unnecessary death. In so far as a man adopted the new and rationalist philosophy he could be compared to an actor who, after spending a lifetime playing Hamlet and Othello and King Lear, retires to keep a country pub. All was thenceforward to go at a peaceable jog-trot. Children were to grow up straight striplings of light, undeformed by repression, unscarred by conflicts, because their parents would hand them over in their earliest years to the care of pedagogic experts. Divorce was not to be reckoned as a disgrace nor as a tragedy nor even as a failure, but as a pleasurable extension of experience, like travel. Furthermore—and this was considered as the sanest adjustment of all—the ardours of patriotism were to be abandoned, and replaced by a cool resolution to place one's country on a level with all others in one's affections and to hand it over without concern to the dominion of any other power which could offer it greater material benefits. It was not out of cynicism that the benefits demanded were material: it was believed that the material automatically produced the intellectual and the spiritual. These reasonable steps having been taken, there was to follow harmony. The only peril was that it might become too sweet.

But the five senses had evidently not been rightly understood. Such children as were surrendered by their parents to expert treatment, complained against that surrender as if it had been any other kind of abandonment. They quarrelled with the pedagogues as much as they would have quarrelled with their parents; but, the bond of the flesh being absent, there was something sapless in their quarrels, and there was less energy engendered. Sexual life was not noticeably smoother than it had been. The epic love of marriage and the lyric love-song of the encounter both lost much by the pretence that they were the same. Nor, as patriotism was discredited, did peace come nearer. Indeed, the certainty of war now arched over the earth like a second sky, inimical to the first. If harmony had been our peril, we were preserved from it, both within and without. For it was plain that, as Christian philosophy had so harshly averred, the world was a stage on which an extraordinary drama, not yet fully comprehended by the intellect, was being performed; and its action was now an agony. But, owing to the adoption of the rationalist philosophy, some of the actors filling the most important parts were now incapable of speaking their lines. It appeared that *Hamlet* and *Othello* and *King Lear* would be no longer cathartic tragedies but repellent and distressing farces if the leading characters had, in the climactic scenes, been overtaken by the delusion that they had retired and were keeping country pubs.

So the evil moment of fascism came and was clear: not surpassed in evil since the days of the barbarian invasions. The devil of nationalism had been driven out of man, but he had not become the headquarters of the dove. Instead there had entered into him the seven devils of internationalism, and he was torn by their frenzies. Then what is against all devils came to his aid. The achievement (which, as yet, is unfinished, since peace does not reign) was accomplished by a continuance of the drama in spite of the difficulties created by the rationalist philosophy. Since the actors cast to play the leading parts would not speak, the action was carried on by the peoples who used to walk to and fro at the back of the scene, softly laughing or softly weeping, or simply quietly being. Now these people streamed across the continents, inscribing their beliefs on the surface of the earth by the course of their flights, and on the sites of their martyrdoms. They defeated fascism by not being Fascist. They showed the contrast between fascism and non-fascism so clearly that the world, wishing to live, defended their side because it could be seen that they were the representatives of life. As they exorcized the devils from the body of Europe they seemed to affirm certain values. It was perhaps true that the origin of man was in criminality, for once a community refused to make the effort of seeking the company of godhead it certainly became criminal. It was perhaps true that hedonism is an impotent gospel, for now it could be seen that pain rather than pleasure is the happiness of many men. As fast as those who ran to save their lives ran those who ran to slay them, even if their pursuit, pressed too hard, might change them into fugitives whose own lives were in danger. Now the scorned bonds of the flesh asserted their validity. It was the final and unbearable misery of these flights that husbands were separated from their wives, and parents lost sight of their children. The men who performed the cruellest surgery on these families, who threw the husband and wife into the gas chamber while the children travelled by train to an unknown destination, had themselves been brought up to contemn their own ties of blood. The anguish of the divided was obviously holy. The contentment of those who felt no reluctance to divide was plainly damned.

In this day of exposition those who made the other sacrifice of the near for the far, and preferred other countries to their own, proved also to be unholy. The relationship between a man and a fatherland is always disturbed by conflict if either man or fatherland is highly developed. A man's demands for liberty must at some point challenge the limitations the state imposes on the individual for the sake of the mass. If he is to carry on the national tradition he must wrestle with those who, speaking in its name, desire to crystallize it at the point reached by the previous generation. In any case national life itself must frequently exasperate him, because it is the medium in which he is expressing himself, and every craftsman or artist is repelled by the resistance of his medium to his will. All men should have a drop or two of treason in their veins, if the nations are not to go soft like so many sleepy pears. Yet to be a traitor is most miserable. All the sane men described in this book were sad as they stood their trials, not only because they were going to be punished. They would have been sad even if they had never been brought to justice. The earlier traitors, who had hired themselves to the Nazis, were to the superficial view sadder than the later. They had forsaken the familiar medium; they had trusted themselves to the mercies of those who had no reason to care for them; knowing their custodians' indifference, they had lived for long in fear; and they were aware that they had thrown away their claim on those who might naturally have felt affection for them. The Communists had experienced none of these things, and were still persuaded that the bargain they had driven with the U.S.S.R. would be to their own advantage. But the earlier traitors had not perceived the extent of the breach with moral tradition that the Nazis had hoped to make, and they sometimes redeemed their treachery by flashes of loyalty to that moral tradition. Ronald David, for instance, might have escaped all punishment for his connection with the British Free Corps had he not voluntarily confessed it in order to gain permission to give evidence for one of his fellow-traitors whom he believed he could clear of a serious charge. The later traitors could not warm themselves by such deeds. The only loyalty they knew was to the Communist Party, which laid on them a discipline forbidding them to use their own wills, and binding them to alien and utilitarian ends. So, wholly without human glory, they would go on till they learned that strangers, as King Solomon put it, were filled with their wealth, and their labours were in the house of a stranger, and they mourned at the last when their flesh and body were consumed. As a divorce sharply recalls what a happy marriage should be, so the treachery of these men recalled what a nation should be: a shelter where all talents are generously recognized, all forgivable oddities forgiven, all viciousness quietly frustrated, and those who lack talent honoured for equivalent contributions. Each of these men was as dependent on the good opinion of others as one is oneself; they needed a nation which was also a hearth, and their capacity for suffering made it tragic that they had gone out from their own hearth to suffer among strangers because the intellectual leaders of their time had professed a philosophy which was scarcely more than a lapse of memory, and had forgotten, among much else, that a hearth gives out warmth.

THE END

Printed in Great Britain by
Billing and Sons Ltd., Guildford and Esher
G4574